Bill Roark
Ryan Roark, CCIM

Concise Encyclopedia
of Real Estate
Business Terms

Pre-publication
REVIEWS,
COMMENTARIES,
EVALUATIONS . . .

"**W**hether you are a real estate student, real estate professional, or a first time home buyer, the *Concise Encyclopedia of Real Estate Business Terms* is an excellent source of information! There are hundreds of real estate terms that are explained in this book with easy-to-understand definitions. The book is very useful and provides example forms of leases, closing checklists, purchase agreements, and lease/purchase agreements. This book is a great tool for the advancement of our industry!"

Crystal C. Acreman
Realtor,
Century 21 Shackelford-French,
Louisiana

"**A**n excellent reference for anyone involved in the real estate business, whether the person is a practitioner or a consumer. This work is truly an encyclopedia, not a dictionary, offering readers opportunities for more complete understanding. It is of particular value to those who are educating and training real estate professionals. The book is full of meaningful and practical examples of working documents for aspiring professionals. The entries are well organized and contain the proper balance of information to be encyclopedic yet concise. This is an excellent launching point for learning of real estate. The approach of using a work such as this produces students who have been exposed to a comprehensive set of terms and their meanings."

Michael Harford, JD
Wake Forest University School of Law;
Professor of Management
and Past Chairholder of Real Estate Studies,
Morehead State University

Concise Encyclopedia
of Real Estate
Business Terms

BEST BUSINESS BOOKS®
Robert E. Stevens, PhD
David L. Loudon, PhD
Editors in Chief

Doing Business in Mexico: A Practical Guide by Gus Gordon and Thurmon Williams

Employee Assistance Programs in Mananged Care by Norman Winegar

Marketing Your Business: A Guide to Developing a Strategic Marketing Plan by Ronald A. Nykiel

Customer Advisory Boards: A Strategic Tool for Customer Relationship Building by Tony Carter

Fundamentals of Business Marketing Research by David A. Reid and Richard E. Plank

Marketing Management: Text and Cases by David L. Loudon, Robert E. Stevens, and Bruce Wrenn

Selling in the New World of Business by Bob Kimball and Jerold "Buck" Hall

Many Thin Companies: The Change in Customer Dealings and Managers Since September 11, 2001 by Tony Carter

The Book on Management by Bob Kimball

The Concise Encyclopedia of Advertising by Kenneth E. Clow and Donald Baack

Application Service Providers in Business by Luisa Focacci, Robert J. Mockler, and Marc E. Gartenfeld

The Concise Handbook of Management: A Practitioner's Approach by Jonathan T. Scott

The Marketing Research Guide, Second Edition by Robert E. Stevens, Bruce Wrenn, Philip K. Sherwood, and Morris E. Ruddick

Marketing Planning Guide, Third Edition by Robert E. Stevens, David L. Loudon, Bruce Wrenn, and Phylis Mansfield

Concise Encyclopedia of Church and Religious Organization Marketing by Robert E. Stevens, David L. Loudon, Bruce Wrenn, and Henry Cole

Market Opportunity Analysis: Text and Cases by Robert E. Stevens, Philip K. Sherwood, J. Paul Dunn, and David L. Loudon

The Economics of Competition: The Race to Monopoly by George G. Djolov

Concise Encyclopedia of Real Estate Business Terms by Bill Roark and Ryan Roark

Marketing Research: Text and Cases, Second Edition by Bruce Wrenn, Robert Stevens, and David Loudon

Concise Encyclopedia of Investing by Darren W. Oglesby

Concise Encyclopedia of Real Estate Business Terms

Bill Roark
Ryan Roark, CCIM

**BEST
BUSINESS
BOOKS**

Best Business Books®
An Imprint of The Haworth Press, Inc.
New York • London • Oxford

For more information on this book or to order, visit
http://www.haworthpress.com/store/product.asp?sku=5637

or call 1-800-HAWORTH (800-429-6784) in the United States and Canada
or (607) 722-5857 outside the United States and Canada

or contact orders@HaworthPress.com

Published by

Best Business Books®, an imprint of The Haworth Press, Inc., 10 Alice Street, Binghamton, NY 13904-1580.

PUBLISHER'S NOTE
The development, preparation, and publication of this work has been undertaken with great care. However, the Publisher, employees, editors, and agents of The Haworth Press are not responsible for any errors contained herein or for consequences that may ensue from use of materials or information contained in this work. The Haworth Press is committed to the dissemination of ideas and information according to the highest standards of intellectual freedom and the free exchange of ideas. Statements made and opinions expressed in this publication do not necessarily reflect the views of the Publisher, Directors, management, or staff of The Haworth Press, Inc., or an endorsement by them.

Cover design by Marylouise E. Doyle.

Library of Congress Cataloging-in-Publication Data

Roark, Bill.
   Concise encyclopedia of real estate business terms / Bill Roark, Ryan Roark.
      p. cm.
   Includes bibliographical references and index.
   ISBN-13: 978-0-7890-2341-4 (alk. paper)
   ISBN-10: 0-7890-2341-5 (alk. paper)
   ISBN-13: 978-0-7890-2342-1 (soft : alk. paper)
   ISBN-10: 0-7890-2342-3 (soft : alk. paper)
   1. Real estate business—Dictionaries. 2. Real property—Dictionaries. I. Roark, Ryan. II. Title.

HD1365.R63 2006
333.3303—dc22   2005032861

This book is dedicated to my wife, Janice, whose patience and understanding during the sixteen months of preparation have made this work possible.

Bill Roark

To my mother, Janice, whose love and care have been a constant source of inspiration and guidance.

Ryan Roark

ABOUT THE AUTHORS

William E. (Bill) Roark, BA, is past president of the Northeast Louisiana Board of Realtors and past director of the Louisiana Association of Realtors. He formed Tri-State Properties in 1975 as a commercial real estate company and has had the opportunity to represent some of the country's leading restaurants, retailers, and industrial manufacturers. He is co-host of "Taking Care of Business," a live weekly real estate news and information talk radio program.

William R. (Ryan) Roark, BS, CCIM, has been structuring real estate investments and managing real estate portfolios since 1999. He is a member of the National Board of Realtors and is co-host of "Taking Care of Business," a live weekly real estate news and information talk radio program.

CONTENTS

Authors' Note

The opinions and statements herein reflect the viewpoints of the authors. While a great deal of care has been taken to provide accurate and current information, neither the authors, editors, nor staff assume responsibility for the accuracy of the data or information contained herein. The general information and conclusions presented are subject to local, state, and federal laws and regulations, court cases, and any revisions. This publication is sold for educational purposes only with the understanding that the authors, publishers, and editors are not engaged in rendering legal, accounting, or any other professional advice or service.

Concise Encyclopedia of Real Estate Business Terms
© 2006 by The Haworth Press, Inc. All rights reserved.
doi:10.1300/5637_a

AAA TENANT

In retail or office leasing, tenants may be rated according to their credit history as judged by a recognized credit rating bureau and to their stock value or net worth. Many AAA tenants, often referred to as *triple "A" tenants,* will be treated somewhat different from an "A" tenant or "B" tenant. A triple A tenant may receive a better lease rate, have the deposit waived, or not be required to personally guarantee the lease.

Triple A tenants are most often national tenants with a strong credit rating, a history of stable business, and multiple store or office locations.

A lessor may be willing to invest additional dollars in tenant improvements for the triple A tenant. Many triple A tenants are considered anchor tenants. An *anchor tenant* is one who will attract both a large volume of shoppers in retail centers and other retailers to the center. In office leases a triple A tenant may provide prestige to a building that will in turn attract other tenants. Regional or national banks are often considered anchor tenants to an office building.

Triple A tenants in shopping centers will often place requirements on the number, placement, and type of out-parcel tenants permitted. They may also limit the placement or number of other tenants who sell competitive products.

ABSORPTION RATE

When a market becomes overbuilt, it is important to calculate the amount of time it will require to absorb the excess product. If the economy is strong and interest rates are at moderate to low levels and appear to be stable, there is a tendency to overbuild in segments of the real estate market. Overbuilding can occur in any market segment but

Concise Encyclopedia of Real Estate Business Terms
© 2006 by The Haworth Press, Inc. All rights reserved.
doi:10.1300/5637_01

primarily is confined to apartments, office space, retail space, motels/hotels, or spec homes.

At times, depending on the geographical location, we have all seen overbuilding in one or more of these market segments will occur. When it does, there is an effort to calculate the length of time it will take the market to absorb the overbuilding. For example, if there is a 30 percent vacancy in office space and the market can absorb only 10 percent of the vacant space, then the annual absorption rate is 10 percent. At the 10 percent absorption rate, there would be a three-year oversupply of office space to reach a theoretical 100 percent occupancy.

ABSTRACT

The public records doctrine requires that all instruments affecting third parties be filed in the public records. The summary of a search of all the instruments that affect a particular party is an *abstract,* sometimes referred to as an *abstract of title.* Such instruments include deeds, transfers, mortgages, liens, and any other filing in the public records that may affect the title adversely.

However, any other sales, contracts, judgments, mortgages, etc., that are not filed in the public records will not be a part of the abstract. Therefore, when the sale of property occurs, it is important that the deed be immediately recorded along with the mortgage to place any third parties on notice.

The period of time covered by an abstract can vary widely but must cover at least the period of time from the previous sale that showed the owner and all mortgages placed against the property along with any liens, judgments, and other instruments that may affect the title.

ACQUISITIVE PRESCRIPTION

A property that is not acquired by a deed or recorded title but rather over a period of time through adverse possession that meets all legal requirements is an acquisitive prescription. Acquisition through acquisitive prescription or adverse possession by maintaining continuous possession for the required period of time acquires good title.

For example, if the law requires uninterrupted possession for a period of ten years, the person who meets this requirement can be granted good title by the means of acquisitive prescription.

Acquisitive prescription supercedes any claim of ownership based on title. Ownership does not depend on written title but on acts of adverse possession that meet legal requirements.

ACRE

An acre is a standard measure used to describe land mass, consisting of 208.7 feet × 208.7 feet, which equals 43,560 square feet or 160 square rods. When converted to liquid measurements, 1 cubic foot of water per second equals 450 gallons per minute or about one acre-inch per hour. An acre-foot of water equals an amount required to cover one acre of land to a depth of one foot, which is 325,850 gallons or 43,560 cubic feet of water. An acre-inch of water equals 27,154 gallons.

Land descriptions are most often written as divisions of a square mile or 640 acres. When divided into quarters, the description can continue to divide into ever smaller sections. For example, a forty-acre tract can be described as the southeast (SE) quarter of the Southeast (SE) quarter. This is written as the SE4 of the SE4 of a certain section that consists of a square mile or 640 acres.

AD VALOREM

A tax assessed on real estate based on the assessed value of the property, which is different from the market value, is called *ad valorem*. The county tax assessor determines the assessed value from the market value he or she places on the property.

It is the responsibility of the tax assessor to determine the market value of each property within his or her jurisdiction, generally a county or a parish. From the assessed value a tax is assigned based on the millage rate of each subdistrict within the jurisdiction. One mill is the tax rate per 1,000 of assessed value. One mill per 1,000 calculates at $1.00 of taxes per $1,000 of assessed value. For example, if the assessed value is $5,000 and the millage rate is 85 mills, multiply the 85 mills by 5. The annual tax for that property would be $425.

For residential property, there may be a homestead exemption for homes of a stated value for which all such property is exempt. For example, if the homestead exemption is $50,000 and the value of the property is $100,000, only $50,000 is considered toward the assessed value.

For commercial and industrial property, there is no homestead exemption. Such property may have an assessed value of 10 percent of the market value of the land and 15 percent of the market value of the buildings. This property is then taxed at the millage rate applicable to all property within the subdistrict. Property owned by nonprofit entities, such as schools, churches, and governmental agencies, are exempt from all forms of property taxes.

ADD-ON CHARGES

In addition to the monthly rent charge, a lessor may pass on other costs to the lessee on a pro rata share basis. These charges can include property taxes, insurance, and common area maintenance costs. They are generally included as a monthly charge to the lessee. They may be stated as a cost per square foot (SF) of the leased space. The cost is based on the percentage of the total space that a lessee occupies.

For example, if the total space is 100,000 SF and the lessee occupies 5,000 SF, the pro rata share for this lessee will be 5 percent. If the total of these costs is $12,000, the pro rata share to this lessee will be $600 per year which may be paid at $50 per month in addition to the lease amount.

The lease will almost always provide for an annual adjustment based on the actual increase in the cost for the preceding year. It may, however, provide for an annual cap on the increase not to exceed, for example, 5 percent annually.

Add-on charges are most common in shopping centers, where multiple tenants share the cost on a pro rata basis. However, they can also be found in office space or other commercial leases.

ADJUSTABLE RATE

Adjustable rate is typically used in conjunction with mortgages. An adjustable rate mortgage (ARM) allows the interest rate to be changed at specific intervals, usually in relation to one of the standard interest rate indexes (LIBOR [London Inter Bank Offering Rate], prime rate, etc.). These types of loans normally have an interest rate cap placed on them above which the interest charged could never rise. For example, an investor may purchase property with an ARM whereby the beginning interest rate would remain in place for two years and then be adjusted in relation to an index every year thereafter. ARM loans carry a lower annual percentage rate than fifteen-year and thirty-year fixed rate loans.

AGENCY

Agency is the relationship created when a property owner trusts the sale or lease of his or her property to another person, generally called a *real estate agent*. It is likewise created when a buyer trusts the purchase of real estate to someone else, generally also a real estate agent. However, in both instances, the relationship could be formed with an attorney or trustee. The person with whom the responsibility is placed becomes a fiduciary and assumes the responsibility of representing the other party's interest. For example, if the fiduciary party represents the seller's interest only, they are known as the *seller's agent*. If the person represents both the buyer's and the seller's interest in a fiduciary capacity, they are known as a *dual agent*.

The agency or fiduciary responsibility requires that the agent act in a manner that represents the other party's interest. This may require not revealing some information such as a price that the seller has stated he or she will consider if it is below the listed price or the price that a buyer is willing to pay above the price offered.

The agent must also advise the other party of certain responsibilities the agent may have assumed. In the case of the seller, if there is a defect with the property, the agent is required to reveal this in writing to a potential buyer. The agent is also responsible for explaining any terms within the agreement that a buyer or seller may not understand, such as specific performance, deposit, assignment, or contingencies.

The agency relationship is always created in writing, with beginning and ending dates, such as a listing agreement. A dual agency relationship is created when an agent enters into an agreement with the owner to sell the property and then with the buyer to represent him or her in the purchase of the same property. A buyer's agency agreement authorizes the agent to be the sole and exclusive agent of the buyer in the purchase of, for instance, a home or a commercial building.

Agency does not always imply responsibility for payment. For instance, the seller may pay a buyer's agent even though the agent only represents the buyer. Agency does, however, always imply fiduciary responsibility.

ALTERNATIVE MORTGAGE

There are a number of mortgage instruments that are structured different from the fixed rate, level monthly payment mortgage that is standard in real estate financing. These types of mortgages are sometimes called *alternative mortgages* and may go under a variety of names but are commonly referred to as *AMI* (Alternative Mortgage Instruments) *mortgages.*

Some of the mortgages included in the AMI category are variable rate mortgage (VRM), reverse annuity mortgage (RAM), and graduated payment mortgage (GPM). A mortgage may call for interest-only payments for a specified time period, annual or semiannual payments, interest to be adjusted at a specified time, or reduced principal payments rather than level payments with a specified balloon payment to make up the principal deficit at an agreed upon time.

The advantage of the alternative mortgage is that it can be structured in any manner acceptable to the mortgagee and mortgagor. Such mortgages enable many properties to be sold to a purchaser who would otherwise be unable to meet the requirements of a standard level pay, fixed rate mortgage.

AMORTIZED LEASE

An amortized lease is a lease that has payments based on an amortization schedule in which the lessee is given credit for the principal paid. The lessee is given the option to purchase the property at a future date with the purchase price based on the remaining principal balance. For example, if the purchase price is $100,000 with an 8 percent interest rate and a fifteen-year term, the payments would be $955.65 per month. The lease payment then becomes $955.65. If the lessee is given the option to purchase at the end of five years, the purchase price will be $78,766.39 based on an amortization schedule with the lessee given credit for the principal paid based on the amortization schedule. If the lessee does not exercise the option to purchase, the lessor may continue the lease at the same payment for the fifteen-year term; or, depending on the lease agreement, the lessor may have the right to increase the rent payment.

Amortized leases are generally triple net leases, with the lessee responsible for maintenance, repair, or replacement of all systems as well as property taxes and insurance costs. Such leases may be used for commercial and residential properties.

APPRAISAL

The following definition is provided by *The Appraisal of Real Estate*, tenth edition, published in 1992 by the Appraisal Institute. An appraisal is

> [t]he most probable price, as of a specified date, in cash or in terms equivalent to cash, or in other precisely revealed terms for which the specified property rights should sell after reasonable exposure in a competitive market under all conditions requisite to a fair sale, with a buyer and seller acting prudently, knowledgeably and for self-interest and assuming neither is under undue duress.

For further discussion, consult *The Appraisal of Real Estate* tenth edition, pages 18-22.

Appraisal is the opinion of value provided in writing by a trained specialist in real estate values. Such specialists have generally been through numerous courses or seminars and received certification by a state authority or other appraisal institute or society. Many colleges and universities offer courses or degrees in real estate appraising. There are generally annual educational requirements in the law and requirements by the lending institutions to be acceptable for mortgages.

An appraisal is designed to reflect what a buyer in a particular market is willing pay for a certain property. There are three accepted approaches to determine value.

The comparable sale approach looks at the most recent sale of comparable properties in a particular area. Although no two properties are exactly alike, the most recent and most comparable sales can be used to determine what a buyer will pay. This is probably the most accurate test of value.

The reproduction cost approach is what it would take to construct a similar building today with adjustments for depreciated value. The depreciated value is a factor of the condition of the property and obsolescence in construction design and materials used.

The income approach is the consideration of the rental value should the building be placed for rent. The income approach considers the expected rental income should the property be rented based on similar properties currently rented. The expected income is then factored into a sales price that takes into consideration maintenance, debt service, insurance, and any anticipated management services.

Some of the factors that influence value are the location of the property, its obsolescence in design, any deferred maintenance, the condition of the surrounding neighborhood, and the projection of future deterioration of the general area caused by age or neglect. The cost of improvements added by an owner, especially in residential properties, may or may not be reflected in an increased appraisal value. For example, an extra bedroom and bath added to an existing home may have cost 30 to 50 percent more than the value they added to the appraisal. Painting or wallpaper may add little, if any, to the actual appraisal value even though it makes the residence more sellable.

Because appraisals reflect the opinion of one person, at times there can be significant differences of opinion among appraisers. Based in part on the comparable sales used, the value given to deferred maintenance and the personal opinion of a particular appraiser can vary as much as 30 percent. However, as a general rule, most appraisals will vary by less than 5 percent when done by equally trained and experienced appraisers.

The importance given to market conditions, such as high interest rates, which lead to fewer buyers, or high inflation and lower interest rates, which attract more buyers, will impact most appraisals.

APPURTENANCES

Appurtenances is a legal term to designate anything outside the property itself that adds to its enjoyment or value. Obvious examples are buildings, driveways, roads, parking lots, and fences. However, rights-of-way and water use rights can also be considered appurtenances.

Unless specified otherwise, all appurtenances are considered part of the land and pass to a new owner when the real estate is sold. For example, a farmer who owns 200 acres of grazing land adjacent to an interstate collects $400 per month from a billboard he leases on his property. If he wants to sell his farmland to another farmer but still collect the leasing fee from his sign, he must specifically state his intention in any legal document involving the sale of his land. Also, it is almost certain that the land beneath the billboard will need to be registered with the county separately from the rest of the farmland so there is no confusion about the billboard's ownership.

AS IS–WHERE IS

In a purchase agreement, the phrase "as is–where is" is used to indicate the buyer's acceptance of the property and the improvements as they are and without any obligation on the part of the seller to make repairs. If the contract contains an "as is" clause, the buyer assumes all obligations for any repairs or replacement required to make the property habitable or usable for the intended purposes. "As is" agreements are generally used after the buyer has had adequate time to inspect the structure and systems, i.e., heating, air, plumbing, electrical, roof, and foundation, of the property and has determined the cost for repairs, replacement, or alterations.

However, this does not release the seller from revealing any known defects or problems with the property to the buyer. This is usually done in writing to protect the seller. If, after the buyer is given written notice, the buyer decides to accept the property "as is–where is," then the seller is released from any further obligations to the buyer. If the buyer later discovers additional problems with the property, he has no recourse against the seller provided the seller had no previous knowledge of such problems. The buyer has signed away any right of future recourse against the seller for any problems that may surface in the future. The seller is providing no warranties of any kind to the buyer either present or future.

ASSESSMENT

A valuation placed on property for the purpose of ad valorem taxes is an assessment. The assessment may be levied on property to cover the cost of a public improvement that benefits the property owner such as water and sewer, sidewalks, etc. When the cost of installing such services provides a benefit to the property owner a public authority may assess the property a tax to cover the cost of installation and maintenance. Most often the assessment is an annual cost sufficient to amortize the debt over an extended term of years. Sometimes such an assessment is called a *special assessment* with the funds dedicated for a particular improvement.

Assessment may also apply to owners of a condominium to cover their proportionate share of the common expenses or any new improvements.

ASSESSOR

The administrator of a taxing or an assessment jurisdiction who is responsible for the evaluation of real estate is an assessor. Typically, an assessor, or what is commonly referred to as a *tax assessor,* is responsible for placeing real estate on a tax roll for the purpose of evaluation at fair market value and taxation.

The assessor will typically adjust the fair market value periodically to reflect increases or decreases. The real estate is then placed on the tax roll for tax purposes in accordance with the millage rate assigned to that jurisdiction for purposes of ad valorem taxation.

If in the opinion of the property owner the property has been assessed too high, there is an appeal process available for the purpose of reducing the fair market value and subsequently the property taxes. Changes in fair market value may be the result of comparable sales data, changes in the market, or an improvement that the property owner has made.

An assessor may be elected or appointed. Generally, the actual collection of the taxes from property owners is performed by another government entity.

ASSIGNMENT

The transfer or the right of transfer of the rights or obligations of one party to another is called *assignment*. Buyers may incorporate the right of assignment in a purchase agreement that will give them the right to transfer their obligations to a third party. That third party may be a corporation, partnership, or another individual. The right of assignment may be with or without the sellers' approval. It may also require that the buyer remain obligated to the completion of all the terms and conditions of the agreement even though he or she has the right of assignment.

In a lease agreement, the lessee may have the right to assign his or her obligations to a sublease tenant with or without remaining as obligator to the lessee. In a sublease, the original lessee may agree to also remain responsible for the lease along with the sublessee as additional security for the lessor.

A mortgagor or borrower may be asked by the mortgagee or lender for an assignment of the rents in the event the mortgager defaults in the payment of the mortgage. This provides the mortgagee with the right to collect the rents and apply them first to the mortgage payment. Most often this is a standard clause in all mortgages on income property.

ASSUMPTION OF MORTGAGE

If a buyer assumes an existing mortgage, the buyer becomes equally liable for the debt with the original borrower. The assumption of the debt must be in writing; however, it is not necessary for the buyer assuming the debt to sign the original mortgage.

A buyer may not assert that the assumption of the mortgage is invalid even though the mortgage required the consent of the mortgage holder whose consent was not secured. By the act of assuming the mortgage the buyer waives the requirement of consent. Neither can the buyer assert that the assumption was invalid because it was in violation of the mortgage.

The assumption of the mortgage by a buyer does not release the original borrower from responsibility for the debt. Even the consent of the mortgage holder to the assumption does not release the original borrower from responsibility for the debt. The assumption of a mortgage does not affect its ranking to any other mortgage that may be placed on the property even when the mortgage holder consents to the assumption.

In some mortgages such an assumption may be prohibited and grant the lender the right to call the remaining balance on the mortgage due and payable immediately.

AUTHENTIC ACT

An authentic act is executed before a notary public, or someone authorized to perform that function, in the presence of two witnesses, signed by the parties who executed the document, by each witness and the notary. The execution does not have to be at the same time and place or in the presence of the same two witnesses provided that all parties to the contract, all witnesses, and both notaries sign. The notary and witnesses must be present when the parties to the contract sign.

The notary is not required to explain to the parties what they are signing. It is presumed that the parties have read and understand what it is they are signing.

AVERAGE DAILY ROOM RATE

Average daily room rate (ADR) is used as a measure to value hotel and motel properties. ADR is arrived at by dividing the total guest room revenue by the total number of occupied rooms. For example, if the total number of rooms was 100 and the total revenue for a 30-day period was $90,000, the ADR is determined at by dividing the $90,000 room revenue by 30 to obtain at the average daily rental and then dividing that by the number of total guest rooms. In this example, the ADR is $30.00.

The ADR considers all the guest rooms available, not just the rooms rented. Although the actual rented rate per room in the earlier example may be $50.00 per night, the ADR is only $30.00. A hotel/motel buyer may be interested in the average number of rooms rented per night and the actual rented rate of each room, but the valuation for the purpose of a potential purchase is more influenced by the ADR.

Because hotel rental properties offer a wide range of prices based on number and type of beds per room along with number of occupants per room, the potential buyer knows that the fixed cost of operation for the property is based on the total number of rooms and the total room rent collected over a specified time period. The ADR is usually calculated over a twelve-month average because actual room rent revenue may experience significant fluctuations depending on the day of the week and the season of the year.

The ADR may give a potential buyer an indication of how much he or she can improve the total income based on a market analysis of comparable properties within the market area. The ADR has become perhaps the most accurate standard of hotel/motel value of all criteria a potential buyer can use.

AVERAGE DAILY TRAFFIC

Vehicular traffic access routes are often an essential ingredient to the success of retail and restaurant businesses. The measurement of average daily traffic (ADT) is important in the decision of where to locate. Locating in proximity to large volumes of ADT can mean the difference between success and failure of a business. For instance, most national restaurants project that 15 percent to 20 percent of their business will come as a direct result of a high ADT count. Retailers also attribute a significant percentage of their business to daily traffic volume. This then becomes a major consideration in the determination of a new location.

High ADT volume provides high exposure to the business and is an indicator of easy accessibility for the public. Any site location study will include the ADT count. For most state and interstate highways, these counts are available through the local department of transportation. Cities also have available traffic counts for major inner-city traffic arteries.

BALLOON MORTGAGE

A balloon mortgage is a mortgage that is not fully amortized during the agreed upon term of the mortgage. The principal and interest payments of the mortgage are not sufficient to fully amortize the debt during the mortgage term. The principal may not be fully amortized, but the interest for the entire mortgage is always calculated as part of the monthly payment. This type of mortgage provides for lower payments by the debtor during the term of the mortgage. The final payment required will then pay off the remaining principal balance. This type of mortgage is used sometimes in the purchase of income property, when the projected income is not sufficient to pay for the ordinary expenses such as taxes, income, maintenance, and projected vacancy plus cover the mortgage payments under a fully amortized mortgage.

The mortgagee and mortgagor may then agree on a lower mortgage payment based on amortizing a certain percentage of the mortgage for an agreed upon term with the balance of the principal debt becoming due and payable with the final payment, called the *balloon payment*. This is often accomplished by refinancing the property or selling the property at a price adequate to cover the remaining balance due.

Lenders are more likely to accept this type of mortgage during periods of high inflation when the rents and appreciating value of the property are more likely to provide the borrower rent increases and a high appreciation of the property value.

BINDING EFFECT

A contract that binds all parties to the terms and conditions agreed to within the contract is said to have a binding effect on all parties. A

Concise Encyclopedia of Real Estate Business Terms
© 2006 by The Haworth Press, Inc. All rights reserved.
doi:10.1300/5637_02

legal document such as a purchase agreement or lease when appropriately executed by the buyer and seller or lessee and lessor binds each party to perform according to the terms of the contract. This binding effect on each party is stipulated through such terms as specific performance. Under a specific performance clause, each party agrees to perform certain actions. If one party defaults in his or her performance, the other party has specified remedies such as forfeiture of deposit, stipulated damages, or legal recourse through the courts.

For example, if a buyer signs a contract to purchase property and then decides to not finalize the purchase without cause as stipulated in the contract, the seller may legally force the sale to the buyer through the binding effect of the contract as spelled out in a performance clause or other such language contained in the contract.

Each party to the contract is bound by the terms of the contract to complete his or her obligations as spelled out in the contract. Failure to do so may result in legal action by the other party.

BOND FOR DEED

A bond for deed is a contract to sell property in which the buyer makes the installment payments to the seller or the seller's agent, and, after the payment of an agreed upon sum, the seller or the seller's agent delivers title to the buyer. If the buyer fails to make the payments as agreed upon, the seller may cancel the bond for deed by proper notification. The seller must give proper notification to the buyer that he or she is in default. Generally the seller must give notice before a specified time, such as 45 days, of his or her intent to cancel.

A company or bank authorized to hold the deed in trust and receive payments usually acts as the trust agent and charges a small fee for the service. After the fees are deducted, the payments are forwarded to the seller. Some states may require the refund of all previous payments if the bond for deed is canceled. However, the seller may recover a reasonable rental amount from the buyer prior to the cancellation. Most bond for deed contracts stipulate what the rental amount will be in the event of cancellation.

BREAKPOINT

Retail leases often contain a clause for percentage rent if sales exceed a specified dollar amount. The percentage rent may be calculated to go into effect over a specified amount of sales, known as the *breakpoint*. The breakpoint is determined by dividing the annual rent by the percentage rent agreed upon. For example, if the annual rent is $30,000 and the percentage rent agreed to is 2.5 percent over the breakpoint, then the breakpoint is determined by dividing the 2.5 percent into $30,000, which is $1,200,000. When sales reach $1,200,000, the 2.5 percent percentage rent is charged for any sales over the $1,200,000 amount. In this example, if sales were $1,500,000 for the year, the additional percentage rent would be $7,500. If sales were $2,000,000, the additional percentage rent would be $20,000.

By using the breakpoint calculation, the retailer is provided an initial level of sales to cover his or her normal operating costs and cost of goods sold. If sales exceed this amount, the lessor participates through percentage rent in the additional sales.

Although percentage rent may not come into play in the early years of a long-term lease, it can provide substantial additional rent to the lessor in the later years of the long-term lease.

BROKERAGE FEE

The brokerage fee is a fee charged by a real estate agent to handle or broker the sale or purchase of real estate. Often it is referred to as the *commission* charged and is based on a percentage of the sales price. However, it may be a flat fee agreed to between seller and agent. The brokerage fee is agreed to in writing and incorporated as part of the listing agreement or, in some cases, the buyer's agency agreement.

The brokerage fee is required by law to be paid to the real estate broker, who then pays the agent who worked with the buyer or seller. It is paid at the closing of the sale or escrow. However, the fee may be paid over time, as is often the case in a lease. The brokerage fee may be paid over the term of the lease and/or any renewals exercised by the lessee. Alternatively, part of the fee can be paid at the lease execution and the remainder over the term of the lease and any renewals. In any event, the amount of the payment is always stipulated in writing, and the method by which it is to be paid is always identified.

The brokerage fee is generally paid by the seller or lessor unless the agent has an agreement with the buyer or lessee through a buyer's agent or tenant representation agreement to pay the fee.

BULK SALES LAW

The sale of real estate that includes merchandise, equipment, or inventory, such as the assets of a business, may require compliance with a bulk sales law. This law requires that the seller's assets and creditors be listed and that notice to the creditors of the sale and advertisement of the sale be completed prior to the sale. If failure to comply is proven, the purchaser may be liable to the creditors for any outstanding debts. A purchaser may want to escrow funds from the sale to make certain all creditors are paid in full at the time of closing.

BUY/SELL AGREEMENT

The buy/sell agreement, sometimes called a *real estate purchase agreement,* is the written document that lists all the terms and conditions under which a buyer is willing to purchase and the seller is willing to sell a particular property. Generally, according to real estate law only written agreements are legally binding. Any oral agreements between buyer and seller in most states are not recognized as binding on either party. Exceptions to this may be conditions of the property, particularly defects, that were known by the seller but either not revealed or denied orally by the seller. In such cases, these may be interpreted such as to affect an otherwise legally binding agreement.

The buy/sell agreement states the full legal name and address of all parties to the agreement. The buyer states the terms and conditions under which his or her offer to purchase is made. The document contains either a full legal description or an abbreviated legal description that identifies the property in addition to a municipal address if available. In the case of a parcel of land, acreage, or a vacant lot to which no municipal street address has been assigned, a legal description defines the property. Often in such cases a property plat or survey is attached for further identification.

The price the buyer is offering and how it is to be paid are stated. The method of financing or payment is identified as cash, seller financing, or financing by a mortgage through a lending institution. If financing is by the seller, the terms and amount of the financing requested by the buyer are specified as to amount, interest rate, and length of term (stated in months or years, called the *amortized term of the mortgage*). The seller may also be given the right to call for full payment at a time prior to the fully amortized term of the mortgage, commonly known as a *right to call*.

The seller is asked to make certain warranties as to the good condition of the title. If problems are discovered with the title, the seller is provided a specified time, such as thirty days, to clear the title or the agreement is voided. The seller may also make other warranties as to the working condition of all systems, i.e., plumbing, electrical, HVAC (heat and air-conditioning), roof, exterior, foundation, and structure.

A buyer gives a deposit with the agreement to indicate his or her sincerity. The deposit is usually held by a third party, such as a real estate broker, attorney, or title company. The deposit may be considered as earnest money, which is applied to the purchase price at closing. Any contingencies are stated, such as subject to financing, subject to owner financing, subject to transfer of mineral rights to buyer, etc. The buyer is given a "due diligence" period to inspect the property and report in writing any problems or deficiencies that are discovered. Prior to closing, the seller must correct any deficiencies if the sale is to close. Many states now require a property condition form be completed and made a part of the agreement.

By law, if an item is attached to the building, it remains with the sale unless specified to be removed by the seller prior to closing. Such items may include chandeliers, window air-conditioner units, kitchen ranges, or any other items agreed to by buyer and seller. The agreement does not include items such as furniture and refrigerators, which are not attached and do not go with the sale.

The seller may accept the buyer's offer, counter the offer, or reject the offer. Any changes made by the seller to the buyer's offer must be initialed by buyer and seller in order to remain binding on all parties. Otherwise, the buyer is released from his obligation to buy. Most buy/sell agreements have a specific performance clause binding the buyer and the seller to the terms of the agreement. The agreement will also contain a date on or before which the sale must occur; otherwise the entire document is null and void. The agreement also gives the seller a time in which to accept the offer; if not accepted in the given time, the buyer's offer is void.

BUYER'S AGENT

An agent that agrees to represent only the buyer's interest in a sale is the buyer's agent or a designated agent for the buyer. An agreement may be signed by buyer and agent in which the buyer designates the agent as his sole agent in the purchase. The agreement may appoint the agent as the exclusive agent for the buyer. Some agreements may bind the buyer to pay the agent even though the buyer found the property he wishes to purchase through his own efforts.

A buyer's agent has fiduciary responsibility to the buyer to represent only his interest in the purchase, even though his commission may be paid by the seller.

CALL

Call is a term used in mortgages giving the mortgagee the right to demand the remaining principal balance due and payable immediately by the mortgagor. Generally, this right may only be exercised by the lender in the event of default.

Some mortgages may also contain a right to call the mortgage to be paid in full after a certain term of the mortgage. For instance, the mortgage may be amortized over a fifteen-year term, but the lender may have the right to call for the remaining principal balance to be paid in full after the fifth year. In this case, the lender may or may not call for payment of the remaining principal balance by the borrower depending on the past payment history by the borrower and the current interest rate. Often the lender may adjust the interest rate but leave the other terms of the mortgage intact. This will require an increase in the monthly payment if the interest rate is increased.

CAPITALIZATION RATE

The value of an investment property can be measured by a formula called the *capitalization rate.* This method converts income into an estimate of value. The higher the income and the lower the capitalization rate, the greater the estimated value of the property. The income is based on net income before mortgage payments are deducted. To determine the value, divide the income by the capitalization rate, also called the cap rate.

For example, if the net income from an investment property is $100,000, the following CAP rates would yield the following values (rounded to the nearest thousand):

Concise Encyclopedia of Real Estate Business Terms
© 2006 by The Haworth Press, Inc. All rights reserved.
doi:10.1300/5637_03

CAP Rate	Value
8%	$1,250,000
9%	$1,111,000
10%	$1,000,000
11%	$ 909,000
12%	$ 833,000

The cap rate does not take into consideration the cost of deferred maintenance or renovations required, which are other factors that can affect property value. Although a cap rate is useful, other factors must also be considered, such as changes occurring to the general area where the property is located. An investor must also consider the long-term income prospect. For example, an investment property may have a steady level of income now, but if the general area is in decline what is the prospect of maintaining that income in the future? The cap rate is a reliable value indicator for today but cannot predict a future value, which will be influenced by a number of factors other than current income.

CAPITAL GAINS

The amount of taxes owed at the time real estate is sold is based on the capital gain or loss. The capital gain or loss is the amount the property is sold for minus the original purchase price. There may also be an additional amount deducted from the sale price if the owner has added capital improvements during the time of ownership. Capital improvements may be an addition to the investment property, such as covered parking for an office building or apartment complex. Items that are not considered capital improvements include carpet, painting, and ceiling fans.

Also, to qualify for capital gains, an asset must be held for a period of time set by the Internal Revenue Service, generally one year or longer. If the property is not held for the required period of time to qualify as a capital gain, then the sale of the asset and any profits realized may be taxed as ordinary income at the rate at which the seller's other ordinary income is taxed.

The tax rate on capital gain income is lower than the taxpayer's ordinary income rate. Ordinary income, but not capital gain income, is taxed at the same rate the seller is taxed for salary and other non-investment income.

CASH FLOW

Cash flow is the term used to express the return on a real estate investment after all direct and indirect expenses are paid. Expenses include but are not limited to mortgage payments, property taxes, insurance, repairs, replacement costs, management, outside services such as janitorial or parking lot cleaning, utilities, accounting, and any other costs related to operating, owning, and maintaining the property.

Cash flow is positive if after all expenses there is a cash return on the investment and negative if there is a cash loss on the investment. Investment returns can also be expressed as a cash flow after tax on the positive cash flow or pretax if calculated without consideration of any taxes due on the profit or positive cash flow generated.

Cash flow to an investor is the investor's final evaluation of the real estate investment. However, other considerations may be important to the investor, such as tax write-offs or tax shelters. Even if the investment has a negative cash flow, the tax write-off may be considered in the final analysis.

Investments that have a negative cash flow can be profitable in later years when increased rents or income move the investment from a negative cash flow to a positive cash flow. Also, cash flow does not take into consideration the appreciation in property value, which can be substantial over a period of several years.

CHATTEL PROPERTY

Chattel property is personal property apart from real estate owned by an individual; it is the property owned other than real estate that would be considered a part of an estate. For example, automobiles, furniture, jewelry, furs, clothes, etc., are chattel property. Chattel property can be divided into two categories: personal and real. Personal property is the possessions of an individual. Real chattel property is intangible personal property rights that may be created through leases, options, easements, etc.

In some states or taxing jurisdictions, personal property may be taxed based on its assessed value. With such taxation, an individual may be required to declare all personal items with a value in excess of a certain amount. A tax may then be collected in accordance with the millage rate applicable to that jurisdiction. In other cases, the tax may simply be a percentage of the value of the personal property.

CLOSINGS

The two types of closings are live closings and escrow closings. In a live closing, the parties appear at a specified time and place to sign documents and pass funds. Live closings are more common in some states than in others. At an escrow closing, the documents are signed by buyer and seller, generally at a title company, and submitted to an escrow agent, who records the documents in accordance with written instructions. The parties do not appear before the escrow agent at closing.

CLOUD

Cloud describes a condition of the property title that will affect the sale of the property. A cloud is anything that prevents the passing of a clear title. It is most often caused by the lack of a clear chain of title to the property. However, a cloud may be any number of issues that obscures ownership or may cause dispute of ownership in the future.

For example, if a property owner has died, there are many heirs, and the property is sold without a signature on the deed of any one of the heirs, there is a cloud on the title. If a mortgage against the property has never been cancelled, there is a cloud on the title. When an improvement such as a home, garage, or other building has been constructed by an adjacent property owner over the property line, an encroachment is created that places a cloud on the title.

If the cloud is insignificant, many times a title company will insure without making the cloud an exception in the sale of the property. However, if the title company notes the cloud as an exception in its policy, any future disputes or lawsuits arising from this cloud are exempted from the policy of title insurance. Mortgage companies, many times, will not accept a policy of title insurance if there is a cloud on the title that is an exception to the policy.

COLLATERAL

Any security that is offered by the borrower as a guarantee that the financial obligation will be paid in full is called *collateral*. A loan on real estate will almost always require the property as collateral to guarantee repayment. However, a lender may also require a first or second mortgage on additional real estate, known as *additional collateral*. Other forms of assets, such as stocks, bonds, certificates of deposit, or anything else in which the borrower has equity or value, may also be offered as additional collateral.

A lender may consider as additional collateral other real estate in which the borrower has equity. However, most lenders will only consider real estate whose appraised value is more than 20 percent above the amount owed on the property.

For example, if the borrower has a property with an appraised value of $100,000 and the loan on the property is $85,000, the lender will generally not consider the property as additional collateral.

When one or more additional properties are offered as collateral, it is called *multiple collateral* or sometimes *cross-collateralization*. Often in a multiple mortgage there will be offered not only the properties that are to be mortgaged but additional properties as collateral to secure the mortgage. The lender will then not release any of the properties offered as collateral until the mortgage has been paid in full, unless previously agreed to at the time the mortgage is made. For instance, the lender may agree that once the mortgage is paid down to 60 percent of the original loan amount certain properties will be released as collateral to the mortgage.

COLLATERAL MORTGAGE

A collateral mortgage is a form of a conventional mortgage. The owner of real estate creates a collateral mortgage and at the same time executes a collateral mortgage note. In addition, a promissory note is executed, usually in favor of any future holder. The collateral mortgage is paraphed ne varietur by a notary to identify the note with the act of mortgage. The collateral mortgage is recorded in the public records.

This type of mortgage is made to secure loans that may be made in the future and pledged to the creditor to secure the indebtedness up to the amount of the collateral mortgage. The actual debt is evidenced by a "hand note." The hand note states the actual amount of the loan, the interest rate, and the terms of repayment. If the borrower defaults, the creditor may enforce the collateral mortgage note that is pledged to secure the hand note and foreclose against the real estate mortgage.

For example, if the borrower pledges a collateral mortgage against real estate he or she owns in the amount of $100,000 and executes two hand notes in the amount of $20,000 each at different times, the actual debt is only $40,000.

COMMISSION

Commission is sometimes referred to as a *broker* or *realtor fee* that is paid out of the seller's proceeds unless otherwise provided for in the purchase agreement. A commission is usually expressed as a percentage of the sale price and is always a negotiated fee between the agent and the party, generally the seller, who is to pay the fee. The commission is always paid to the real estate company or broker who then pays the agent an agreed upon percentage of the commission collected. Most often the commission is paid by the seller and may be split with a portion paid to a cobroker even though the cobroker represented the buyer as his or her exclusive agent.

The commission may also be a flat fee or a graduated percentage fee as opposed to a fixed percentage of the total sale price.

COMPARABLES

Comparables is a term most often used in the appraisal of real estate. A trained professional appraiser will use comparable properties that have sold in the process of establishing the value of a property to be sold or financed. Comparables represent as near as possible a mirror image of the subject property. They are located in the same area or an area that is substantially the same as the other property. The comparables will as far as possible have the same lot size as well as the same number of bedrooms, bathrooms, and square feet of living area. Other factors important in a comparable are the presence of a carport or garage and its capacity, whether the house has a fireplace and how many, whether the house is located on a lake or beach or near a railroad track, whether the property has ever flooded, whether it is in an area where similar properties are deteriorating, and whether it is located on a high-traffic street.

Other factors that must be compared are obsolescence, deferred maintenance, condition of the neighborhood, location of the property such as a corner or interior lot, and best use. When properties are compared, an appraiser must also consider eye appeal. Although this is a subjective term, it implies whether or not a majority of potential buyers will find this property generally appealing. In highly specialized properties, the search for comparables may reach beyond the general vicinity into a much broader geographical area. Finding recent sales of comparables for unique properties requires a skilled and experienced appraiser.

Generally, a comparable is considered only if the sale of the property has occurred within the past twelve months, unless a time adjustment is applied.

CONDOMINIUM

The individual ownership of a portion of a building is called a *condominium*. Generally, a condominium property has numerous units all individually owned. All owners possess a deed to their property, pay their own taxes independently, and may sell, lease, or mortgage the unit they own. All halls, lobbies, elevators, public bathrooms, and the land underneath are considered common areas and are owned jointly among all the owners. These rules and all others are spelled out under a condominium regime that all owners are bound to upon buying into the property. This document provides for the maintenance and upkeep of all common areas, including parking lots and elevators, and distributes this cost among all the owners in the form of a monthly fee. In general, all owners have a vote in any changes to the governing rules, and the process for making changes would be outlined in the original document.

Condominium developments have for the most part been associated with residential property, but it is now an increasingly popular method to distribute the cost of office and industrial buildings. Condominiums can be built new or converted from existing structures. A key difference in condominium buildings is that every unit must be registered separately with the city/county/government and have separate taxes and utility meters. For example, an owner of a ten-year-old office building would like to sell the building for maximum profit but still keep his or her small suite of offices for personal use. By registering the building with the city as a condominium development and providing the extra utility meters for every unit, he or she incurs significant expenses. However, the total price received for selling all of the smaller condominium units should be higher than the price for the total building, and the owner can retain the space he or she is currently using.

CONFIDENTIALITY AGREEMENT

If a seller is asked to provide information regarding his or her business that he or she considers confidential, the seller may request the buyer to sign a confidentiality agreement prior to providing such information. Sometimes a buyer or a seller may request that the terms of their agreement be kept confidential prior to closing after which the sale becomes public knowledge through placing the deed in the public records.

Terms of a confidentiality agreement vary according to the requirements of a buyer or seller. However, in the sale of a business, the seller may require confidentiality for a limited time such as twelve months or even longer if for some reason the sale does not close. In such cases there is always a penalty for disclosure. The penalty may be expressed in a dollar amount or simply provide the seller with legal recourse if the confidential information is revealed to anyone other than those specified in the agreement. Confidential information is often required by the buyer to determine what offer he or she is willing to make and must be revealed even before an offer to purchase is made.

For example, a business may be required to reveal the gross sales, expenses, and even a customer list. Without a confidentiality agreement and provided the sale does not close, a prospective buyer may use such information to the detriment of the seller. This is especially true if the prospective buyer is a competitor of the seller.

Sometimes a prospective buyer is required to sign the confidentiality agreement before it is ever revealed which business it is that is for sale because a seller may not wish to make public to the employees that he or she is interested in selling.

CONSIDERATION

The price agreed upon between a buyer and seller for the sale of real estate is called the *consideration*. In any transfer of property, there must be a consideration agreed to by both parties. A purchase agreement will always state the price agreed to by buyer and seller, which is the consideration.

The consideration is usually stated in a dollar amount, but there may also be an exchange of property, company stock, another item of value, or any combination of these. For the transfer to be legal, there must be a consideration.

For example, a seller may agree to exchange for another property with or without other consideration. A business may be purchased for a consideration of a dollar amount plus stock in the purchasing company. It may also include stock options that grant the seller the right to purchase additional stock in the purchasing company in the future generally at a agreed upon price.

Also, the agreed upon consideration for the purchase may not always be the final consideration for the property. For instance, if a buyer agrees to purchase a property and in the course of due diligence discovers structural damage to the building, the cost to repair such damage may be deducted from the final consideration, with the buyer taking the property "as is."

CONSTRUCTIVE NOTICE

As part of the public records doctrine, all parties are held to have received constructive notice through the recorded instruments entered into the public records as affects real estate. One cannot take a single instrument from the public records and disregard the other instruments that are recorded. The records must be considered as a whole, and third parties are bound by what the entire record reveals as relates to a particular property.

The search of public records is done in chronological order and includes all instruments filed into the records as a history of the recorded documents for a property. It is the responsibility of the third party to accurately research all instruments that affect the property, and the buyer is considered to have purchased at his or her own risk any property if the entirety of the records are not properly researched.

CONTINGENCY

A contingency is a specific condition that must occur for a contract to be valid. Most real estate purchase agreements contain at least one condition, often many, that allows a buyer to make an offer on property based on a set of assumptions. For example, a buyer may want to pay $200,000 for an office building as long as the roof, air conditioners, and plumbing have no defects and the bank will agree to finance the building. In the purchase agreement, the buyer would write four contingencies, three requiring the roof, air conditioners, and plumbing to pass inspection and one requiring the bank to finance the property. If a seller agrees to these terms, then the contract is valid, and, should the bank decide not to loan the money or if there is a leak in the roof, the buyer would not be legally bound to buy the property and would receive the deposit or earnest money back.

Contingencies can be written for anything and everything. Buyers may add a contingency that their own property must sell before they purchase the new property. Financial rates and terms, environmental studies, owner financing, and approval of leases are some of the more common contingencies found in purchase agreements. However, all contingencies are merely a request for the seller to agree. If a seller receives two purchase agreements for a similar price, he is more likely to agree to and sign the one with the fewest contingencies.

CONTRACT FOR DEED

Under this type of sale, sometimes called a *land contract sale* or *bond for deed,* a seller will sell the property and finance all or a portion of the purchase but not deliver the deed to the purchaser until sometime in the future when the total purchase price is paid. The purchaser will generally pay a portion of the purchase price when the contract is signed. Thereafter, the purchaser will pay installments as called for in the contract until the entire purchase price is paid, at which time the seller will deed the property to the purchaser.

If the purchaser defaults on the agreed upon payments, the seller may cancel the contract. This type of contract protects the seller's interest in the unpaid balance and provides, according to the terms of the contract, a foreclosure procedure much more simple then if the seller had deeded the property to the purchaser and then had to foreclose.

The buyer is obligated to deliver the deed to the property provided the purchaser completes his obligations in accordance with the contract. There are companies that for a small fee will collect the payments from the purchaser, pay the taxes and insurance, and forward the balance of the payment to the seller. They will hold the deed from the seller until the terms of the contract are fulfilled by the purchaser and then deliver the deed.

COUNTEROFFER

When an offer to purchase is received by a seller for less than the asking price with or without special contingencies or conditions, the seller may accept the offer, counter it, or reject it. If the offer is countered, the seller may change the purchase agreement or other conditions to what is acceptable and initial by each change and then sign the agreement. The agreement is then binding on the buyer only if the changes are initialed by him.

A more appropriate method of countering a purchase agreement is to use a counteroffer form to list the changes to the offer that the seller wishes to make. The seller will then sign the counteroffer form and submit it to the buyer for acceptance by signing it.

COVENANTS

A covenant is any agreement between parties outlining the relationship in legal terms and actions promised to take place or to refrain from doing. Covenants have an unlimited number of uses, but for real estate purposes the restrictive covenants on land are the most important. Restrictive covenants can be placed on any property and may specifically prohibit certain uses, structures, styles, or businesses. By registering the land and restrictive covenants at the courthouse, an individual may continually control certain aspects of the land for an indefinite amount of time. Anything may be restricted as long as it has not been declared discriminatory by the U.S. Supreme Court. For example, one wants to sell land to a city and have agreed to a good price because the land will be used for a children's home. By including a covenant in the deed to the land stating that the property must be used for "community social services" one can be sure that one's intentions are carried out.

CROSS-EASEMENT

In the development of a large retail center where there is more than one owner of the site and the properties are adjacent, the owners may agree to a cross-easement for easy access from one owner's property to the other. Such an agreement is made so that both owners have ease of access across each other's property to accommodate customers or shoppers.

With a cross-easement agreement, sometimes referred to as an REA (reciprocal easement agreement), each owner agrees not to place an impediment such as a barrier that would prevent the ease of access from one property to the other. Such an easement is permanent and obligates any future holder of the property to honor such an agreement. A cross-easement agreement may or may not include the open parking of any customers or shoppers on the other owner's property. For example, if a restaurant purchases property that does not have adequate parking space, the seller may grant a cross-easement access, which includes the right to use existing parking to meet the restaurant's requirements. Such an agreement may also be required to meet parking requirements set forth by the city or another governing entity.

CURATIVE WORK

Curative work is a legal term that describes the efforts of an attorney to cure problems that may exist with the title. Such work is required prior to closing in order for the buyer to receive a clear title. A title to the property may have a problem, sometimes referred to as a *cloud* on the title.

Curative work may be as simple as having a previous owner who may have had an interest in the property but who failed to sign the deed sign an affidavit declaring that he or she agreed to the sale. It may require the legal resolution of an encroachment issue in which a driveway or building encroaches on the property being sold. Whatever the legal issues that prevent a clear title from being passed to the new owner, curative work is required to ensure the new buyer a clear title.

A purchase agreement will usually grant the seller a period of time to clear the title if any curative work is required. If the curative work cannot be completed in the time period provided, the agreement may be canceled by the buyer unless an extension is granted.

CUSTOMER

In real estate terminology, a buyer is referred to as the *customer.* The customer is the prospect or buyer who looks for a property to purchase. A real estate agent refers to this prospect as a customer. As in other situations, the customer develops a relationship with the agent. That relationship between the agent and the customer is based on professionalism, trust, integrity, knowledge of the market, and the ability of the agent to provide the customer with adequate service to meet his or her needs and desires.

As in any other customer/agent situation, the relationship is not exclusive. An individual may be the customer of more than one agent in the process of finding the right property. Also, customers may change agents at their discretion if they determine the service received is not meeting their expectations or for any other reason. The term *customer* in real estate is used in a broad sense to define any person with whom the agent is working to find a property.

DATION

Dation is a transaction in which a debtor returns the property to the lender who is willing to accept the property in full payment of the debt. The dation is completed upon execution of the instrument that returns the property to the creditor.

A price is required to complete the dation; it is the amount that the creditor accepts as full payment of the debt. A dation requires the mutual consent of debtor and creditor. A debtor cannot require a creditor to accept the property in dation for payment of the debt.

For example, if a debtor owes $10,000 on a property that is valued at $50,000, the creditor may readily accept a dation as full payment of the debt.

DEBT SERVICE

An item identified as an expense factor in any analysis of an investment property is debt service and includes the interest and principal payment required to meet the mortgage payment. Debt service is the amount required for the periodic payment to cover interest on and retirement of the remaining principal balance of the mortgage. Debt service may also be referred to as the *mortgage debt service.*

The debt service on an investment property is not constant in the case of a floating interest rate, which can change monthly, or in the case of a mortgage with periodic adjustments in the interest rate, which can occur annually or at periods agreed to in the mortgage, such as after every three years.

In the calculation of expenses allocated to an investment property and a projection of present and future expenses, any adjustment in the interest rate must be considered in future expense calculations. However, since any increase in the interest rate may not be known until

Concise Encyclopedia of Real Estate Business Terms
© 2006 by The Haworth Press, Inc. All rights reserved.
doi:10.1300/5637_04

such time as the adjustment, an investor will need to use his or her best judgment in the calculation of future debt service costs when projecting future return on the investment. Debt service in adjustable rate mortgages may significantly impact the return on investment especially in times of rising interest rates.

DEFAULT

Any failure to fulfill the terms of an agreement is considered a default. In real estate, default is most often used to describe the failure of a borrower to meet the terms, especially the periodic payment of principal and interest on a mortgage. When this occurs, the borrower is declared in default of the agreed upon repayment terms as specified in the mortgage agreement. The lender may, at his or her option, agree to postpone declaring the borrower in default of the mortgage for a period of time if payments are not made. However, if the borrower cannot in time bring all payments of principal and interest current, the lender will declare the borrower in default of the mortgage.

When the lender declares the borrower in default, he or she may exercise several options available in the mortgage agreement. The lender may be lenient and restructure the loan with payments that the borrower can meet. The lender may exercise the option to call the remaining principal on the mortgage due and payable immediately. If the borrower cannot meet this demand by the lender, the lender may take possession of the property and offer it for sale. When sold, the lender may seek recourse against the borrower in the form of a deficiency judgment for any difference between the amount the property was sold for and the amount of the remaining balance on the mortgage. If a deficiency judgment is granted by a court of law, the lender may seek to collect the deficiency amount from any other assets of the borrower.

DEFECT

A building that has a structural deficiency may be considered a defect. If a defect is present and the seller or agent has knowledge of such a defect, it is required by real estate law to be revealed to the buyer prior to the closing. The buyer can then decide to require the seller to remedy the defect prior to closing, accept a payment or reduced price to remedy the defect himself or herself, accept the property in "as is" condition, cancel the purchase agreement, or proceed to close.

If the buyer discovers the defect during the period of "due diligence," the buyer may also require the seller to correct the defect, accept a reduced price, accept the property in "as is" condition, or cancel the agreement. These options are almost always provided for as remedies for a defect in the purchase agreement.

If a defect is discovered by the buyer after closing, the buyer must prove the seller and/or his or her agent had knowledge of the defect prior to closing. In such cases, the buyer must seek recourse through a court of law and prove that the seller or the seller's agent had knowledge of the defect prior to closing and did not reveal the defect to the buyer.

If a property is sold "as is" and the seller states in a property disclosure form any and all defects of which he or she has knowledge and the buyer purchases the property with full disclosure of all known defects, the buyer has no recourse after the closing even though additional defects may be disclosed.

For example, if the seller discloses that the property has a cracked slab and the buyer proceeds to close with full knowledge of the defect, the buyer has no recourse against the seller after the closing.

DEMOGRAPHICS

The detailed information of a specified geographic area is called its *demographics*. This information is used by retailers, restaurants, and other businesses to determine the size of their market potential. Demographic studies may be for a trade area, a zip code area, a city, a county, or within a specified distance from the property. Often a radius of three, five, ten, fifteen, or thirty miles is used for the latter option.

Demographics include the population, the number of households, and the per capita and average household incomes. More detailed information may be included, such as the number and percentages of Caucasians, African Americans, Hispanics, and Asians. Other information included in more extensive demographics is the number of retail workers, and the per capita retail sales broken into types of sales, such as cars, grocers, general merchandise, and tires. Age groups are generally included in categories of infants to five years old, six years to ten years old, eleven years to seventeen years old, eighteen years to twenty-five years old, etc.

The price of homes in the given area may be included, with categories from $20,000 to $1 million broken into ten or twelve groupings. Income information may also be included, from 0 to $500,000 and up, specified in eight to ten categories.

Much of the information is gathered from the ten-year censuses conducted by the federal government. Most demographic studies show the last census population, the previous census population, and the projection for the next census based on the expected increase or decrease in population.

There are a number of companies that provide these studies at a cost per radius covered. For instance, a study for one radius, such as three miles from the specified location, may be one price, and a two-, three-, five-, and ten-mile radius study may be more expensive. One can also purchase a computer disk that will contain information by zip codes for one or more states.

Demographic studies are generally updated after each census to provide the most recent information.

DEPRECIATION

Depreciation is the lessening of value due to age, use, etc. All improvements, whether to homes, apartments, office buildings, or shopping centers, in time will show the effects of age, obsolescence, use, and deterioration. This lessening of value may be countered by rising real estate values greater than the depreciation.

The Internal Revenue Service has recognized depreciation as a cost in the ownership of all types of investment property. This recognition has established a thirty-nine-year life for investment property and allows an annual equal depreciation from the purchase price of that portion of the price attributed to the improvements. Depreciation is deducted as a cost from the net profit each year. However, upon the sale of the property, the depreciation allowed must be recaptured in whole or part by the seller.

For example, if an investment property has been held by the seller for 13 years and depreciated each year from the $100,000 value of the improvements, the seller must recapture $33,000 of the depreciation in whole or in part. An accountant or certified public accountant can best calculate the amount of depreciation the seller must recapture.

DESIGNATED AGENCY

Many states now require that a real estate professional be a designated agent for the buyer or seller. However, with permission, he or she may also act as a dual agent in a transaction representing both the buyer and the seller. A designated agent represents either the buyer or the seller in a transaction. By acting as a designated agent, he or she represents the interest of the seller (the client) or the buyer (the customer). As such, the agent is required to represent only the best interest of the party he or she is representing and cannot represent both parties in the transaction.

Designated agency is designed to clarify who the agent represents in the transaction. The agent's responsibility and loyalty are only to the party the agent is representing in the transaction. For example, if the agent is representing the seller and the seller tells the agent he or she is not willing to reduce the price of the property but actually would accept a lesser price, the agent is not permitted to reveal this to the agent of the buyer unless specifically permitted, preferably in writing, to the buyer's agent. On the other hand, if the agent represents the buyer and is given an offer less than the listed price but told if not accepted he or she would be willing to raise the offer to a higher price, the agent cannot reveal this to the seller's designated agent.

Designated agency is an attempt to clarify whose interest the agent is representing. In the past, there has existed much confusion on the part of both buyers and sellers as to who represented their interest.

DISCRIMINATION

As defined in the Fair Housing Act of 1968, most forms of discrimination are prohibited by federal law. Generally defined as a refusal to sell to or otherwise penalize a buyer or lessee for reasons of race, gender, creed, age, or handicap, discrimination in other forms may exist. For example, if a buyer or lessee has two children and wishes to rent a three-bedroom apartment that is not listed as exclusively for senior citizens, a violation of the Fair Housing Act may be considered if he or she is refused.

The Fair Housing Act was enacted by federal legislation to prevent all forms of discrimination, particularly in real estate, sales or leases. It is the recognition that an otherwise qualified buyer or lessee may be refused a sale or lease due to the prejudice of the seller or lessor. If an agent does not or will not show all houses that meet the requirements of the buyer or lessee and either steers the buyer or lessee or refuses to show property in a particular area he or she may be charged with discrimination under the Fair Housing Act. Agents must make clear their obligations with regard to the Fair Housing Act to any seller who lists property with them for sale or lease.

DISMEMBERMENT OF OWNERSHIP

The rights of ownership can be divided into three categories: use, enjoyment, and disposition. Each is vested in a different person, as in the case of usufruct. A person may possess ownership and usufruct, referred to as *naked ownership*. However, the ownership and disposition may be vested in one party, and the use and enjoyment may be vested in another, called *usufruct*.

For example, party A may own the property. Party B may have the use and enjoyment for life through a usufruct. However, when party B dies the usufruct reverts to party A, who then possesses naked ownership.

DOMINATE ESTATE

An easement that has been granted is referred to as the *dominate estate*. When an easement is granted, it may affect the value and or the marketability of a property. Many easements are granted in perpetuity, or without end, such as a utility easement for the purpose of installing utility lines. The owner of such an easement has the right to enter the easement to make necessary repairs or add additional construction. If the easement is granted to allow the owner to remove something for profit, it is referred to as an *ancillary easement* as in the case of removing dirt or gravel.

When the easement is granted for a specific purpose only and can only be used for that particular purpose, it is referred to as an *affirmative easement*. In such cases, the easement may have a limited term, ending at a specified time. At the end of such a term, the easement disappears, and the servient estate regains the use of the property designated for such an easement.

An easement, or dominate estate, can affect the value of the servient estate especially if the land use changes and the easement prevents the intended use of the property. For instance, if an easement for access has been granted to an adjoining property owner and the owner wishes to build over the easement, the value of the property may be diminished. The dominate estate easement has then reduced the value of the servient estate.

DOWN PAYMENT

The down payment is a portion of the purchase price paid at closing that represents the buyer's equity in the property. The down payment does not always have to be cash. In some instances equity in other property or other assets are pledged as the down payment. For example, if the property sells and appraises for $100,000 and the loan to value ratio is 80 percent, the buyer will need to place 20 percent or $20,000 as a cash down payment or some other form of asset acceptable to the lender.

If the property appraises for much higher than the loan required, the lender may agree to waive the down payment and consider his security in the property as adequate for the mortgage. In rare cases the lender may consider the net worth of the buyer sufficient that a down payment is not required.

At the closing the price paid to the seller will be a combination of the loan proceeds and the down payment plus any security deposit placed in escrow at the time the purchase agreement is signed to apply toward the purchase price. Together these amounts will pay the seller in full.

DUAL AGENCY

Most states now require that a real estate agent who wishes to represent both buyer and seller have both parties acknowledge such in writing. The agent will have the seller sign his or her acknowledgement at the time the property is listed. The buyer is required to sign when the agent begins the process of working with the buyer to find a property or in some states upon first contact.

Prior to dual agency agreements there existed much confusion as to who the agent was representing. Many buyers were under the impression that an agent represented them when in fact the agent was representing the seller. Many buyers who after the sale discovered the agent was in fact representing the seller filed litigation for nondisclosure.

Dual agency agreements do not generally address the issue of who pays the commission to the agent. Therefore, a dual agent may represent both buyer and seller with only the seller responsible for payment of the commission.

A dual agent owes a fiduciary responsibility to both buyer and seller. The agent agrees to not reveal to the other party any confidential information. For example, if the seller has listed the property at $100,000 but tells the dual agent that he or she will accept $80,000, the dual agent cannot reveal this information to the buyer without violating his or her responsibility to the seller.

DUE DILIGENCE

In a purchase agreement, the buyer may be granted a period of time in which to complete his or her inspection of the property, called the *due diligence* period. This period is usually thirty to ninety days. During this time, the buyer may enter the property or ask vendors to go onto the property to inspect in areas of their expertise. Systems inspectors may include a heat and air conditioning service company, a plumber, an electrician, a structural engineer, or a roofer. The vendor will then provide the buyer with a written report of the inspection.

The buyer may also choose to use a property inspection company qualified to inspect the property in a large number of areas and provide a comprehensive detailed report. In the sale of commercial property, an environmental testing company is often used to complete a

Phase I or Phase II report. In a Phase I report, the historical use of the property is investigated to determine if its use may be cause for contamination. In a Phase II report, the actual soil and construction materials are tested to determine if there is soil, groundwater, or construction material contamination.

In recent years, concern about mold has expanded the search to include specialists who will determine if mold exists and, if so, recommend a remedy. This is a growing area of concern in certain areas of the country.

If any of the inspectors reveal problems with operating systems, structures, or contamination, the buyer reports them to the seller during the due diligence period. Generally, the seller is then given a specified time to remedy the problems. Depending on the agreement signed by the buyer and seller, the seller may have the option to remedy any problems or to cancel the sale. In some commercial purchase agreements, the warranty of the seller extends beyond the closing. In this case, should the buyer discover problems subsequent to the closing, the seller remains liable even after the closing.

DUE ON SALE CLAUSE

Most mortgages contain a clause that stipulates that if the property is sold to another person without the written consent of the mortgage holder, the mortgagee may call the mortgage due and payable. However, the sale of one co-owner to another co-owner when both are liable for the mortgage does not trigger the due on sale clause. A community property sale from one spouse to the other where full ownership is acquired and the acquiring spouse receives complete ownership and assumes the mortgage debt does not violate the due on sale clause.

DURRETT RULE

The Durrett rule was established by the U.S. Court of Appeals in Durrett v. Washington National Insurance Company and deals with foreclosure sales conducted within one year of the debtor filing for bankruptcy. The ruling affects a foreclosure sale when the debtor does not receive a reasonably equivalent value for his or her property.

In such cases the sale can be set aside by the bankruptcy court. The court in this case decided that a reasonably equivalent value of the property was 70 percent or more of the market value at the time of foreclosure. If the sale is less than 70 percent of value it can be set aside as a fraudulent transfer.

As a result of the Durrett rule most creditors will bid at least 70 percent of the value of the real estate to avoid the sale being set aside should the debtor later file for bankruptcy. Many title opinions and title insurance policies will make a "fraudulent conveyance" exception if the property was acquired through foreclosure.

EARNEST MONEY

The deposit given by a purchaser at the time of executing a purchase agreement on a property is always considered as earnest money unless stipulated otherwise. An earnest money deposit provides the seller or purchaser the right to cancel the contract. The purchaser may cancel the agreement by forfeiting the deposit. The seller may cancel the agreement by returning to the purchaser double the amount of the deposit.

A purchase agreement may negate the presumption that a deposit is earnest money by adding language in the agreement that the deposit is not to be considered earnest money. A more popular method of negating the effect of a deposit considered as earnest money is by providing the seller or purchaser with a specific performance clause in the agreement.

Present law is somewhat unclear on the payment of option money when the payment is made subsequent to the exercise of the option. For example, if party A grants an option to party B and provides that the deposit will be made after party B exercises the option, then it is unclear whether the deposit is earnest money or not absent specific language in the option agreement.

ECONOMIC FEASIBILITY

The evaluation of a property for its potential for return on investment is called *economic feasibility*. When referring to new construction, it is the construction cost, both soft costs such as architectural and engineering fees, and hard costs, such as material, labor, and land costs. When the total cost is added up, this becomes the cost to build. This cost is then financed and amortized, which is a large part of the feasibility evaluation. To this cost is added taxes, insurance, maintenance re-

Concise Encyclopedia of Real Estate Business Terms
© 2006 by The Haworth Press. Inc. All rights reserved.
doi:10.1300/5637_05

serve, vacancy projection, management cost, landscape maintenance, and any other related expenses.

These costs are then balanced against the projected income both new and in the future. A pro forma is prepared that shows the estimated current income and projected out, generally for five years. The projection takes into consideration future increases in both income and expenses. Generally future income increases are a factor of inflation. Future expenses, such as principal and interest payments, if based on a fixed rate mortgage, will remain unchanged. However, if financed on an adjustable rate mortgage, increases must be projected based on an increased interest rate. Other expenses such as maintenance must be increased as the property ages, while inflationary increases are added for all other costs.

When all the above factors are considered in a pro forma, it will determine if the investment has economic feasibility. Most investors will base their decision to invest in a property, whether new or existing, based on this projection. Sometimes a property can be made economically feasible that otherwise would not be by using financing that is interest only in the early years or one that includes a mortgage that is not fully amortized with interest only on the unamortized balance.

By determining economic feasibility, an investor can evaluate his or her desired return on investment weighed against the risk involved and the cost associated with the investment.

ENCROACHMENT

The term *encroachment* means to trespass on the rights of another party. In real estate the most prolific form of trespass is when a party constructs across the property line and onto the property of the adjacent property owner. Such construction may be permanent, as in a home or a building, or more temporary such as a fence.

A property survey will reveal any encroachments across property lines. When a permanent structure has been constructed as an encroachment, the usual solution is for the encroached upon property owner to sell that portion of the property to the encroaching party. However, in extreme cases the party encroached upon may demand that the structure be removed.

ENCUMBRANCES

The right of a party other than the owner in property is an encumbrance. This right may actually increase or decrease the value of the property and most often is permanent but may also be temporary. The term means to burden something. The most popular encumbrances are restrictions, easements, and reservations.

Although an encumbrance may burden the property, it does not prevent the seller from conveying the property to a buyer with clear title. However, any encumbrances to the property will be passed to the new owner and as such restricts the new owner's property rights. For example, if the property is encumbered with a twenty-five-foot utility easement, the property owner may not place a building over the easement even though he or she owns the property the easement is on. Therefore, the encumbrance reduces the property owner's rights to certain uses of the property.

EQUITY

The debt on a property subtracted from the market value of the property leaves the equity. Market value is usually determined by an appraisal—an evaluation based on comparable properties that have sold in the same geographic area within the past twelve months adjusted for any existing differences. Adjustments can include, for instance, subtracted value for additional age or added value for larger lot size.

Although estimated value can be determined by an appraisal, the actual value can only be determined by what a buyer is willing to pay. Once a true value is determined, one factor that determines equity has been established.

Another factor is the remaining debt against the property. This is determined by securing a mortgage pay-off balance, which will show the actual amount currently due to liquidate the debt with the mortgagee. This will include any unpaid interest, late fees, and interest penalties assessed.

A third factor that determines true equity is any deferred maintenance required to sell the property. This is a factor often overlooked by a seller when calculating equity. In some instances, substantial repairs required may reduce the actual equity by several thousand dollars. This could include a cracked slab, painting, roof replacement, or other such expensive items. Many of these items will not add value to the property but will provide salability.

ESCALATION CLAUSE

An escalation clause is a clause in a legal document such as a lease that provides for an increase in payments to a lessor under certain pre-agreed upon events. Generally, an escalation clause is inserted to protect the lessor from an increase in expenses that the lessor has agreed to pay. The lease may state that if the lessor experiences an increase in taxes, insurance, maintenance, management, or utility costs, he or she may charge the lessee his pro rata share of these costs based on the square footage of the lessee's occupancy to the total square footage available within the building.

An escalation clause is designed to protect the lessor from increases in his or her cost to operate a building or property. Generally, a mortgage holder will insist that such a clause be included in the lease to give more security in the event the borrower experiences increases in the operating cost of the property that could endanger his or her ability to pay the monthly mortgage note. To affect the escalation clause, the lessor may have to provide proof to the lessee of the increase in costs related to operating the property.

An escalation clause may also be placed in a mortgage to call for all principal and past due interest to be paid immediately provided the borrower has defaulted on his agreed payments. In this event, the borrower must find a new source of financing or risk losing the property to the mortgagee.

ESCHEAT

The government possesses the power to secure clear title to a property from an individual after death if it is determined there is no will and no heirs. This governmental power is called the *power of escheat.* Without a will to place the ownership of the property into the ownership of another entity or individual and without any heirs to which the ownership is passed, the government possesses the power to place ownership in the appropriate governmental entity. Without such powers and under the conditions mentioned, the property would be without ownership and an ascertainable chain of title.

Ownership through the powers of escheat grants the government all the rights of any legitimate owner. For example, the government may then pass the title to another owner through the sale of the property.

ESTATE AT WILL

The occupancy of a property for an undetermined period of time that can be terminated by one or both parties is termed *estate at will.* Occupancy of a building or land under such an agreement is somewhat rare; however, under some circumstances it may meet the needs of both lessee and lessor. Because the agreement can be cancelled at will, generally by either party or occasionally by agreement of both parties, the term is left indefinite. If cancellation is at the discretion of the lessor, the lessee is left without a term of occupancy and can be asked to vacate at any time.

Generally, such an agreement is conditioned on the required action of the lessee. Such condition may require the lessee, for example, to maintain the property in good condition. If the lessor determines the lessee is not maintaining as expected, he or she can, at will, terminate the agreement. Under other circumstances, the lessor may wish to sell the property but agrees to a lease until such time as a buyer can be secured. Upon securing a buyer, the lessor will then issue a notice to vacate to the lessee. Another example is the lessee who seeks a temporary location until a more suitable facility can be acquired or a new building can be constructed. In such an agreement, the estate at will is at the discretion of the lessee, and he or she may occupy until such time as another location is secured or new construction is completed.

ESTOPPEL

Estoppel is a legal term used in real estate to establish facts that cannot later be refuted. A document called an *estoppel certificate* is used to establish the facts regarding a lease to be signed by the tenant when an investment property is sold. By having the tenant sign an estoppel certificate attesting to the terms and conditions of the lease, the tenant cannot later deny or attempt to change the conditions of the lease.

Estoppel legally prevents someone from asserting, saying, or acting different from his or her previous assertions. The estoppel document establishes the facts in a matter whether, it is a lease, option, buy/sell agreement, etc., that cannot be changed at a later date. For example, if a person signed a ten-year option to purchase a particular parcel of land and the land owner dies, the option holder may want the administrator of the estate to sign an estoppel certificate with regard to the terms and conditions of the option agreement.

ET AL

Et al is a Latin term that means "and others." Often this term will be used in a purchase or listing agreement in which there are numerous owners. The agreement may be placed in one partner's name followed by et al. However, even though the agreement lists only one name, all owners or purchasers must sign for the agreement to be legally binding.

ET UX

Et ux is a Latin term that means "and wife." An agreement that names only the husband may be followed by et ux to indicate that his wife is part of the agreement. Even though only the husband is named, the wife must sign the agreement to make it binding on both parties.

EVICTION

Eviction is the process by which a lessor terminates the lease agreement with a lessee and regains possession of the space or property. Generally the lease is terminated by the lessor for nonpayment of rent. However, a breach of other provisions of the lease may be cause for the lessor to terminate the lease even though the rent is paid as required by the lease.

For example, if the lease has a nondisturbance clause for other tenants and the lessee creates a situation that disturbs other tenants and after a written notice from the lessor to cease the disturbance continues, the lessor may evict the lessee.

If the lessor has allowed the lessee to consistently pay the rent late, a notice of default must be given by the lessor prior to any attempt to evict. A notice to vacate must be delivered to the tenant with a stipulated number of days to vacate. If the lessee fails to vacate, the lessor can file a rule for possession. If the rent is then paid in full and accepted by the lessor, the eviction is voided.

EXCLUSIVE LISTING

An exclusive listing precludes the owner from listing the property with another agent during the listing term but does not exclude the owner from selling the property himself or herself. If the owner finds a buyer during the term of the listing, the agent is not due a commission under this type of agreement. Generally this type of agreement will provide protection to the agent for any prospect whom the agent has shown the property or presented information to and thereby becomes the procuring source of the sale.

The exclusive listing agreement will include the property description, price of the property, term of the listing, and any other provisions agreed to by the seller and the agent.

The agent may advertise the property for sale but if a buyer goes directly to the seller without contacting the agent the agent will be due no commission per the terms of the listing agreement. The agent is only due a commission if he or she is the procuring cause of the sale.

EXCLUSIVE RIGHT TO SELL

This listing agreement grants the agent the exclusive right to sell the property during the term of the agreement. All prospects are to be referred to the agent by the owner should the owner be contacted by a prospective buyer. This type of agreement may also specify a number of days after the listing expires that the agent is protected should a prospective buyer contact the owner that the agent has become the procuring cause of an eventual sale. The agent is best protected by providing the seller with a list of prospects with whom he or she has made contact.

This agreement will include the description of the property, the selling price, the term of the agreement, and any other terms to which the owner and agent may agree. The agent is due an agreed upon commission if the property sells during the term of the listing regardless of whether sold by the agent or the owner unless the owner and agent have agreed to exclude certain prospective buyers by name in the agreement to whom the owner may sell the property without paying the agent a commission. Generally the exclusion of named prospective buyers from the listing agreement is limited to a number of days from the execution of the agreement. For example, if the owner excluded Mr. Smith for thirty days as a prospective buyer and Mr. Smith decided to enter into an purchase agreement forty-five days after the listing agreement was signed, the agent would be due his commission.

EXECUTION

Execution is a legal term denoting that the proper signatures of all parties to the agreement have been secured. This may require only the signature of the parties or the signature plus one or even two witnesses or even that the signatures of all parties be notarized. Until all parties to an agreement have been secured in the manner required, the document is not considered to be fully executed and binding on all parties to the agreement.

For example, if a purchase agreement requires the signature of buyer and seller plus a witness plus the initial of both parties to any agreed upon changes plus the buyer and seller to initial that they have read each page, until all of this is completed the document is not binding or considered fully executed. A purchase agreement that is not fully executed may leave either party an option to later void the agreement.

Full execution of a legal document is required before it becomes legally binding on all parties to the agreement. Without full execution, the agreement may later be voided by either party.

EXPROPRIATION

Expropriation is the right by law given to public entities to take possession of property from the owner for public use. The term is synonymous with *eminent domain,* which is used also to describe the right of government to take possession of property from the owner. The law gives the government the right to take privately held property for public use or for use by public entities. Without the right of expropriation, roads and highways, along with many other public projects, could not be built.

Under the right of expropriation an offer is made to the owner; however, if a price cannot be agreed to, an appraisal of its fair market value is made. If the owner is unwilling to accept the appraised price, the property is expropriated. This process can take several months to complete. There is also an expedited appropriation called a *quick-take expropriation.* Following an unsuccessful attempt to purchase the property, the government entity may take possession and proceed with construction without waiting for an appraisal or the courts to settle the final price.

Expropriation is often an unpleasant procedure but essential in order that a few property owners do not prevent construction of roads, highways, etc., for the public use. The final decision regarding the amount paid for the property is settled in a court of law. However, the price paid is usually the appraised value unless there is special circumstance that adds value.

EXTRAPOLATION

Making a calculation into the future based on current data is called *extrapolation.* Extrapolation from current data is the process used to predict future performance.

This process is frequently used to predict the future performance of an investment property. For example, if the existing and past performance data of a shopping center shows that the rents have increased by 5 percent per year on average and the expenses have increased by 3 percent on average, we can extrapolate from these data to project the performance of the investment into the future.

This procedure can also be used to project the future performance of new development. If the data from the market area show the current rent of comparable properties to be $15.00 per square foot rent for new office space and rents have increased by 3 percent per year, we can use the extrapolation process to project what the new development rents will be upon completion and project what rents will be in the future.

F

FAIR MARKET VALUE

The price for which a seller is willing to sell a parcel of real estate and a buyer is willing to pay is determined to be the fair market value. It can further be defined as the cash price that can be reasonably anticipated in a current sale under all conditions requisite to a fair market sale. In the establishment of fair value, it must be determined what a prudent seller and buyer may agree upon to sell and purchase a property without any undue circumstances that would influence the sale. An example of an undue circumstance is the threat of a foreclosure on the seller by the lender that holds the mortgage. Other examples of undue circumstances are forced sales and liquidation sales.

An appraiser will use recent comparable sales, adjustment factors, and other calculations to arrive at his or her opinion of a fair market value for a property. Fair market value is also determined by the physical maintenance, the property's ultimate use, and the time required for development.

The determination of fair market value is the process whereby the ultimate sale price of a willing seller and a willing buyer is arrived at. The standard market time for fair market value is generally determined to be no longer than twelve months.

FEE SIMPLE

Fee simple ownership is title of ownership, usually conveyed in a deed, that grants the owner all the rights of ownership in a particular parcel of land along with all the improvements located thereon. This absolute ownership is unencumbered by any other interest claimed by another party. Fee simple ownership, however, is always subject to the limitations of the four powers of government, i.e., taxation, eminent domain, police power, and escheat.

Concise Encyclopedia of Real Estate Business Terms
© 2006 by The Haworth Press, Inc. All rights reserved.
doi:10.1300/5637_06

Fee simple ownership may sometimes be conditional and terminated upon the occurrence of a specified event at a specified time or not at all. At such time as the conditional limitation to fee simple ownership occurs, the grantor, the heirs, or a designated party must act to terminate the estate.

A life estate can exist as a conditional fee simple. Under such a condition, an individual may possess all the rights of ownership for as long as he or she lives. However, upon his or her death, an act by the heirs may revert the property to ownership by another party.

Most property is conveyed under a fee simple ownership that is not conditional and through which the owner possesses absolute control and enjoyment subject to the four governmental powers previously mentioned.

FIDUCIARY

Fiduciary is a term used to describe a relationship in which one person has the responsibility to act for the benefit of another person. A person with a fiduciary responsibility for another is charged with acting in a manner that represents the other person. A guardian acts as fiduciary for his ward, a trustee acts as fiduciary for the individual for whom he or she may hold property in trust, and an executor of an estate acts as fiduciary for the assets of the estate. Likewise, a real estate professional must act in a fiduciary capacity as the representative of buyer and/or seller of property. In such capacity, he or she is responsible to act in the best interest of the party to the contract whom he or she represents.

For example, if a real estate agent lists property, he or she is the fiduciary of the seller. If the seller reveals what is the lowest price he or she will accept but asks the agent to keep that in confidence, the fiduciary responsibility of the agent requires that he or she not reveal this to a buyer or a buyer's agent.

FIXED RENT

Fixed rent is the rent due from the lessee before any add-on charges. A triple net lease will generally list the fixed rent plus add-on charges for pro rata taxes, insurance, and common area maintenance.

Fixed rent is sometimes called the *base rent*. It is most often found in shopping center and commercial building leases.

For example, the monthly rent charges can be expressed in the lease as follows:

Fixed Rent	$1,000
Taxes	$115
Insurance	$30
Common Area Maintenance	$60
Total rent and add-on charges	$1,205

FIXED TERM

Sometimes referred to as the *firm term,* the fixed term is used to establish the initial term of the lease. This term represents the number of years the lessee is obligated for in the lease, not including any option periods he or she may or may not choose to exercise. A fixed term, for example, may be only one year in short-term leases or twenty to forty years or more in build-to-suit commercial leases. During the fixed term in long-term leases of ten years or more the rent may be adjusted based on the consumer price index, the inflation rate, or some other agreed upon factor.

FOR SALE BY OWNER

When a property owner attempts to sell property without the assistance of a real estate professional, it is "for sale by owner" (FSBO). The motivation for the seller is generally to save the payment of a real estate commission.

When placing property FSBO, the owner assumes responsibility for advertising, showing the property to prospective buyers, writing a contract, securing and holding a deposit, securing legal assistance for any title work, securing a survey, and closing the sale. Although many property owners are capable of selling their own property, a lack of knowledge of the legal responsibilities and the procedures of moving the sale to closing can cause complications for the buyer.

An estimated 85 percent of all FSBO sellers will eventually enlist the assistance of a real estate professional.

FORCE MAJEURE

The failure to perform that required by a contract caused by an unforeseen and unpreventable act is a force majeure. Generally such an event is referred to as an "act of God." Such events can include a flood, earthquake, hurricane, or other such natural disaster. The courts have generally ruled that these occurrences legally excuse a party from fulfilling the performance required by a contract. Such occurrences may only delay the performance or permanently prevent the fulfillment of the contract.

Many contracts will stipulate that in the event of a force majeure the obligations as set forth in the contract for the contracting parties are cancelled and consider the contract as null and void. Although such an event is rare, it is advisable when entering into a contract to include such language to cover the occurrence of what is defined by law as an act of God.

For example, if a property owner enters into a purchase agreement in which he or she agrees that all systems will be in working order at the closing on a certain date and an earthquake destroys or severely damages the property, it then becomes impossible to meet the terms of the contract through such a force majeure and the contract will be canceled. This could also apply if the property was damaged or destroyed through a flood, hurricane, or other act of God.

The deposit is returned and neither buyer nor seller has any further obligation to the other. In legal terms, both parties are made whole as if the agreement never existed.

FORECLOSURE

Foreclosure is the legal process of declaring a borrower in default, generally for nonpayment of the mortgage by the mortgage holder. The process begins by legal notification to the borrower that he or she is in default of the loan payments and calling for the repayment of the remaining principal balance of the loan. A suit is filed by the mortgage holder against the borrower for repayment.

The end result, if the borrower cannot repay the loan, is repossession of the property by the mortgage holder. The property may then be resold and, depending on the terms of the mortgage, the mortgage holder may seek a deficiency judgment against the borrower if the property does not sell for the amount of the principal balance that remains on the mortgage. With a deficiency judgment the mortgage holder may attach the judgment to any other assets of the borrower to secure full payment of the mortgage.

FREE-STANDING STORE

A free-standing store is a retail store that is located in a building not attached to a larger structure and contains only a single retail store. Some retailers prefer to be a destination point for shoppers. These retailers believe their product line sells best when the shopper is not exposed to other retailers who offer competitive products in close proximity.

Generally these stores are regional or national in scope or are supported by a strong advertising program or national reputation. Examples of such stores include national furniture, electronics, and appliance stores. They can also include discount general merchandise stores that find it difficult to locate in larger retail centers where regular price stores exist and often object to their proximity.

Some free-standing stores, due to special requirements for service as well as sales, find it difficult to convert normal retail space to their use. An example would be a tire and auto service center that requires service bays generally not found in most retail centers.

G

GENERAL PARTNERSHIP

A general partnership purchase of real estate consists of two or more partners each with a percentage of ownership. The percentage of ownership can be equal or unequal between the partners. Each partner shares according to his or her percentage of ownership in the profits or losses of the investment.

In general partnerships each partner may contribute a capital investment in proportion to his or her percentage of ownership. However, each partner guarantees the mortgage. The profits or losses are distributed in accordance with each partner's percentage of ownership.

For example, there are four partners and one partner owns 30 percent, one partner owns 20 percent, the two remaining partners own 25 percent each and the down payment is $100,000. Each partner will contribute toward this amount according to his or her percentage of ownership. If the profit at the end of the year is $50,000, this is also distributed in accordance with each partner's percentage of ownership. However, if the mortgage is $500,000 and requires personal guarantees, each partner will personally guarantee the mortgage. Even though the partnership agreement may specify differing percentages of ownership, ordinarily the lender will look to each partner to personally and individually guarantee the mortgage.

GRADUATED PAYMENT MORTGAGE

A mortgage with payments that begin below the required amount to amortize the debt over an agreed upon term and increase at specified times during the term is called a *graduated payment mortgage*. The lower initial payments may be related to the borrower's income or to low rental rates for income property that are projected to increase

Concise Encyclopedia of Real Estate Business Terms
© 2006 by The Haworth Press, Inc. All rights reserved.
doi:10.1300/5637_07

over the term of the mortgage. The increased rental income will allow the borrower to make mortgage payments above the required amount to amortize the loan if the payments were level throughout the term of the loan. For example, if the payments are reduced for the initial five years of a fifteen-year mortgage, they will be increased over the next five years of the term to make up the deficiency in payments and then reduced over the final five years to the normal payments to amortize the loan.

Sometimes the initial term of the loan is payment of interest only for a specified time followed by full amortization of the principal over the remainder of the loan. For example, if a fifteen-year term is agreed to with interest-only payments for five years, the remaining ten years of the mortgage must fully amortize the principal plus pay the interest due.

Referred to as a GPM, the graduated payment mortgage it is especially popular during anticipated times of higher inflation that will permit the borrower to raise rents and thereby adjust to higher mortgage payments.

GRANTEE

A grantee is a buyer of real estate who has received a deed certifying purchase of the property. A grantee is one to whom property rights and ownership have been granted through an appropriate form of purchase, generally a deed, trust instrument, or other such document. These documents, when filed in the courthouse, place the public on notice of the buyer's ownership.

GRANTOR

A grantor is a seller who transfers ownership of property to another person or entity as evidenced through a deed, trust instrument, or other such document. When filed in the courthouse, these documents place the public on notice that the seller is no longer the owner of a certain property.

GROSS LEASE

A lease that includes in the monthly rent all obligations for payment by the lessee is called a *gross lease.* The lessor assumes all obligations for payment of taxes, insurance, maintenance, and replacement of systems such as heat, air-conditioning, plumbing, electrical, roof, and structure. Gross leases are generally used for residential single family properties and multifamily properties such as apartments.

The lessee generally has an obligation to return the property upon vacating in the same condition as received minus normal wear and tear. However, during the term of occupancy, no responsibility is placed on the lessee for repair or maintenance of the major operating systems or for their condition upon vacating.

Office leases are generally gross leases as well, with one exception. Because of the extended term of office leases, the lessor often retains the right to increase the monthly rent on an annual basis due to his or her increased costs for taxes, insurance, maintenance, and management. This increase may be assessed as a one time payment, reflected in a rent increase on the anniversary of the lease, or upon some specified date such as January 1st.

Sometimes a modified gross lease is negotiated whereby the lessee assumes obligation for only one or two specified items, such as taxes and insurance.

GROUND LEASE

When a property owner is not willing to sell, he or she can often lease the ground to a lessee. The lessee may then possess the property under the terms of a ground lease and may construct a building on it. Many restaurants, retail stores, and shopping centers are constructed on leased land. Typically, a ground lease may be for twenty years with the lessee granted several option terms for ten or twenty years each. The lessee may then use the property for fifty years or longer.

Often the property is reappraised at the renewal of each option period. The ground rent may then be adjusted as a percentage of the new appraised price. However, under the terms of some ground leases, there may be an arbitrary rent adjustment, or it may be based on some other factor such as the increase in consumer price index during the past lease term.

If the lessee fails to exercise the renewal option, the land plus any improvements that have been made revert to the owner of the property. The owner may then use these improvements at his or her own discretion, such as re-leasing to a new tenant, removing the improvements and re-leasing the ground to a new tenant, or selling the property.

Financing of construction on leased ground generally requires the lessor to subordinate the lease to the mortgagee. If the lessee defaults in the mortgage payments, the mortgagee may then repossess the building but not the land and resell to another user. Generally, the mortgage requires that the ground lessor relinquish any ground lease payments until the building is sold to another owner.

At such time that all the lease renewals have been exhausted, any improvements that have been made become the possession of the ground lessor.

GROUND RENT

A property owner who does not want to sell but is willing to lease property to someone who may then construct a building can enter into a ground lease. Such leases are long term, usually for twenty years or longer, and may contain several options for the lessee to renew the lease. The lessor may or may not be required to subordinate his lease to a lender who loans money to the lessee to construct a building on the property.

Long-term ground leases generally contain rent adjustment clauses every five or ten years based on a new appraisal of the land, the consumer price index, or some other agreed upon standard. Some ground leases with renewal options can cover a fifty- to ninety-nine-year time span. However, once the firm term of the lease and all renewal periods have expired, any improvements made on the property become the possession of the land owner.

Some ground leases may grant the lessee the right to purchase the land at the expiration of the firm term and any renewal options, generally at the appraised value of the land or the land and any improvements.

HABENDUM CLAUSE

A clause used in real estate documents that states the term of the interest conveyed to a buyer or party to the contract is called a *habendum clause*. The interest in the property may be conveyed conditional upon a specified event, such as death, or upon the written revocation of another party as granted in the deed. In either event, a habendum clause spells out what event or events must occur after which the owner or heirs may act to revoke the ownership interest of another party.

For example, a parent may deed a property to a child or to anyone else as long as that person lives. However, should that person die prior to the grantor who deeded the property, the grantor may act to reclaim possession.

In any event, under a habendum clause, a property may be deeded for life, in fee simple, or for some other predetermined event that shall permit the vendor to once again take possession provided the vendor acts in accordance with the provisions within the deed or other legal document.

HARD COSTS

The actual costs of labor and materials for the construction or extensive renovation of a building project are called the *hard costs* or *direct costs*. When a contractor's bid for the project is received, although it will include a limited line item detailing the indirect costs of construction, it is primarily the contractor's bid based on the hard costs associated with the project. Hard costs or direct costs of the project include the following:

heavy equipment used in preparing the site
subcontractor bids
contractor labor and materials
parking lot labor and materials

Concise Encyclopedia of Real Estate Business Terms
© 2006 by The Haworth Press, Inc. All rights reserved.
doi:10.1300/5637_08

These are the costs directly related to the actual construction of the project that are most readily identified.

HAZARDOUS WASTE

The contamination of a property by the dumping or leakage of substances that contaminate the soil or water supply is a result of hazardous waste. Hazardous waste is generally defined as a substance, such as fuel or oil but also includes other substances such as polychlorinated biphenyl (PCB) used in electrical insulators or dichloro-diphenyltrichloroethane (DDT) used as an agricultural poison that may contaminate soil or water sources. The leakage, spillage, or dumping of such hazardous waste substances can harm humans, wildlife, or fish and enter the food chain through consumption of food or water by causing a variety of illnesses, such as cancer, respiratory disease, or other health-related problems.

The federal government in recent years has recognized the seriousness of the problem and taken steps to require testing, cleanup, and prevention of such substances to eliminate their dangers. The Superfund program was established to fund for such cleanup.

Various phases of discovery have been established to provide a systematic method of testing and cleanup. A Phase I environmental test is a visual and historical inspection of the property and its prior use. If there is an indication of possible contamination, other phases are required to test for hazardous waste material and its eventual clean up.

HEAT, VENTILATION, AND AIR-CONDITIONING SYSTEM

This term refers to the heating, ventilation, and air-conditioning (HVAC) system of a home or commercial building. Whether the system is a forced-air system cooled by water circulation or Freon-cooled coils, the heating system is hot water, gas, or electric, the ventilation is a mixed air system that includes outside air or the movement is limited to only circulation of internal air, the system is collectively referred to as an HVAC system.

HIGHEST AND BEST USE

A study that accounts for the most probable use of a property based on its legal, appropriate, and past use to render the best profitability must take into consideration the surrounding area, the population growth, traffic patterns, and other elements of demographics as well as topographic considerations and soil analysis. When all of these elements are combined in a thorough study, they will reveal what is known as the *highest and best use* of a property.

The four critical considerations for the highest and best use are physically possible, legally permissible, financially feasible, and maximum profitability. All four must be included to determine the highest and best use. These criteria will apply to vacant land as well as to developed property. In the process of aging, sometimes a developed property will have undergone changing land values; such changes can lead to the conclusion that the highest and best use is to demolish and seek an alternate use. A study of vacant land will determine whether development of single-family homes, multifamily dwellings, retail space, or some other option, such as agricultural or timber land, will be most profitable.

An appraiser, when determining the value of real estate, will begin by making a determination the highest and best.

HOME INSPECTION

When purchasing a residential property, the buyer will want to inspect the property for unknown defects. Such an inspection will include the foundation, roof, air conditioning and heating system, plumbing, electrical system, and other components.

The inspection may be completed by a company that specializes in home inspections. Many states now require such companies to be licensed to ensure their competence. The inspection company will provide the buyer with a written report for a fee, generally between $150 and $500.

However, the buyer may also choose to use venders such as plumbers, roofers, air conditioning and heating companies, structural engineers, etc., to complete these inspections. These vendors will charge a fee for the inspection. This type of inspection is most often done for purchases of commercial or investment properties, such as shopping centers, multifamily complexes, and office buildings.

When inspections are done by a licensed inspection company, the buyer should inspect the liability policy of the company to determine its responsibility, if any, should it fail to report a defect that is later discovered by the buyer.

HOMESTEAD EXEMPTION

Many states grant homeowners an exemption from property taxes up to a certain value of the home. The requirement for a homestead exemption is that the property owners use the home as their primary residence. A secondary residence or vacation home, even though it may be used equally by the homeowners as a residence, does not qualify. Homeowners must declare only one home as a primary residence and declare that home as exempt from property taxes up to the homestead value .

The value of the home declared as the primary residence under homestead exemption that exceeds the value allowed will be taxed at the rate a property not under homestead exemption law would be taxed. For example, if the maximum value allowed under the homestead exemption law was $75,000 and the value of the home was $100,000, the additional $25,000 would be taxed the ordinary property tax rate, based on the millage.

The value of the home is adjusted either at the time of sale or by a reassessment of property values by the property tax assessor as required by state law. Generally, the tax assessor is required to reassess value of the property tax every four years or some other term set by state law. If the property owner believes the value placed on the property is too high, there is an appeal process that he or she may enact.

Homestead exemption values may be adjusted by the state legislature at its discretion in some states and by public vote in other states. The original enactment of homestead exemption laws by states was to grant low-income property owners of lower value homes relief from property taxes. In time this was changed to include every homeowner up to a stated home value.

IMPROVEMENTS

Structures that are built on land or attached to it are considered a permanent part and referred to as *improvements*. An appraiser or the tax assessor, for purposes of evaluation, may designate a value to the land and another value to the improvements. However, any improvements added to the property become an integrated part of the real estate for purposes of evaluation or sale. Legally the improvements become a permanent part of the real estate.

There are four exceptions to the permanency of improvements. If the owner sells the improvements apart from the real estate, then they may be removed. If a mobile home or portable building has been set on the property but not permanently attached, then it may remain as a moveable property and not attached to the real estate. For a mobile home to become a permanent part of the real estate, its owner must file a certificate of immobility at the clerk of court's office, thereby making it a permanent part of the real estate. The other exception involves destruction of the improvements by fire or by an act of God, such as a tornado. Another exception is when the property owner purposely destroys the existing improvements often in order to build other structures on the property.

IMPUTED INCOME

Investment property purchased by an owner-occupant may be calculated to have imputed income as opposed to actual income based on the rent not paid by the owner. This process is used to determine the total return on investment that an owner-occupant will receive from his or her investment. For example, if an owner buys a fourplex apartment unit and moves into one of the units, his or her actual income may be $1,500 per month from the three units rented at $500 per month. However, to determine the real return, an additional $500 per month is added that the owner does not pay himself or herself in rent. This imputed income of $500 represents the amount the owner has saved by purchasing the property.

When the owner-occupant determines the actual return on investment, he or she will need to consider both actual income as well as imputed income.

IN REM MORTGAGE

A mortgage granted to a borrower that stipulates that the borrower is not personally liable for repayment of the debt is an in rem mortgage. The validity of the mortgage is not affected by providing for such a limitation of the liability against the borrower; however, without language that precludes or limits the liability of the borrower, the borrower remains personally liable for repayment.

In rem mortgages are generally granted only on real estate purchased for large sums and for which the lender determines he or she has adequate security without the personal liability of the borrower.

For example, if a borrower has an in rem mortgage on a $1,000,000 property and defaults with a remaining balance of $800,000, the lender may repossess the property. If the lender sells the property for only $600,000, there is no recourse against the borrower for the deficiency.

INDEMNIFY

The act of indemnification as applied to real estate is to ensure against a possible loss or damage that may be suffered by the buyer or seller. The purpose is to grant a legally binding warranty to the other party against a particular damage that may occur. The person or entity that grants the indemnification is called the *indemnifier,* and the person or entity who receives the indemnification is known as the *indemnitee.*

For example, the seller of a business may indemnify the buyer against any unknown or unrevealed debts against the business should an unknown holder of a debt surface after the closing. Also, a homeowner may indemnify a buyer for a period of time, e.g., ninety days, after closing should a plumbing problem surface after closing. This is most often done if a problem is suspected but not discovered before closing occurs. Although such agreements rarely occur, they can be agreed to by buyer and seller and become part of the closing documents.

INFRASTRUCTURE

Generally, infrastructure includes roads, bridges, water and sewer lines, electric power lines, telephone lines, and other such physical amenities that are either required for a property to be saleable or that the governing entity requires by law for a developer to provide.

There are some exceptions to the legally required infrastructure for such things as water, sewer, and road access. Water may be supplied by a well on the property. Sewer may be provided by a septic or mechanical treatment plant, and road access may be through a private drive onto the property.

The value of property is determined by the degree of infrastructure that supports both it and access to it. For example, having a dirt or grave rather than a paved access road most likely will affect the price at which the property can be sold. If the property owner must provide his or her own water source and sewage treatment, then the value of the property is usually less.

INGRESS/EGRESS

Ingress/egress is the means by which a property is accessed for public or private use. Ingress is access for entering a property, and egress is the means of exiting a property. In the development of a commercial property such as a shopping or retail center, multiple means will usually be provided for ease of entering and exiting the property. This is especially important for larger centers, which may require several entrances and exits to accommodate traffic flow. The ease of ingress and egress is enhanced if the development abuts more than one public street or highway. The success of a development may depend on its ability to handle traffic entering and exiting the property.

In the development of multifamily and condominium properties, especially gated communities, it may be desired to limit access and provide only one means of ingress and egress. Limited access can increase security and decrease the presence of the general public.

INTERNAL RATE OF RETURN

The internal rate of return (IRR) is a method of determining the profitability of an investment property. This method is based on establishing the rate of return, sometimes called the *annualized yield rate*, which an investment will return over the period of ownership. The IRR is the discount rate that produces a profit index of one and a net present value of zero. It is primarily used as a profit indicator to measure the profit from an investment after income taxes, called the *after-tax equity yield rate*. The equity yield rate considers the effect of financing the debt on the cash flow to the investor.

The IRR is another method used by an investor to determine the real profit after all expenses are deducted and after taxes are paid on the profit.

LAND CAPABILITY CLASSIFICATION SYSTEM

The land capability classification system is a system that has been developed by the Natural Resources Conservation Service (NRCS) to determine the limitations of types of soils for agricultural use. This system does not classify soils according to their yield potential but to their potential for damage and to the particular soil needs. For example, a sandy loam soil will have different needs than a heavy clay soil and will require different management and crop considerations.

By developing a land capability classification system, the NRCS hopes to help in the determination of the highest and best use of different soil types for agricultural use. There are subclasses that identify limitations of certain soils related to moisture content and retention as well as prevailing climate within the area. For example, a pewy clay soil is generally poorly drained and found in flood plain areas. It has only moderate fertility and contains elements potentially toxic to crops. Both water and air move slowly through the soil, and it is primarily used for pasture land when agricultural use is possible. On the other hand, a cahaba fine sandy loam soil is well suited to crops but may have low fertility. Therefore, it requires frequent additions of soil additives to achieve good yields of cotton, corn, or soybeans.

By establishing the land capability classification system, the SCS has enabled farmers and others to avoid crop failures and to establish the best use of the land.

LAND CONTRACT

Land contracts are also referred to as *contract for deed* or *installment sales contract,* and they represent a unique method for financing a property. The basic idea is to combine a lease and a purchase agreement into the same document. A buyer typically pays a deposit and begins using the property while making a series of monthly payments; after all payments have been completed the buyer will own the property. Laws applying to land contracts differ among states, with some requiring the title to be held by the seller until all payment obligations have been met and other states requiring the seller to pass title to the buyer after a certain percentage of the payments have been made. There are many variations on this type of sale, including payments set according to an amortization schedule with a portion of the monthly payments designated as interest and another portion allotted to reducing the principal. Many land contracts require a buyer to complete all payments and purchase a property, whereas others state that a buyer may be released from all obligations by forfeiting all deposits and payments as lease payments for the rental of the property. This type of sale is very useful for a buyer who cannot obtain bank financing or for a seller eager to sell a piece of property.

An example of this type of sale is a contract whereby a $300,000 office building could be purchased by giving the seller a $20,000 down payment and amortizing the payment of $280,000 over the course of fifteen years at 8 percent interest.

LEASE

A lease is an agreement in which a person or company gives rental payments to a property owner, and it establishes all the rights and obligations of both the owner and the tenant. There are numerous types of lease agreements. A gross lease consists of a set periodic payment to an owner whereby the owner pays all of the property's expenses (taxes, maintenance, etc.) out of the gross rental income. A net lease requires the tenant to pay a periodic fee to rent the property as well as all other expenses of the property, including taxes, utilities, and insurance. A month-to-month lease may have no formal written agreement, but the tenant makes monthly payments to the owner and the owner is required to give a one-month notice before canceling the lease.

A land lease would give a renter the right to use the land and the build structures on the land if desired. Land leases are typically for long periods of time in order for the renter to fully utilize the functional life of any buildings erected. Generally the ownership of any structures built on leased land will revert to the landowner upon expiration of the lease.

LEGAL DESCRIPTION

The identity of the property sold or leased is described in legal terms to distinguish it from any other property. It can be described by lot, square, subdivision name, township, range and section, or portion of a section. Metes and bounds may be used to further describe a property located outside of a recorded subdivision. Identity of city (if in city limits), county, or parish and state are also required.

Accurate legal descriptions are needed to identify the property a seller is selling and a buyer is purchasing. Municipal addresses, although they may be used in certain documents, are not acceptable apart from the legal description to clearly identify the subject property.

LESION

If a property is sold for less than one-half of its value, the property may be set aside for lesion, legally referred to as *lesion beyond moiety.* Even though the seller willingly and knowingly sold for less than one-half value and acknowledged that he or she was selling at 50 percent below value, a legal action can set aside the sale for lesion.

The law was intended to protect the weak, the unknowing, or the otherwise mentally handicapped from being taken advantage of by others. If the legal action to set aside the sale is successful, the seller may return the amount paid for the property, or the buyer may pay the difference up to the fair market value and retain ownership.

LESSEE

The party that executes a lease with the property owner is a lessee. This person or entity assumes all the obligations of "tenancy" as defined in the lease agreement. The lessee's rights are governed by the terms of the lease.

LESSOR

The owner that leases property to a tenant or lessee is a lessor, sometimes referred to as the *landlord*. The lessor agrees to lease property or, in the case of an office building or shopping center, the "space" to a lessee or tenant. The lessor's rights are governed by the terms of the lease agreement.

LETTER OF INTENT

A letter of intent is an informal and generally nonbinding proposal to purchase property submitted by a buyer to the seller. The proposal will state the price and other conditions and terms that the buyer proposes. The proposal will also state the time to close, any contingencies, such as "subject to financing," and that the proposal if accepted by the seller will be followed by a formal and binding purchase agreement. The proposal will have a place for the seller to indicate acceptance of the proposal.

If the terms of the proposal are not acceptable to the seller, the seller can counter with a different proposal to the buyer. Although this type of negotiation is generally nonbinding on buyer and seller, it does condense to a written form what one or more parties are willing to do in the purchase and sale of the property.

The letter of intent or purchase proposal is most often used in the sale of commercial property. The ease of offering to purchase and the counter by the seller are expedited by the lack of a binding agreement. Once the price, terms, conditions, and contingencies have been negotiated, the buyer and seller enter into a binding purchase agreement with specific performance.

LICENSE

A license is an activity conducted for the public that requires governmental permission. Almost all professions that provide a public service require one or more licenses to be issued by the appropriate governing body. A license is designed to establish standards primarily for education and practical knowledge of the area of expertise that an individual or business intends to offer as a service to the public.

In the area of real estate, the individual who intends to enter the profession needs a licence. This requires a course of study consisting of a set number of class hours followed by an examination. Through this manner the government protects the public from anyone practicing real estate without adequate knowledge to provide a reasonable degree of professional service. A real estate license is designed to test not only the individual's knowledge of real estate sales but also his or her knowledge of the laws that regulate the profession.

The requirements for a real estate license are set by the state which governs the profession through a commission or other type of governing agency.

LIEN

A lien is a claim to hold property to meet a debt or a liability. It may allow a creditor to force the sale of a property in order to pay off a debt associated with the property. A mortgage is an example of a lien on property in the event of default. Liens are prioritized based on the order in which they are recorded at the county records office. A first lien has the right to all monies received by selling a property until it is fully paid off, with excess monies going to pay each successive lien in order. A materialman's lien can be used to satisfy unpaid maintenance work or construction on a property. Generally, when a lien is satisfied there will be a lien release document signed and recorded at the county records office to announce that the lien has been satisfied. Liens are the primary instrument that allows banks to loan money to other parties for purchasing real estate, and they allow banks to have a claim on property without holding the title to the property.

LIFE ESTATE

Life estate is applied to a property that is granted to a recipient to use for the duration of his or her life. With the granting of a life estate, an individual is granted the absolute use and control of the property. The individual is defined as a life tenant. Although life tenants are not the owners by virtue of a deed, they possess the same rights of a tenant through lease. They may not sell or demolish the property, but they do possess the rights of use, occupancy, and control of the property for as long as they live.

Life estates are sometimes used to dispose of property prior to the death of the owner. In such cases, the property may be sold to an heir or other party, with the owner executing an agreement for use as long as he or she lives. Such an agreement, although generally limited to the life of one individual, can be extended to the death of both a husband and a wife. In such a case, upon the death of both parties, the life tenancy ends.

Upon the death of the life tenant or tenants, the use and control of the property reverts to the deeded owner, who then has the same rights as any other owner would possess.

LIMITED PARTNERSHIP

A limited partnership is a type of partnership purchase of real estate in which different partners have different levels of liability. The term *limited partnership* is derived from limiting the liability of one or more partners. This type of ownership divides partners into two types—limited and general.

A limited partner has passive ownership without responsibility for the mortgage or day-to-day operation of the investment. This partner's liability is limited to the amount of his or her capital investment.

A general partner assumes liability to manage the investment and full liability of the mortgage or any other debt the investment may incur.

For example, if an investment has one general partner and five limited partners and was purchased for $1,000,000, with each of the five limited partners investing $50,000 and the balance of $750,000 placed as a first mortgage against the property, the limited partners have a limit on their liability of the $50,000 invested. However, the general partner has liability for the $750,000 mortgage.

The Securities and Exchange Commission has placed a limit on the number of limited partners allowed in order to qualify as a limited partnership.

LIQUID INVESTMENT

An asset that can be immediately converted into cash is a liquid investment. Examples of liquid investments include stocks and mutual funds. Real estate is not considered a liquid investment because of the time often required to convert it into cash.

Even in an active real estate market in which property is selling fast, or when a highly desirable property can be sold in a relatively short time, real estate is not considered as liquid.

When making an investment, if liquidity may be required to convert into cash quickly, an alternative investment other than real estate should be chosen.

LIQUIDATED DAMAGES

Liquidated damages is an amount agreed upon by both parties in advance through a contract should either party breach the agreed upon terms of the contract. The inclusion of liquidated damages in a contract will often prevent litigation through the courts should either party fail to fulfill his or her legal requirements. Liquidated damages, also called *stipulated damages,* in a real estate purchase agreement is a means of setting the penalty for both buyer and seller should either party fail to meet the terms of the agreement.

For example, if a buyer and seller enter into a purchase agreement for a $100,000 property and stipulate $5,000 in liquidated damages, and the buyer refuses to close other than for reasons agreed to in the agreement, the buyer is required to pay the seller $5,000. Liquidated damages are excluded from any contingencies agreed to in the agreement such as subject to buyer securing financing, if financing is not secured by the buyer.

LIQUIDATION

Liquidation is the sale of real estate resulting from the pressure to take profits from creditors or from a declining market. A liquidation sale results in a price for real estate without adequate time to market and find a buyer at a reasonable market price. This is a sale forced on a seller by necessity to convert assets to cash. Proceeds from a liquidation are first used to satisfy all creditors, with any remaining balance distributed to the owner.

Most often a liquidation results from pressure applied by the lender to receive the balance of a mortgage. When this occurs, a lender has usually failed to receive timely payments from the borrower. A lender may also determine that the property is in decline and project that future payments are placed in jeopardy. Additionally, a lender may exercise an option to call the mortgage or to not renew after the initial commitment period. For example, a lender may make a five year loan with a fifteen-year amortization and determine not to renew after the expiration of the five-year term. In this case, the borrower will be forced to pay off the remaining balance either through liquidation or by moving the loan to another lender.

A liquidation price is determined by what price a buyer is willing to pay when a seller is under pressure to sell and there are no other buyers ready to purchase in the limited time frame allotted by the lender or other circumstances in a declining market.

LISTING TERM

A listing agreement must include a beginning and ending date, referred to as the *term of the agreement.* The listing term is negotiable between seller and agent. In addition to the term, many agreements provide for a specific period of time after expiration, the *protective period,* that the agent will be due a commission provided the buyer became interested in the property due to the agent's efforts during the term of the listing. The listing term is referred to as the *primary period,* and the protective period is called the *secondary* or *extension period.*

The courts have ruled that the agent does not have to be the procuring cause or have entered into negotiation with the buyer to be due a commission if sold during the secondary period. However, the agent must have created an interest on the part of the buyer in the property that resulted in the eventual purchase. The courts have further ruled that if the owner has listed his or her property with a second agent, the secondary or extension period is voided. If the secondary period did remain in effect, the owner could then be liable for two commissions, one to the first agent under the extension period and another to the second agent under the primary period.

LITIGATION

Litigation is the act of settling a dispute or foreclosure through a court of jurisdiction. In real estate, when a buyer and seller cannot settle a dispute or default by one party on the terms of the agreement, the other party may choose to seek recourse in a court of law. A lender may decide to foreclose on a loan when a borrower defaults on payments and initiate a lawsuit against the borrower and seek recourse through the courts to force a sale and repay the balance of the loan.

Litigation is initiated through a lawsuit filed in the courts to ask the court to settle the matter and award monetary or other damages against the defendant (the borrower). When a lender forecloses on a loan he or she may request a court of law to order the sale of the property. If the sale does not result in an amount sufficient to pay off the mortgage, the lender may seek a deficiency judgment against the borrower for the amount of the mortgage not repaid through the sale of the real estate. If a deficiency judgment is granted, the lender may then force the sale of other assets owned by the borrower to satisfy the remaining unpaid balance of the loan.

Litigation is generally used as a last course of action. If a seller decides to force the sale of the property to a buyer who has defaulted in the purchase, he or she may be prevented from selling to any other buyer until the court issues a final ruling. Such a ruling by the court may require two to three years to finalize.

LOAN PREQUALIFICATION

When a buyer anticipates the purchase of a property, particularly a home, the buyer may first visit with a lender to determine the amount of loan for which he or she qualifies. The prequalification process is based on information provided by the potential buyer. The financial information provided by the buyer will include income, both husband's and wife's if married, credit card debt and monthly payments, other loans and monthly payments, how long employed, how many in the household, and other recurring or monthly obligations. A deduction is made for the ordinary expenses, which include clothing, food, transportation, etc.

When the total expenses are listed, discretionary expenses, usually listed as a percentage of income, will be deducted. After subtracting from the income all actual and projected expenses, the remaining balance will show the level of mortgage that can be serviced by the remaining income.

By using the prequalification process, a potential buyer will know the amount of mortgage he or she qualifies for based on current income.

LOAN TO VALUE

The amount of the loan as it relates to the value of the real estate that secures the loan is the loan to value (LTV). Lenders generally have set requirements for the LTV based on different criteria. The LTV is a function of perceived risk by the lender. For instance, investment real estate often is limited to 80 percent of the value. However, if the property is to be owner occupied, the LTV may be as high as 90 percent. For residential property that is the primary home of the borrower, the LTV may reach 95 percent or even 97 percent. The logic is that a borrower will more likely pay a mortgage secured by his primary residence than one secured by a property for investment purposes.

As an example, if a property appraises for $100,000, the LTV may be $95,000 or even $97,000 for a primary residence, whereas the loan for an investment property of the same value may be only $80,000. This requires a much higher down payment for property a lender perceives to be of higher risk.

Recently, lenders have begun basing the LTV on the purchase price or appraised value, whichever is less. For instance, if an investor purchases a property for $100,000 but the property appraises for $125,000, the lender will require a $20,000 down payment or 80 percent of the purchase price rather than 80 percent of the appraised value. This required LTV may sometimes be met by the placement of additional collateral by the borrower as security for the loan instead of a cash payment.

MARKET RENT

The rental rate that can be anticipated from an investment property based on the current rent received from comparable properties in a given market is known as *market rent*. A thorough study of like properties will establish what an investor can most likely anticipate as his rental rate.

To establish the market rent, a study of like properties must be completed. Such a study will include properties within the same general market area, their condition and quality, and the supply of like properties within the market and market demand.

For instance, a current market rent study may show a market rent of $10.00 per square foot for comparable properties; however, if the market is oversupplied, the investor may not be able to rent his or her like property for the same amount. Although the market rent will in time reflect what an investor can anticipate for rents, the investor may have to adjust below the market rent. Alternatively, if the demand is higher than the supply, the investor may be able to secure higher than market rent. Although market rent may be an indicator of what an investor can anticipate in rents, other factors must be considered.

The market rent is a rental price that a similar property would bring in the same rental market. Therefore, market rent is a competitive rate. If, for example, most apartments with two bedrooms and one bath rent for an average of $800 in a given area, that price is the market rent. For most real estate markets, the majority of properties would rent very near the market rent, with those in better areas or having more amenities receiving somewhat higher rents and those in less popular areas or with fewer amenities receiving somewhat lower rents. Price per square foot is another factor that can influence market rent, with set amounts for each amenity being added or deducted depending on availability.

Concise Encyclopedia of Real Estate Business Terms
© 2006 by The Haworth Press, Inc. All rights reserved.
doi:10.1300/5637_11

MARKET VALUE

Real estate professionals are asked to provide a seller with a price for the seller's property based on their knowledge of the market, the recent sale of comparable properties, the condition of the property to be sold, and other factors that can influence the sale of this particular property. The establishment of an estimated market value does not constitute an appraisal but rather is an opinion of an estimated price that the seller can reasonably expect to receive. When providing an estimated market value, real estate professionals need to inform the seller that their estimate of a selling price is not an appraisal. Problems occur when this distinction is not made clear to a seller, including misunderstandings between the real estate professional and the seller.

Only a licensed real estate appraiser can provide the seller with an appraisal of the property.

The process of determining the market value for a commercial property (office building, warehouse, shopping center, etc.) is different from that used for residential property. The determination for a shopping center might include taking a weighted average of three distinctly different values. One value can be determined by the prices paid for similar properties with additions and deductions based on size of buildings, size of land, and amenities included. Another value can be determined by the income or rents received from leasing the property with additions and deductions based on amenities and age. Another value can be determined by the cost it would take to rebuild the structures on the property, including buildings, parking lots, fences, etc. All three values may be combined to reach a final market value. Also, it should be noted that two different real estate professionals may reach two different final market values for the same piece of property, although they are generally close to the same value.

MARKETABILITY

The circumstance under which a property can attract potential buyers or tenants will determine its marketable status. Marketability is a factor of market conditions including competing properties through which an individual property has the potential to appeal to buyers.

For example, a residential property may have deferred maintenance that limits its ability to be marketed. Although correcting the deferred maintenance, such as painting or a new roof, may not increase the property's value, it does increase its marketability when competing with other comparable properties in the market.

Marketability is especially critical in new development, such as multifamily or retail centers. A determination must be made on market conditions to absorb the new development, including competing rents, current vacancies, location, accessibility, and growth patterns. A thorough market study will address all of the influencing factors.

If a property or development has adequately addressed all of these issues, it is considered to have high marketability. However, if the factors mentioned above determine that there are high vacancies, the development cannot compete with current market rents, or the projected population growth pattern cannot support a new development, the property may have a low marketability. In such case, the proposed development may have a limited chance of success.

MARKETING PLAN

When commercial real estate will be sold or leased, a plan detailing how the property is to be marketed and the time table for each phase of the plan to be completed is commonly referred to as a *marketing plan*. Such a plan will include the preparation of an informative package to be used in the marketing. This package will contain demographic information, traffic counts, a property plat or building layout, and the price or lease rate. It will also identify the target market on which the marketing will focus, how to reach that market, and what means of promotion are to be used and with what frequency.

A cost estimate is provided for the promotional strategy. A description of any mass media to be used, and at what frequency, and an estimated cost of each source, such as newspaper, television, radio, or magazine, are included. This cost combined with a professionally prepared information package will provide a projected promotional cost for the property.

A marketing plan also incorporates a time table for the sale or leasing of the property. A time table generally starts with completion of the packaging phase. The next item is a time projection as to when certain phases of the promotion will begin and how long they are projected to last. There are also contingency plans if set goals are not met. For example, if after ninety days of marketing, the goal of 25 percent sales or leasing has not been achieved, then the response may be to add television ads to the promotional campaign.

The final phase includes projections for reaching certain goals within a set time frame. There is also generally a preset response if goals are not met within their time table. If sales or leasing is not meeting projections and if there is a percentage deficiency depending on the level of deficiency, the predetermined response may be more advertising, terminating the marketing team, or selling off the project at a drastic price reduction.

When the plan is completed, it should provide a detailed outline for marketing the property, the means to be used, the time table of expectations, the estimated cost, and, finally, the consequences if projections are not met.

MERCHANTABLE TITLE

Merchantable in its simplest form is to be saleable. The title to real estate is considered to be merchantable if it contains no cloud on the title and there is a proper chain of title establishing clear ownership. Some of the issues that might keep a title from being merchantable include encroachment of an improvement over the property line, a chain of title in which the current owner does not have proper ownership, or a previous sale in which not all the owners signed the deed or gave power of attorney to someone to sign for them.

Any cloud on the title that cannot be cleared is considered acceptable provided an established title company will insure the title without the defect being made an exception to the policy. Although this does not clear the cloud on the title, it does provide merchantability to the title.

MERIDAN

Meridan is a method of land identification used throughout the United States. This method begins with the prime meridian running north and south from the north pole to the south pole. Further meridians are identified lines moving every 30 degrees in an east or west direction from the prime meridian and always in a north/south direction. Further divisions of the meridian sections are townships and ranges.

All land is divided first into meridians, then into townships and ranges, and then into sections.

METES AND BOUNDS

A property not included within the boundary of a plated subdivision may be described by metes and bounds. Metes are measures of length, such as feet, yards, and rods; bounds are boundaries natural or artificial. In a metes and bounds description, a picture of the property is drawn beginning with a reference to a recognizable point called a *commencing point.* The distance from this point to another point is described as the *point of beginning* of the parcel to be described. The boundaries of the subject property are then outlined from the point of beginning.

METROPOLITAN STATISTICAL AREA

The federal government has divided the country into areas based on population density. A metropolitan statistical area (MSA) is defined as a city with at least 50,000 people. An urbanized area is one that has at least 50,000 people with a total metropolitan population of at least 100,000. A primary MSA must contain more than 1 million people in an urban county or a group of counties with strong economic ties. The federal government established the MSA standards in 1980.

Statistical areas are important to retailers when determining new locations or to industries when determining sizes of labor forces. By using the statistical area data available, a customer base or potential labor force can be readily determined.

Statistical areas are determined by federal census every ten years. Growth patterns as well as out-migration can reclassify an area into another statistical division when new census data become available. Also, the creation of economic ties with new places can enlarge the statistical area, thus changing the classification. Reclassification into a larger area can be important in securing new retail and industrial growth that had previously been impossible to secure.

MILLAGE RATE

Millage rate is a term used in the calculation of the amount of property taxes due from each piece of property. Each state determines its percentage of fair market value (FMV) to use for property taxation. Some states assess property at 100 percent of the FMV while others assess property at a percentage of FMV (i.e., 10 percent).

In calculating the amount of property tax, the number of mills (voted by the people) along with the assessed value (percentage of fair market value used to assess property) are the determining factors. One mill is one one-thousandth (.001); therefore, 1 mill equals $1 per $1,000 taxable assessed value. Twenty mills equals $20 per $1,000 taxable assessed value. For example, if the FMV of a home is $100,000 and the assessed value is 10 percent of the FMV, the property has an assessed value $10,000. If there were a 20-mill tax, then the property tax would be $200 (not withstanding any exemptions). For example: $10,000 × .020 = 200$.

MINERAL RIGHTS

Minerals contained in or under the ground are in some states considered to have a separate value from the property. Other states treat the minerals as inseparable from the land. Minerals include oil, gas, gravel, coal, and all others that may be extractable. When mineral rights are separated from the property, they can be held by a party other than the property owner and purchased and sold apart form the land. In such instances, the minerals may be sold to another party with the exclusive right to extract them from the property.

In some states the law sets a time limit on the holder of the mineral rights to begin extraction. If no extraction activity is begun during the prescribed time limit, for example, ten years, then the mineral rights revert to the property owner of record. If any extraction has begun during the prescribed period, the mineral rights remain with the holder as determined by law.

MITIGATION

By law, mitigation is the responsibility of an injured party to make every reasonable effort to reduce the damages he or she suffers. In real estate, mitigation is used to reduce the flooding effect when wetlands are developed and thereby removed from their capacity to hold water. The mitigation process requires that other property within the same drainage district be excavated to contain not only what that property would normally retain in water but also an amount equal to what the property to be developed would retain in drainage water. This amount is generally measured in an acre-foot, defined as the volume of water equal to an amount required to cover one acre of land to a depth of one foot.

MORTGAGE

There are three types of mortgages: conventional, legal, and judicial. A conventional mortgage is created by contract and is the most common. A legal mortgage is created in favor of minors, interdicts, and absentees on property in favor of their tutors and curators as security for administration. Judicial mortgages are the result of a judgment. A judicial mortgage acts as a lien, such as that created by bankruptcy.

Mortgages may also be divided into special and general. A special mortgage encumbers only specified property, such as a home or rental property. A conventional mortgage is a special mortgage against only a specific property. A general mortgage is a mortgage against all the property owned by the debtor. A judicial or legal mortgage is considered a general mortgage and encumbers all the property owned by the debtor.

MORTGAGE BROKER

A person who searches for qualified borrowers and/or willing lenders for a fee is a mortgage broker. Brokers generally have knowledge of the requirements for borrowers established by each of the lenders they work to place loans with as well as the loan parameters set by the lenders. For example, some lenders may only make loans on apartment complexes, and others may only loan on shopping centers. A lender may also set parameters on both the minimum and the maximum loans they will consider. The lender may also specialize in construction or bridge loans and require a permanent loan be placed with another lender. Some lenders specialize in second mortgages, while others specialize in 100 percent mortgages and still others in nonrecourse loans.

A mortgage broker understands each of the lender's requirements and will search for borrowers who meet the requirements. A mortgage broker collects a fee, generally expressed as a percentage of the loan. The fee is paid by the borrower at the time of closing. Some mortgage brokers will also charge a packaging fee to prepare the package for the borrower to be presented to the lenders. The packaging fee has come under legal investigation because some mortgage brokers have charged the fee to a number of clients but seldom if ever produced a lender willing to make a loan.

MORTGAGE CANCELLATION

When a mortgage has been fully satisfied, the mortgagor should receive a document from the mortgagee stating that the mortgage has been paid in full. This mortgage cancellation agreement is then filed in the court records to cancel the debt against the property. Although the mortgagor and mortgagee may recognize that the mortgage has been paid, without such a cancellation being filed in the public records, the mortgage will still be shown as a debt against the property. Often a mortgage is paid but a cancellation is not filed, and it will still be shown as a debt against the property when the owner attempts to sell to another buyer.

Mortgage cancellation is an important and necessary step in the mortgage process to ensure that only current existing and unpaid mortgages are shown in the public records against any property.

MORTGAGE INSURANCE

If a property is financed with a loan to value in excess of 75 percent the lender will require insurance to cover default by the borrower. The insurance is based on the additional risk by the lender. The insurance covers the lender's additional risk above 75 percent of the loan to value. Up to the 75 percent loan to value a lender interprets the loan as a safe loan because in the event of a default by the borrower the property could almost always be sold to cover the remaining balance of the loan even after foreclosure fees are paid. Such insurance applies to residential as well as commercial loans.

For example, if the loan is 90 percent of the loan to value, then the private mortgage insurance is added to the payment. However, when the principal of the loan is paid down to the 75 percent original loan to value, the insurance payment is no longer required. Because many lenders do not track each loan, it is often required of the borrower to request that the private mortgage insurance premium be cancelled.

Private mortgage insurance will cover the loss by the lender of an amount in the excess of the 75 percent loan to value. For example, if the original loan was $100,000 and represented a 95 percent loan to value and the borrower defaulted on payment of the mortgage with a $90,000 remaining principal balance, the private mortgage insurance would cover the $11,000 over the 75 percent loan to value ratio.

MORTGAGE SATISFACTION

When a mortgage is paid in full, a lender will issue a certificate marked "paid in full." This certificate, or mortgage cancellation, is filed at the appropriate courthouse to place the public on notice that the mortgage on the property is cancelled. It is important that such a cancellation be filed in order that a future search of the public records will show that the mortgage no longer exists against the property.

If a property is sold and a new owner secures a mortgage, a cancellation document will also be filed to provide a public record that the mortgage that previously existed against the property has been satisfied.

MOVABLE PROPERTY

In the course of selling or buying improved real estate, a dispute may arise over whether an item is considered a movable or a fixed part of the property. A widely accepted definition for movable property is any item not fixed or attached to an immovable part of the building or residence. If an item has been attached to a wall, ceiling, or floor so as to make it part of the property in a more or less permanent manner it is considered an immovable part of the property.

For example, a bookcase attached to a wall and made a part of the building or residence would be an immovable item. However, if the bookcase was free standing and not attached to a wall it would be considered a movable item or movable property. Likewise, an air conditioner placed in a window that can be easily removed is considered movable, while light fixtures are considered immovable.

Often, however, a buyer and seller will agree as part of the negotiations that an item normally considered as immovable may be removed by the seller. For instance, a buyer and seller may agree that a particular chandelier, an immovable light fixture, may be removed by the seller. When this occurs the purchase agreement needs to specify any items normally considered as immovables that may be removed by the seller to avoid any confusion at a later date.

NEGATIVE AMORTIZATION

Negative amortization is a financing structure whereby the monthly payments on a loan are less than the amount required to amortize the loan. In this situation, the amount owed on a loan becomes larger each month due to unpaid interest until at some future date the payment is increased or the loan is paid off. The advantage of this type of loan is the lower initial payment, and some buyers may even gamble that the property will appreciate in value at a faster rate than the increasing amount owed. An index-adjusted loan may incidentally create a negative amortization situation if the interest rate it is tied to rises enough to create more interest due than a fixed monthly payment. However, many index-adjusted loans use variable payment amounts to prevent such a situation.

NEGOTIATE

To negotiate is to bring a buyer and seller or lessee and lessor to an agreement in a real estate transaction. The process often involves a third party to act as intermediary. This intermediary is often a real estate professional experienced in the art of negotiation. The real estate professional may represent the interest of the buyer or seller or lessee or lessor or, under a dual agency agreement, both parties. As the fiduciary, a real estate professional is required to act with integrity and honesty toward both parties in a transaction whether he or she represents one or both.

Negotiation in a real estate transaction will involve price but also extends into other areas of disagreement. To conclude a sale or lease, both parties to the transaction must agree that they have received an acceptable level or fairness. A negotiator may need many years of experience to be able to conclude a sale or lease that includes difficult or unique issues. The value of a real estate professional acting as a third

Concise Encyclopedia of Real Estate Business Terms
© 2006 by The Haworth Press, Inc. All rights reserved.
doi:10.1300/5637_12

party fiduciary agent is his or her ability to structure a final contract to which all parties have achieved an acceptable level of agreement.

NET LISTING

A net listing is a seldom-used form of listing property that guarantees the owner a stated price for the property. The agent will receive any amount over the stated price that the property sells for. The agent assumes the risk that the property will sell for more than the amount the owner is to receive; if it does not, the agent receives no commission even though he or she is the procuring cause of the sale.

This type of agreement may not be legal in some states because it often leads to disputes between owner and agent that result in litigation. An owner who agrees to a net listing may later claim that, because the agent was more knowledgeable of property values than the owner, he or she was taken advantage of by the agent. This usually occurs when the property sells for an amount substantially above the amount the owner has agreed to receive.

A net listing must be carefully prepared, with the agent providing comparable sales to educate the owner on the current value of the property. The agreement must also specify whether the amount the owner is to receive excludes any other costs the seller may have, such as pro rata taxes, deed preparation, title, or survey costs.

NET OPERATING INCOME

Net operating income (NOI) is a popular method investors use to measure the performance of a real estate investment. The NOI is the amount that remains after all operating expenses are deducted from the actual or anticipated net income. Often an investor will use the NOI to calculate the value of an investment when considering a purchase. This method does not include the mortgage debt service and depreciation as expenses. For example, if the expenses, which include taxes, maintenance, insurance, management, utilities, and any other direct costs, are $100,000 and the income is $150,000, then the NOI is $50,000. The $50,000 NOI must then cover the debt service plus any profit an investor expects to make on the investment.

Replacement or repair services may or may not be included in the NOI. It is best if they are not included because it is a subjective expense factor that may not be supported by actual future cost.

When preparing a pro forma for a future or existing real estate investment, the NOI is considered in determining what debt service the project can support and what net return on investment can be anticipated. In this situation, future income and expenses can only reasonably be determined based on other comparable properties. If no other comparables are available in the market area, then an available data approach must be used based on the best and most recent information available.

NET PRESENT VALUE

The net present value (NPV) is often used as a benchmark to determine the value of an investment. To determine the NPV, cash flow is calculated as the total sum of all present income or cash flow against the present value of all capital expenses, sometimes referred to as *negative cash flow.* Negative cash flow includes the initial down payment, other associated costs to purchase the property, and all expenses incurred in operating the property.

If the NPV is used to calculate the value of an investment property, a positive NPV indicates a sound investment while a negative NPV may show the investment to be unacceptable. A zero NPV will indicate that the investment is marginal and may need additional cash infusion to make it profitable. This method is one of several used by investors to determine value.

NONBINDING AGREEMENT

A proposal that sets forth the price, terms, and conditions under which a buyer is willing to purchase a property but does not obligate the buyer to purchase and that the seller accepts is called a *nonbinding agreement.* Also called a *purchase* or *lease proposal,* its intent is to set forth the general terms for purchase or lease. Usually such a proposal will be followed by a binding agreement if the general terms are found acceptable.

In any nonbinding agreement the intent is to present a proposal that if accepted will be the basis of a future binding agreement. The purpose then becomes the outline of an agreement that can be entered into. Generally the buyer will give the seller a period of time to accept the proposal. If the seller finds the proposal to be unacceptable, the seller may counter with his or her own nonbinding proposal back to the buyer in which the seller has set forth the price, terms, and conditions to the buyer that he or she find acceptable.

Nonbinding agreements are intended as a prelude to establish acceptable terms to be followed by a binding purchase or lease agreement.

NONEXCLUSIVE LISTING

Property owners may sign an agreement with an agent to sell property but retain the right to sign an agreement with other agents or to sell the property themselves. Under this type of agreement, the agent is only due a commission if he or she produces a buyer at a price acceptable to the seller and before another nonexclusive agent has produced a buyer or the owners have found a buyer themselves and entered into a purchase agreement.

A nonexclusive listing will identify the property, the price, and the term of the listing. The agent may or may not be permitted to place a sign on the property.

Nonexclusive listings grant the agent the right to advertise the property, show the property to a prospective buyer, and prepare a purchase agreement. However, the agent is not given any exclusive right to sell the property. A commission is earned by the agent only if he is the procuring cause of the sale and does so before the owner or another nonexclusive agent produces a buyer.

NONRECOURSE LOAN

A loan in which the mortgagee agrees that the sole security for the loan will be the real estate mortgaged is referred to as a *nonrecourse loan*. It is also called an *in rem* loan, which means against a thing, not a person. If in the judgment of the mortgagee or lender the real estate is of sufficient value above the amount loaned, the personal guarantee of the mortgagor or borrower may not be required.

In the event of a default by the borrower, the lender may repossess the property but not hold the borrower personally liable for repayment of the loan. The lender agrees that his or her only recourse is against the property.

The lender must evaluate the property, the potential for success of the investment, and the ability of the borrower to operate the property in a judicious and profitable manner.

Generally, a nonrecourse loan will have a higher interest rate, a higher prepayment penalty, and a lower loan to value ratio than one with recourse. Nonrecourse loans are usually made through specialized lenders, such as an insurance company. They will also usually have large minimum loan amounts, such as $1,000,000, and are made against large investment properties. The lender will evaluate the investment for its profit potential as well as the borrower for his or her past performance with investment properties. The lender must consider the value of the property as sole security for the loan in the event of default by the borrower. In case of default, the lender will repossess the property and consider its resale potential as the only security for the loan.

Only a small percentage of loans made are nonrecourse loans because they are considered more risky than a normal recourse loan with personal guarantees.

NOTARY PUBLIC

A person who has passed a notarial test and thereby becomes authorized to give legal authenticity to documents is a notary public. Many legal agreements require a notary to authenticate the signatures of all parties to the document. A notary is required to witness the signature of the party to the document needing notarization. The purpose of a notary is to give legal authenticity to the signature and to protect the parties from fraud.

A notary seal is required by some states to certify the notarization, but not by all states. It is illegal for notaries to notarize signatures that they have not personally witnessed. Notaries can lose their license if it is proved that they have notarized an unwitnessed signature. A notary is authorized to witness acknowledgements and sworn affidavits, which may be filed at a courthouse and entered into the public records.

NUISANCE

A nuisance is that which interferes with the use and enjoyment of private or public property. A nuisance may be a source of annoyance to others that prevents their enjoyment or creates discomfort. Nuisances are categorized as public or private. A public nuisance is one that interferes with the public interest. A private nuisance is one that destroys, devalues, or injures a person's property. Such nuisances interfere with the lawful use and/or enjoyment of property or deny the common rights of an individual or the public.

Examples of nuisances are uncontrolled barking dogs, dangerous animals, and excessively loud music.

NULL AND VOID

An action or lack of action that cancels any agreement, particularly as related to the purchase or lease of real estate, is referred to as *null and void*. Agreements between two parties in a sale or lease of real estate often contain language that cancels the agreement under certain predetermined circumstances that have been agreed to by both parties, sometimes referred to as *conditions* or *contingencies* of the sale or lease. When such contingencies or conditions have been agreed to at the time of execution of the agreement and are not met, the agreement may be considered null and void without either party having any recourse against the other.

Examples of contingencies or conditions that may cause a contract to become null and void are buyer's inability to secure financing, discovery of systems not in working condition that the seller is unable or unwilling to repair or replace, problems with the title that cannot be removed in a reasonable time, or presence of substances that violate the requirement that the property be free of environmental contamination.

When a contract becomes null and void, it is as if the agreement had never existed, and each party is made whole as if the agreement had never been made.

OCCUPANCY

Occupancy is the number of units or square feet occupied compared with the total units or square feet available. Usually this is expressed as a percentage of the whole. An investor who intends to purchase an apartment complex, office building, or shopping center will want to know the current and past percentages of occupancy for the property. The historical trend of occupancy will provide an investor with an occupancy pattern to determine existing or past problems that may be corrected to increase occupancy.

Occupancy is a barometer used by an investor to determine the profitability of a property as well as its upside potential for profits. Many investors view low occupancy as a potential for future profits provided the investor believes a higher occupancy is possible with corrective action. Generally a property with low occupancy is sold at a reduced price and represents a future potential for profit. Many times low occupancy is the result of deferred maintenance, dated décor, lack of popular amenities, or failure to provide adequate marketing. If an investor determines these deficiencies can be corrected with proper attention and repairs or renovation, he or she may complete the purchase, allowing for additional capital expenditures or promotion to raise the occupancy level.

Occupancy is an important factor in an investor's determination to purchase as it directly affects the profit or potential profit of an investment property.

OPEN-END MORTGAGE

When a mortgagee lends money based on a ratio of assets to debt and the mortgagor may from time to tome borrow additional funds as long as it does not exceed the ratio agreed upon, this is an open-end mortgage. Generally, an updated appraisal of the mortgagor's assets

Concise Encyclopedia of Real Estate Business Terms
© 2006 by The Haworth Press, Inc. All rights reserved.
doi:10.1300/5637_13

is required to establish that the ratio has not been exceeded. However, other proof can be provided through inherited assets, the sale of assets that lowers the ratio of debt, or the increased value of assets such as stocks or mutual funds.

The open-end mortgage is favored with multiple-property investors. If a property is sold, it immediately provides additional funds for use in the purchase of other properties.

OPEN LISTING

In an open listing contract to sell property, the seller pays the agent an agreed upon fee, usually a percentage of the sales price. However, the seller may sell the property himself or herself or accept a contract from another agent and owe the original agent no fee if either the other agent or the seller sells the property. This type of agreement does not give the agent any control over the sale of the property. However, if the agent produces a sale, the agent will be paid a commission or fee.

Agents do not prefer open listings because they may work to sell the property and receive no fee or commission if it is sold by the seller or another agent. If the agent does produce a buyer on price and terms acceptable to the seller, the seller is contractually obligated to pay the agent.

OPERATING STATEMENT

An operating statement is a financial statement that uses the gross income and the total expenses over a given period of time to arrive at the net operating profit or loss of an investment property. The statement will include the time period that is covered in the report, generally a calendar or fiscal year. Actual costs are included, such as taxes, insurance, utility costs, mortgage payments, and management fees. Maintenance reserve or projected expenses are not included.

An operating statement is valuable to an investor who is considering the financial return for the given period. If the operating statement, which includes only actual income and expenses, shows a consistent loss, then it is considered a poor investment even if depreciation and other tax benefits erase or at least minimize the loss. An operating statement is a good measure of how the investment is performing.

OPTION

A contract between buyer and seller that grants the buyer a period of time in which to decide if he or she wants to purchase the property is called an option. The option must contain an ending date, a price to be paid for the property, and a consideration paid at the time the option is signed. The seller is obligated to the person holding the option until the option expires and cannot sell the property to anyone else. The person holding the option is not obligated to purchase the property; however, this person will lose the option deposit if he or she fails to complete the purchase. If the buyer completes the purchase, the option deposit is applied to the purchase price.

In an option contract, there are no conditions under which the buyer will receive a return of the deposit. However, in a modified option contract, a seller may agree to return the deposit under certain conditions, such as a title problem that cannot be cleared in a reasonable time or discovery of environmental contamination.

Options are often used in new developments to tie down the property until a determination can be made as to the viability of the project.

ORDINANCE

A law, usually local, that provides public regulation for the use of property is an ordinance. Local governments enact laws to regulate the use of property for the public good. Violation of an ordinance by a property owner can result in a fine or other penalty to the property owner.

Examples of public ordinances are zoning, setback distances from a public right-of-way, landscaping requirements for commercial property, construction standards, or provisions for public access to buildings and restrooms in accordance with the Americans with Disabilities Act of 1990.

A property owner who violates an ordinance will receive notice from the appropriate governmental agency requiring conformity to the ordinance, or in extreme cases, a "cease and desist" requiring compliance. If the property owner does not take appropriate action, a hearing may be scheduled to determine if a violation has occurred and to assess a penalty, fine, or other remedial action.

It is incumbent on property owners to acquaint themselves with all ordinances that affect their property, including, but not limited to, zoning, building standards and, setback lines for construction. Failure to do so has resulted in severe consequences for property owners.

OTHER CONDITIONS

A purchase agreement for real estate will often list conditions under which the sale is to be completed that apply only to this purchase and are outside of the usual terms of an agreement. These other conditions must be agreed to by buyer and seller at the time the agreement is signed. The conditions apply to a specific property purchase and are limited only by the agreement between buyer and seller or laws in effect at the time. Local, state, and federal laws cannot be violated by the other conditions. Sometimes called *special conditions,* they may provide circumstances under which the sale may not be completed by buyer or seller. They can also relate to a unique privilege granted by one party to the other. An example is when the buyer grants the seller the right to remove a family heirloom chandelier that would normally be a part of the sale.

Other conditions can void the sale if the buyer is unable to close the sale within, for example, 90 days. In such a case, if the sale is not completed by the buyer, the agreement becomes null and void with no further obligation of either buyer or seller to the other and a full refund of the buyer's deposit.

PARTIAL RELEASE

A clause that states that upon payment of a specified amount toward the principal reduction a portion of the property held for collateral to secure the loan will be released is a partial release clause. This clause is most often found in mortgages secured by property to be used for residential or commercial development into lots for sale. Upon the sale of a lot, the lender agrees to release the lot from the mortgage provided an agreed upon portion of the sale price is used to reduce the mortgage principal.

For example, if the developer borrows $500,000 for the development of the property into lots that includes the price of the land and the development costs and the lots sell for $25,000 each, then upon the sale of each lot the lender may agree to release the lot from the mortgage for the payment of $15,000 toward the remaining principal balance of the loan. With this release, the developer can provide a clear title to the buyer. Without such a release, the lot could not be sold with a clear title free of the original mortgage.

The partial release clause may also be used if a property owner wishes to sell at some time in the future a portion of the property covered by the mortgage. This clause permits the owner who has paid a large portion of the mortgage to sell a portion of the property free and clear of the blanket mortgage that originally was secured by the entire property.

PARTICIPATION MORTGAGE

A mortgage in which the owner participates in the income and/or profits from the sale is a participation mortgage. It can also be a mortgage in which the indebtedness is held by more than one lending institution. As an incentive for a lender to make a loan, the borrower may offer a percentage of the return from both cash flow and sale pro-

Concise Encyclopedia of Real Estate Business Terms
© 2006 by The Haworth Press, Inc. All rights reserved.
doi:10.1300/5637_14

ceeds to the lender. This type of mortgage is often made when the borrower's financial strength and/or down payment is less than the lender desires, but the project has the potential for above-average return and resale value. Rather than make a nonrecourse loan without personal liability to the borrower or a subpar loan based on standard requirements of the lender, the lender may offer to participate in the project's potential profits.

When such a loan is made, the lender generally becomes a quasi-partner in the project and closely monitors its progress and income and expenses. Such participation may extend for a specified term after which the project must be sold or refinanced and the lender removed as a participant. If refinanced, the project is appraised, and the lender's percentage of ownership is bought out with proceeds from the new mortgage.

The other definition of a participation mortgage occurs when a lender does not wish to assume the entire risk of the mortgage or the loan exceeds the limits of the lender's regulation for a single loan. For example, if a lender's limit for a single loan is $1 million and the loan needed is $1.5 million, the lender may bring in a participating lender to loan the additional $500,000 required.

PARTITION

If a property is held by co-owners such as in a partnership and one owner desires to sell and another owner does not, one of the owners may seek a division of the property through legal action. If approved by the appropriate court of law, the property is divided into separate parcels according to the percentage ownership of each co-owner. For example, if three co-owners together own 120 acres of land each with an equal percentage of ownership, the legal separation may divide the property into equal forty-acre parcels, thus severing the unity of possession. Each partner may then sell or retain his or her parcel.

This action generally occurs when the co-owners cannot agree or are unwilling to buy one or more of the other partners out of ownership. In such a case, one or more of the partners may ask the court to intervene and partition the property into separate ownership.

PERCENTAGE LEASE

Generally, a percentage lease is used with retail property but can also be used with other property, such as farmland. The lessor may receive a specified base rent and a percentage of the gross sales or income derived from the business or operation by the lessor. The percentage is based on a percentage of sales or income over a specified amount. The payment is a lump sum due at a specified time annually and is accompanied by proof of sales or income provided by the lessee with the payment. The percentage can be increased if sales or income reach a preagreed upon level.

For example, the lessee and lessor agree that the base rent will be $2,000 per month plus 2 percent of annual sales over $1 million and 3 percent of annual sales over $1.5 million, sales reach $1.8 million, and the percentage rent is due every February 15th for the past calendar year's sales. According to these terms, the lessee would pay $24,000 in monthly rent plus 2 percent of $500,000 or $10,000 plus 3 percent of $300,000 or $9,000 for a total rent of $43,000 for the year. However, if annual sales reach only $900,000, the lessee's annual rent would be only $24,000.

Percentage rent reduces the lessee's risk and allows the lessor to participate in the additional sales and subsequent profits of the lessee. By making the percentage rent an annual payment based on sales, it permits the lessee to make the payment from his or her additional profits.

PERCOLATION

The measurement of the amount of water that a particular soil type can absorb is called *percolation*. Soils heavy in clay will have less ability to absorb water than sandy soils. The absorption rate is important in calculating the type of foundation and the footings required in certain types of construction.

A test of the ability of the soil to absorb a given amount of water in a certain time period is called a *percolation test*. Health departments will conduct such a test to determine the amount of land required to effectively operate a septic system for waste removal. Because a septic system operates on the ability of the soil to absorb water, the greater the absorption rate, the shorter the field lines are required to be. The field lines are installed to slowly leak the water from the septic system into the soil, where it is absorbed.

A sandy soil may only require 50 feet of field lines, whereas a heavy clay content soil may require 100 feet or more. The septic system is designed according to the ability of the soil to absorb the water without it ever reaching the surface. A septic system that allows areas of standing wastewater may have insufficient-sized field lines or, in the case of older systems, a broken or deteriorated field line. With age, field lines can deteriorate to the point of collapsing and then have to be replaced. This is generally the case in older systems where there is surface wastewater. In newer systems, surface wastewater is generally the result of an insufficient length of the field line to allow the particular soil type to absorb the water.

PERPETUAL EASEMENT

A perpetual easement is one that does not have an expiration date. However, many easements are granted for a particular time period, after which the easement expires.

If an easement is granted in perpetuity, it lasts forever and is conveyed with the sale of the property to a new owner. It continues to be conveyed no matter how many times the property is sold. Because in time the use of the property may change, perpetual easements can be a burden to the landowner, who may wish to, for instance, construct a building over the easement. In such cases, the only recourse that may be available to the landowner is to buy out the easement from the easement owner.

An easement can diminish the value of the property if a change of use is desired. For instance, if a perpetual easement was granted by a landowner who now wishes to sell the property for the development of a shopping center, the easement will not permit the development because it would be required to be built over the easement. The owner must negotiate to move the easement or to buy it out from the easement owner. If this is not possible, the shopping center cannot be built and may thereby lower the market value of the property.

PHYSICAL LIFE

The expected life of a building is designated its *physical life*. When constructed, a building may be assigned a physical life of fifty years. However, circumstances such as neglected maintenance can reduce this life expectancy by a considerable number of years. Also, uncontrollable situations, such as an act of God, for example, an earthquake, can affect the physical life expectancy.

As an example, a deteriorating roof left unrepaired for an extended period may result in such further deterioration in structural supports that the cost to repair is greater than the cost to demolish and reconstruct. In such case, the physical life may be reduced to only a few years or even to zero years.

Physical life is a measurement of the time a building will last as opposed to its economic life, which is the number of years a building will contribute to the property value. Although a building may remain standing for some time, it may no longer have an economic life. The remaining physical life must be considered in a determination of its real market value.

The estimated life expectancy of the total component of a building from construction to the ultimate decay and dilapidation is considered the term of its physical life. The physical life of a building, as opposed to the economic life that measures the term that a building can produce income as an economic source, is measured by the life span rather than the economic span of a structure.

Physical life is related to both the quality and type of construction as well as the manner in which it has been maintained. Physical life can be greatly extended through timely maintenance of the structure.

PLANNED UNIT DEVELOPMENT

A large tract of land that is divided into smaller than normal lots for development is a planned unit development (PUD). Open areas for parks or landscaping are included in the PUD as compensation for the smaller than usual lots. The lots are then sold individually for residential, commercial, or industrial use to individual owners. The large open areas or parks are owned jointly by the lot owners, and generally a fee is collected from each property owner or a fund is setup by the developer to maintain the open areas. Sometimes these areas are donated to the city, county, or some public entity in return for maintaining the areas.

In a PUD, the developer must calculate the return on the investment from the lots to be sold. Generally, there is a higher rate of return from a PUD than from a normal development because of the additional lots available for sale. PUD developments may utilize zero lot lines or other such size limitations to obtain more lots per acre than are usually permitted.

POTENTIAL GROSS INCOME

The total potential income of an investment property before vacancy or expenses are considered is the potential gross income (PGI). This is often the beginning point an investor will use to evaluate the possible return an investment will yield. If a property has 100 rentable multifamily units with 40 one-bedroom units that rent for $500 per month and 40 two-bedroom units that rent for $600 per month, and the other 20 units are three-bedroom units that rent for $700 per month, the investment PGI for this property is $58,000 per month or $696,000 per year.

If vacancy is projected at 10 percent, then the remaining balance to pay for all other expenses would be $52,200 per month or $626,400 annually. An investor may then determine what the operating expenses, taxes, insurance, maintenance, and mortgage payments must not exceed to produce the desired return on investment. However, this can only be determined by first knowing the PGI.

The PGI is especially important for projections involving new construction or renovation of an older building because past performance data are either not available or are not a reliable indicator. In the case of renovation, the rent after renovation may be significantly higher than the present rent, and therefore the will not indicate the PGI after renovation.

POWER CENTER

A retail shopping center that is defined by the amount of total square feet and the number of retail anchor stores can be defined as a power center. It is different from a regional shopping center, which generally is larger and has more anchors and more specialty stores.

A power center will have more than 250,000 square feet of leasable area and contain at least three or four anchor stores that occupy more than 75 percent of the total leasable area. The term is derived from the number of retail anchor stores that generally occupy more than 50,000 square feet each and have the capacity to draw large numbers of shoppers.

POWER OF ATTORNEY

In the event a buyer or seller will not appear personally at the closing to sign the closing documents, a power of attorney must be prepared and signed by the nonappearing party granting authority for another person to appear and to sign in his or her place. The closing attorney will need to review the document for its appropriateness under the existing state law.

A power of attorney can be general or specific. If a general power of attorney is granted, it will need to specify the acts that the agent is granted the right to perform. If a special or limited power of attorney is granted, it will need to specify the act for which it is granted, including, in the case of real estate, a legal description of the property that is to be conveyed or mortgaged.

The legal authorization may be specific and granted only for a limited time and for a specified action, or it can be granted for an unlimited time and to cover any actions required by the individual.

People who are or know they will soon become unable to act for themselves can grant an unlimited power of attorney, giving another person the legal authority to act for them in all situations. In all cases, the power of attorney can be revoked by the grantor at any time.

PREDIAL SERVITUDES

Predial servitudes may be created by title, such as an agreement between the servient and dominant estate, by prescription, or by destination of the owner. When created by title, it becomes an alienation of a part of the property, often created in the act of sale. An example is the reservation of a right of passage. However, it is possible to create a servitude by verbal agreement if the property owner acknowledges the servitude and the owner of the servitude makes use of the servitude.

Predial servitudes are extinguished by prescription of nonuse for ten years or a shorter period of time if the parties agree. A predial servitude must be recorded in the public records to notify third parties. A predial servitude is inseparable from the property to which it is attached and remains in effect regardless of a change of ownership of the estates owing or due the servitude. A predial servitude is sometimes called an *appurtenant easement.*

PREPAYMENT PENALTY

Some loans are made in which the borrower cannot pay the loan principal in full until the expiration of the amortized schedule without a penalty; this penalty is called a *prepayment penalty.* A prepayment penalty is designed so that lenders can secure their rate of return and monthly income throughout the term of the loan. In some states prepayment penalties are prohibited.

If a borrower secures a mortgage for $50,000 and agrees to repay the mortgage in 120 equal payments at 10 percent interest and the interest rate drops to 7 percent, the borrower may wish to prepay the loan. However, if the mortgage contains a prepayment penalty of 10 percent, the borrower must not only pay the remaining principal balance but an additional 10 percent of the prepaid principal balance.

Prepayment penalties are perhaps most often used when an individual sells a property and carries the mortgage. The owner may be using the monthly payment as a source of continuing income required to meet his or her living expenses and not want the borrower to pay the mortgage off early. A prepayment penalty will help ensure that the borrower continues payments throughout the term of the mortgage.

PRESCRIPTION

A property that has been in the possession or under the control of someone who is not the deeded owner for a period of time prescribed by law may receive legal title through prescription. Possession may be by actual use, such as use of a driveway, or it may be land fenced in by the adjoining property owner for the number of years prescribed by law. This differs from an easement in that the deeded owner never gave permission through the granting of an easement.

Generally, property granted by prescription must be fenced or otherwise assumed to be in the possession of the other party for a period of ten to thirty years, depending on the statue of law that defines the prescribed period. Prescription requires that the deeded owner did not legally object to the possession whether the owner had knowledge or not. Many times the possession is discovered through a survey completed by the legal owner. However, if the prescribed number of years have passed prior to his or her knowledge and objection, the other party may seek legal title to the property and receive a deed through a court of civil procedure. Such legal action then prevents the original owner from recovery of the property and grants the party possessing the property a title by prescription.

PRESCRIPTIVE EASEMENT

If an easement has been used for an extended period of time, usually ten to thirty years, with no objection from the property owner, it may be prescribed by a law known as *prescriptive easement.* To prescribe by law, an easement must be used and unchallenged by the property owner for this extended period of time. If the owner then objects after it has been prescribed by law, the user may seek to establish the easement as permanent through a judicial process.

For instance, if a user has had access to the property though an unrecorded but unchallenged easement for the time prescribed by law without an objection from the property owner, it may be legally recognized as a permanent easement by the court. If, however, the property owner revokes the use of the property as an easement prior to the prescription period, the user has no recourse through the courts to establish it as a permanent easement.

For example, if property owner A has allowed property owner B to use an access through his property for a period of nine years and the prescriptive period is ten years, property owner A may refuse property owner B the further use of this access in writing without any recourse. If, however, the period of use has exceeded the ten year prescriptive period, property owner B may seek a permanent access easement through a court order.

PRETAX CASH FLOW

Cash flow from an investment property that is calculated before any tax consequences are considered is called *pretax cash flow*. When all expenses are deducted from the total income, including mortgage payments, property taxes, insurance, maintenance, and management expenses, the amount remaining before taxes on the cash flow profit are considered is the *pretax profit*. Because taxes on any profit may be significant, a pretax cash flow may significantly differ from an after-tax profit.

For example, if the pretax cash flow is $250,000 and the tax rate is 20 percent, the after-tax profit would be reduced to $200,000. This is also called *before tax cash flow* or *equity dividend*. Although pretax cash flow may be important in certain calculations, it does not represent the return on investment until the after-tax profits are calculated. Only then can the actual profit from the investment be calculated.

PRICE LEVEL ADJUSTED MORTGAGE

A mortgage in which the interest rate remains constant but the principal balance is adjusted for inflation is called a *price level adjusted mortgage*. This type of mortgage provides the lender the advantage of adjusting the principal based on current inflation. The adjustment is generally made on the anniversary of the loan each year based on the inflation factor over the past twelve months.

For example, if the original loan was $100,000 and the inflation rate was 10 percent, and assuming the principal reduction was $15,000 during the first year, the adjustment would be 10 percent of the remaining principal balance of $85,000. The new principal balance would be $93,500, and the monthly payments would be recomputed to reflect repayment of the loan over the remaining term at the same interest rate.

This type of loan can be significantly impacted in periods of high inflation but only slightly affected in periods of low inflation. With this loan, the lender agrees not to adjust the interest rate over the entire term of the loan but instead to adjust the principal balance annually.

PRIVATE MORTGAGE INSURANCE

When a lender loans more than 75 percent or 80 percent of the value of the property, private mortgage insurance (PMI) is required to protect against default by the borrower. The PMI is purchased and paid for by the borrower to insure the amount in excess of the 75 percent or 80 percent of the loan. This applies to both residential and commercial loans.

Generally, a lender determines that a loan below 75 percent or 80 percent is a safe loan based on the value of the property, the borrower's financial strength, and, in the case of commercial/investment loans, the projected cash flow of the investment. However, above this projected safe limit, a lender may require insurance to cover the additional risk.

Mortgages that require PMI have a provision that once the loan is paid down to the 75 percent or 80 percent of loan to value ratio then the insurance is no longer required, and the borrower's insurance premium is dropped from the payment. For example, if a lender loans $90,000 on a property that appraised for $100,000, the loan is 90 percent of the loan to value and may require PMI insurance. After a period of time when the borrower has made on-time payments to reduce the loan to $75,000, the insurance payment is no longer required. However, in most cases, the borrower must request that the PMI be discontinued in order for the lender to no longer collect the PMI payment.

The use of PMI has created the possibility for many borrowers to secure 90 percent or even 95 percent loans and allows the lender to feel secure with this loan to value ratio.

PRO FORMA

When an investment property is purchased, it is helpful to project not only the current income and expenses but also what can be reasonably anticipated in the future. This projection of future income and expenses is called a *pro forma,* literally, how the investment is expected to perform into the future. Generally, a pro forma is projected three to five years into the future or longer. This is especially helpful when a property is purchased that is underperforming with high vacancy or below market rents.

A pro forma projects not only the income when higher rents can be anticipated in the future but also how that additional income offsets higher expected expenses. A pro forma will show the performance of the property during each year of the projection. For example, it may be anticipated that ordinary rents will increase 3 percent to 5 percent each year and that a higher than normal vacancy can be reduced to a normal vacancy. Increased expenses, such as taxes, insurance, utilities, and other operating costs, must be considered. An increase in expense may also be projected as a 3 percent to 5 percent increase per year. A completed pro forma will provide a purchaser with a reasonable expectation of return on the investment through the years covered. Although a pro forma is only a projection of anticipated income and expenses and cannot cover the unexpected, such as an abnormal increase in taxes or insurance, it is a useful tool for the real estate investor in calculating future return on investment.

PRO RATA SHARE

Tenants in a multitenant building may be required under terms of the lease to share in the landlord's cost of insurance, taxes, management, maintenance, and utilities, collectively referred to as *operating costs*. These costs when passed on to the tenant are sometimes referred to as *add-on charges*. Leases will often call for a base rent as so much per square foot for space the tenant occupies in the building plus a pro rata charge calculated as an additional charge per square foot of occupied space or a percentage of the leasable space. Together they will make up the total charge to the tenant.

Leases will also provide for an annual adjustment to the per square foot charge based on any increases in the operating costs. These additional costs are known as *adjustment charges* over the base rate and passed on to the tenant on a pro rata basis of square feet occupied to the leaseable space. The tenant's share of the operating cost is calculated as a fraction. The leased area of the tenant's space is the numerator, and the gross leasable space of the building or shopping center is the denominator.

As an example, if the tenant leases 2,000 square feet and the total leasable area is 100,000 square feet, then the tenant's fraction of the total is 2 percent. If the operating costs are $50,000 per year, the tenant's share is 2 percent × $50,000 or $1,000 divided by 12 months and added to the monthly base tenant charge. This increase may be passed on to the tenant as a one-time charge to be paid each year on a specified date or added to the monthly rent plus pro rata charges.

By using the annual "adjustment charge," landlords protect themselves from increases in the operating charges that may occur over the term of the lease.

PROPERTY CONDITION DISCLOSURE

In many states a seller must complete a disclosure of the condition of the property as part of the process of placing the property for sale. This disclosure form must then be presented to any prospective buyer.

The property disclosure will include such information as the time of purchase, condition or age of roof, any plumbing leaks, known termite damage, previous flooding, etc. The information is intended to disclose to the buyer past problems experienced by the seller and the actual condition of the property the buyer is purchasing.

This disclosure form may be required in some states only for residential property. Commercial property often uses a due diligence period for the buyer to investigate the condition as well as requires any knowledge or previous reports to be furnished by the seller to the buyer.

PROPERTY INSPECTION

A property inspection is a thorough examination of a structure to ensure that it is sound and to reveal deferred maintenance, inoperable systems, municipal code violations, and similar problems. Property inspections are part of the due diligence period in real estate transactions and allow buyers and sellers to agree on the terms of a sale before a great amount of time and expense have been spent. Normally, if a property does not pass inspection, the buyer is refunded any deposit and the seller is left with nothing for the time wasted. However, after a property inspection is approved and accepted by the buyer, the buyer is generally obligated to purchase the property assuming all other contingencies are met. Typically, inspections include a thorough report on the foundation, roof, air-conditioning and heating systems, electrical system, and drainage.

PURCHASE AGREEMENT

The purchase agreement, also known as a buy/sell agreement, is entered into by a buyer and seller to set forth the price, terms, and conditions in which the buyer agrees to purchase and the seller agrees to sell a certain property. The agreement will identify the buyer and the seller by their appropriate names and addresses. It will state the agreed upon price and the method of payment i.e., cash or owner financing, along with all other terms and conditions.

The agreement will state the seller's warranties, such as all systems to be in operating condition and any other conditions related to the title or property. The agreement will state any contingencies by the buyer, such as subject to securing financing.

Other items generally covered in the agreement include the date of closing, specific performance, amount of deposit, and when occupancy is to be granted.

When signed by both buyer and seller, the agreement becomes a legal document enforceable by either party according to contract law applicable in the state in which it is executed.

PURCHASE MONEY MORTGAGE

A mortgage in which the seller carries a portion of the purchase price is called a *purchase money mortgage* (PMM) with this type of mortgage, the seller may take a first mortgage or a second mortgage for a portion of the purchase price. In either event, if the purchaser defaults in repayment according to the terms of the PMM, the seller or mortgagee may foreclose on the mortgage. If the seller has taken a second mortgage, he or she must pay off the first mortgage or make other arrangements with the first mortgage holder as a condition of the foreclosure.

For example, if the seller has taken a $20,000 second mortgage behind an $80,000 first mortgage, the seller must satisfy the first mortgage holder as a condition of the foreclosure should the seller default on repayment of the second mortgage. If the seller carries the entire first mortgage, with default by the buyer the seller may foreclose and regain possession of the property.

A PMM is generally used to reduce the amount of cash down payment by the borrower in the purchase of property. The incentive for the seller is that it may allow him or her to sell more quickly and even at a higher price. The seller also earns interest on the mortgage that may equal or exceed what could be received by reinvesting the money in a cash sale.

PURCHASE PROPOSAL

The purchase proposal is often referred to as a *letter of intent*. Usually drafted in a less formal and nonbinding form than a purchase agreement, it is not intended to set forth the entire agreement but rather outline the basic conditions by which a purchaser is willing to purchase a property. The purchase proposal is submitted by a purchaser to determine if the price and preliminary terms are acceptable to a seller.

The purchase proposal does not bind the purchaser to buy the property or, if accepted, does not bind the seller to sell. However, if accepted by the seller, it provides a time limit, usually thirty days, in which a binding agreement will be executed by buyer and seller. The formal purchase agreement to follow will provide more specific obligations of the buyer and seller and become the final and binding agreement.

For example, the purchase proposal will state the price offered by the buyer, the time for due diligence, conditions under which the purchaser is willing to enter into a binding agreement, and other general conditions of the purchase. Purchase proposals are more commonly used in the purchase of commercial and investment properties.

RANGE LINE

Range lines are government land survey lines that extend due north and south at six-mile intervals and are numbered east or west from the principal meridian. Range lines are used to form the east and west boundaries of townships.

RATE OF RETURN

An investment is generally evaluated based on the ratio of net income to the initial investment. This ratio is most often expressed as percentage of return. The rate of return may be expressed as a percentage return on an annualized basis or over the term of the investment. The appraised value may establish a value limited by the economic life of the property in calculating a long-term rate of return. An annual rate of return may be calculated by using the annual net income from the investment to the capital invested.

For example, if an investment has an annual net income of $20,000 and the capital investment was $80,000, then the rate of return would be calculated as a 25 percent return. The investor balances the rate of return from any investment against what he or she may receive as a return on another type of investment and the risk calculation. When an investor determines that the risk factor is greater than or equal to the rate of return, the investor will generally choose another investment vehicle.

To determine the real rate of return on an investment, it must be adjusted for inflation. For instance, if the rate of return is 10 percent and the inflation factor is 5 percent, then the real rate of return is only 5 percent. The advantage of real estate investments over, for example, mutual funds is that the investment must also be calculated to include the inflation value of the investment held. For instance, if the real rate

Concise Encyclopedia of Real Estate Business Terms
© 2006 by The Haworth Press. Inc. All rights reserved.
doi:10.1300/5637_15

of return adjusted for inflation is 5 percent, theoretically at least the real estate held would have appreciated 5 percent in value.

REAL ESTATE INVESTMENT TRUST

Real estate investment trust (REIT) is the purchase of real estate by a large group of investors. REITs are regulated by the Securities and Exchange Commission. A REIT must include no fewer than 100 investors. The REIT must disclose a resumé of the officers of the REIT along with a complete financial information and details of the real estate holdings.

REITs have become a popular method of investing in large commercial real estate. Generally a REIT will specialize in a type of commercial real estate holding, such as hotels, shopping centers, office buildings, or apartment complexes. The investor's loss is limited by his or her initial investment. The investor will share in the tax write-off of any loss and receive a proportionate share of any profits.

Many REITs have become public companies that sell shares of stock on a stock exchange. These shares are bought and sold the same as other stocks.

REAL ESTATE OWNED

When a bank or lending institution acquires real estate through a procedure of foreclosure or as an investment, it is referred to as real estate owned (REO) property. A bank may purchase a property for future expansion, such as for opening a branch, and hold the property in inventory as an REO property subject to federal regulations on the amount of time the property may be held. However, most property owned by banks or lending institutions are acquired through a process of foreclosure on loans that have defaulted.

When a foreclosure is instituted against a borrower who has defaulted on loan payments, the bank will begin a legal process to repossess the property. After completion of the legal process, the property by judicial order is deeded back to the bank and placed in its REO portfolio. The bank will usually then proceed to find a buyer through its own efforts or place the property under a listing agreement with a real estate company that will proceed to market the property and find a buyer. Until such time as a buyer is found and the property is deeded to the new buyer, it is held in the bank's REO portfolio. If the property does not sell for the amount owed, the bank may proceed to secure a deficiency judgment against the original owner who defaulted for the difference in the amount sold and the remaining balance owed. However, the property must be sold for a minimum two-thirds of the appraised value. If the property is sold without benefit of appraisal, it must be sold for an amount to cover all costs and mortgages.

REAL PROPERTY

Real property includes all the rights, interest, and structures attached to the land inherent in the ownership of property. Real property is defined by many states as synonymous with the term *real estate.* Real property is the real estate, with or without structures, that is transferable through public records from one owner to another. It is represented by the individual parcels or larger tracts of property owned by the individual, partnership, or corporate entity. Real property is further defined as property other than personal property, such as furniture, fixtures, equipment, or jewelry, owned by an individual and identified as portable as opposed to real estate, which is not portable.

REALTOR

Realtor is a registered trade name that identifies a real estate professional who is a member of the National Association of Realtors (NAR) and any of its affiliated local and state Realtor boards. A Realtor has been licensed to sell, manage, and lease real estate through a state licensing commission and maintains his or her license usually renewable annually. A real estate professional may be licensed to sell, manage, or lease real estate and not be a Realtor or member of the NAR.

A Realtor subscribes to the code of ethics and bylaws of the local and state boards of Realtors. If a Realtor violates any portion of the code of ethics or bylaws, he or she can be summoned to appear before the appropriate committee and in extreme cases evicted from membership.

Realtors are offered education courses to further their professional practice in such areas as fair housing, dual agency, risk management, and contracts. As the real estate profession has grown in large numbers, the NAR is credited with moving real estate brokerage into a nationally recognized profession nationwide.

REALTOR COMPENSATION

Any compensation paid by a seller to the real estate broker is regulated by the contract between the seller and the Realtor, as agent. The amount of compensation, generally expressed as a percentage of the sales price, is a negotiated fee between seller and realtor.

However, a Realtor may agree to a net listing in which the owner agrees to accept a minimum amount from the sale. The Realtor receives as compensation any amount over this. The compensation to the Realtor is the difference between the minimum amount the seller agrees to accept generally less the costs and expenses of the sale to the seller.

An accepted custom among Realtors is to co-broker a sale with another licensed real estate professional. In the absence of a written split of the total compensation received, it is general practice to divide the compensation equally between the Realtor representing the seller and the Realtor representing the buyer.

RECAPTURE RATE

Recapture rate is calculated as the return on investment divided by the cash investment expressed as a percentage of return. When an investment property is purchased, there is a cash investment in the form of a down payment. This cash infusion becomes the basis on which the rate of return is calculated, generally expressed as a percentage of return.

For example, if the down payment is $100,000 and the investment returns a cash flow profit of $20,000 in any year, the recapture rate for that year is expressed as a 20 percent return or recapture rate. This rate of recapture will vary from year to year as additional capital may be invested in the property and the cash flow profit changes.

When originally used as a term to calculate return on investment, real estate depreciation was assumed to determine the investment as a constantly declining value. However, in recent years, the recapture rate has been recalculated to express the generally increasing value of the investment over depreciation and to include the other factors that must be considered in determining the true recapture rate.

Although it is true that depreciation must be recaptured when the property is sold, the recapture rate will generally be positive if the property returns a cash flow profit.

RECIPROCAL EASEMENT AGREEMENT

When one property owner grants an adjacent property owner a right for customers to cross his or her property and this right becomes reciprocal, the agreement is called a reciprocal easement agreement (REA). This is especially important in retail shopping centers, where an out-parcel owner may need to have his or her customers drive across the shopping center parking lot. Without such an agreement, an owner could construct curb restrictions that prevent access.

An REA agreement is especially important when a large-use retail store or supermarket and a development for smaller retail stores are constructed adjacent to each other. Often a retail shopping center developer will sell the adjacent property he or she owns to a supermarket for development. Both the developer and the supermarket will enter into an REA agreement whereby both agree to connect parking lots and not construct any barriers that would prevent free flow of traffic from one parking lot to the other. This is a convenience to the customers who shop at the center and helps the retailers who locate in the center by providing them with additional customers due to the ease of traffic flow.

RECOGNIZED GAIN

When a property is sold or exchanged, the amount over what was paid for the property, plus any capital improvements, less any taxable deductions is called the *recognized gain* from the sale. The recognized gain may vary greatly from the actual equity received at the time of the sale. Recognized gain relates to tax consequences and not to actual monies received at time of sale.

To arrive at the recognized gain, one must start with the equity and subtract the initial cost of the property, any special tax credits applicable, any capital improvement costs, etc. To this calculation, one must add back the depreciation taken over the term of ownership.

For example:

Sales Price	$1,000,000
Less: Mortgage Owed	−$400,000
Equity	$600,000

To arrive at the recognized gain, calculate as follows:

Sales Price	$1,000,000
Less:	
Price Paid	−$500,000
Tax Credits	−$45,000
Capital Improvements	−$200,000
	$255,000
Add back depreciation recaptured	+ $75,000
Recognized Gain	$330,000

In this example, there may be other deductions applicable that will further affect the recognized gain for tax purposes from the sale of the property. An accountant can best calculate the recognized gain.

RECORDING

Public records exist in every county and parish for the purpose of providing constructive notice to the public. The recording of a mortgage deed, judgment, or any other legal document is considered public notice, and the information is available to anyone who searches the record.

Filing of the mortgage deed, etc., gives protection to the buyer or mortgage holder. This recorded instrument will notify any other buyer or lender of the current status of the property as to the owner and mortgage. A title or mortgage search is usually completed prior to the passing of title or execution of any mortgage against any property.

If a property is sold and the deed is not filed, there is consequently no public notification as to the current owner. In rare instances, the property may be sold to a second owner without knowledge that the property has previously been sold. It then is left to the courts to determine legal ownership through the production of documents by the rightful owner.

When a deed is filed it establishes through the public records the rightful owner or owner of record. This act of recording is governed by state law and provides protection for the owner.

REDHIBITION

Redhibition is a legal recourse used to void a sale when a defect in the property is such as to render its use impossible or so imperfect or inconvenient that the buyer would not have purchased had he or she been aware. Although it may be assumed that the seller was aware of the defect, even if the seller were not aware, the legal recourse of redhibition is available to the buyer.

An example of a defect that would allow a purchaser to exercise the right of redhibition would be a leaking roof, termite damage, faulty air-conditioning or heating system, nonworking sewage system, leaking gas or water pipes, or a cracking foundation.

A component that is old and may need replacing in the future does not constitute a cause for redhibition. A roof that is old and may need replacing but is not currently leaking and for which the seller made no warranty is also not cause for redhibition.

The prescriptive period for an action in redhibition is one year from the date of sale if the seller acted in good faith or one year from the discovery of the defect if the seller acted in bad faith.

REDLINING

The act of refusing to sell property to any qualified buyer in certain areas is called *redlining*. The term originated from an imaginary line drawn around specified areas in which specific races were not shown or sold property. This practice has become illegal by federal laws. Before such federal laws were enacted the practice was widespread and amounted to blatant discrimination. With the states unwilling or unable to act, federal laws were passed to prohibit the practice.

Not only did the practice involve the sale of property, but also was practiced by loan institutions by refusing to make loans to qualified buyers in specified areas. This practice resulted in many otherwise qualified buyers being unable to secure a loan.

REGIONAL SHOPPING CENTER

A retail shopping center that because of its size and mixture of tenants draws customers from beyond its normal geographic area is considered a *regional shopping center.* The tenant mixture of apparel, furniture, services, general merchandise, and often recreational facilities provides a broad appeal and draws from a large geographic area. It is designed to draw from a customer base where many of the products and services are not available such as from smaller towns and rural areas.

A regional shopping center is anchored by one or more department stores that offer a wide variety of products and occupies 100,000 or more square feet. As a general rule, regional shopping centers will have between 500,000 and 1 million square feet of leasable area. The retail area may be contained in an open walk area or in an enclosed area, known as a *shopping mall.*

Regional shopping centers are almost always located in cities of 100,000 people or more. However, they may be developed with a view toward attracting a customer base from a geographic area of 300,000 population up to 1 million. Such centers can require a land area of 50 acres to 100 acres or more. The large land size is required for the retail development and for the customer parking required to accommodate such a large customer draw.

RENEWABLE MORTGAGE

A renewable mortgage is a mortgage in which the lender has the right after a specified time to require payment of the entire principal, to adjust the interest rate, or to alter the original terms of the mortgage. At the lender's option, the terms of the mortgage may be renewed for a specified period at the current interest rate. However, if the mortgage payments have not been made timely or for any other reason at the lender's option, the lender may require full payment of the mortgage.

For example, if the term of the loan is fifteen years with a five-year call option by the lender at a 6 percent interest rate, the lender may at the end of the five-year period adjust the interest rate to a current rate of, for example, 8 percent and renew the loan with a second call period of another five years. In such case, the monthly payments will be adjusted to reflect the payment of the remaining principal at the 8 percent interest rate over the balance of the remaining ten-year term. At the expiration of the second call term of five years, the interest rate may be adjusted again depending on the current interest rate for like mortgages. The monthly payments would then be adjusted again to reflect the new interest rate over the remaining five years of the original fifteen-year mortgage.

Renewable mortgages are especially popular with lenders in times of low interest rates to protect the lender when interest rates rise. Such mortgages are sometimes called *rollover mortgages*. The lender retains the option at his or her discretion to call the loan, renew the loan, or renew with new terms and interest rates.

RENEWAL OPTION

As part of a lease agreement, an option to renew may be granted to the lessee. The option is not mandatory as part of the lease but is granted as an option that the lessee may or may not choose to exercise. A renewal option is usually granted by the lessor for a specified term and may include more than one renewal option term. For instance, a lessor may grant two option renewal terms for a period of three years each. If the first option term is exercised, the lessee has the right to also exercise the second renewal term.

Renewal options can be granted with an option to renew at the same rent or with an increase in rent specified as either a dollar amount over the previous lease period or as a percentage increase, such as a 15 percent increase. Options may also be based on the consumer price increase (CPI). In such instances, if the rent was $1,000 per month for the previous lease period and the CPI increased 15 percent over the term, then the renewal option rent would be $1,150 per month during the term of the renewal option.

Renewal options grant the lessee a choice to renew the lease but obligate the lessor to renew the lease if the lessee exercises the option. The lessor will grant the renewal option because a lessee is reluctant to sign a lease for, for example, three years without the option, not knowing what the rent will be or if he or she can even remain in the space after the initial term expires.

If a renewal option is granted and the lessor wishes to lease to another tenant, the lessor is legally bound to renew the lease if the lessee exercises his or her option or buy out any renewal options granted.

RESCISSION

A purchaser who has entered into an agreement may be entitled to rescind the agreement and thereby any obligation to purchase for reasons of error or fraud. A purchaser's right to rescind or cancel an agreement may be based on whether he or she would have entered into the agreement had he or she had knowledge of the true condition or nature of the property. A buyer cannot give legal consent when such consent was the result of error or fraud.

In the case of rescission due to error, the buyer may invalidate the agreement if it is proved that he or she would not have entered into the agreement had he or she known and that the error was known or should have been known by the seller. If the error was by fraud on the part of the seller and had the buyer known he or she would not have entered into the agreement, the buyer may rescind the agreement.

In the case of zoning or building restrictions, although they do not constitute a title issue, the buyer may exercise rescission if the restrictions prevent him or her from using the property for the intended purpose. Especially is this true if the seller knew of the buyer's intended use and was aware that the zoning or building restrictions prohibited the buyer from using the property as intended.

The right of rescission is not based on title defect but on whether the purchaser would have entered into the contract to purchase had he or she been aware of the true nature of the property.

Rescission may be ordered by the courts even if the sale has been completed and title has been passed to the new owner.

RESORT PROPERTIES

When the primary inducement for purchasing a lot, condominium, or home is the recreational facilities available, it may be classified as a resort property. A resort property may offer a single recreational inducement, such as a public or private lake for water-related activities, or multiple recreational activities, such as tennis courts, golf courses, ski facilities, and bike or hiking trails. A clubhouse with restaurant is often a part of the amenities offered.

A surcharge or maintenance fee may become an obligation of the buyer. Such fees are used to maintain the recreational facilities for the property owners. The maintenance fee may be a one-time charge or, more often, a monthly or an annual fee paid by all property owners. If the fees are not paid by the property owner in accordance with the terms of the agreement between the resort owner and the property owner, the resort owner may be permitted to place a lien against the property to secure payment. If the property owner sells the property, the lien is required to be satisfied prior to passing title to another owner. In some instances, the resort owner may have the right to foreclose on the property and to force a sale in order to satisfy the payment of past due fees.

If maintenance fees are charged to the property owner and the facilities are not maintained, the property owners have legal recourse against the resort owner. In rare cases, the courts have ruled that the resort owner is in default and the resort has been purchased by the property owners, who then establish a board of directors and assume ownership of the resort.

RESTRICTIONS

A subdivision in which a buyer decides to build or purchase may contain certain restrictions to which he or she is obligated to comply. These restrictions include size of the structure (usually stated in square feet), fencing, architectural design, percentage of brick or other material to be used on the exterior, size and location of carport or garage, landscaping, height of structure, and setback requirements for all sides of the structure from the property lines. In the case of commercial structures restrictions can limit where parking is allowed, amount and type of landscaping, and architectural design.

Another restriction that is commonly placed on residential and commercial structures is the prohibition, or, if allowed, the design and conformity of, additional structures not connected to the main structure, such as storage buildings. Often this restriction will require that the additional building be of the same exterior material as the main structure and conform to the same architectural design.

RESTRICTIVE COVENANT

A restrictive covenant is any restriction on the use, occupancy, size, placement, or architecture of buildings or other improvements that may be placed in the deed. Such restrictions may be used to help ensure the value of the property for present and future buyers. When restrictions are a part of the deed they become binding on the current owner and on all subsequent purchasers. If the highest and best use of a property changes, a restrictive covenant can prevent an alternative use of the property. For instance, if a restrictive covenant is placed on a property allowing only single-family homes to be built and, in the future, the best use of the property is for multifamily or commercial development, such a restriction will prevent the alternate use.

Restrictive covenants can be used for any purpose to restrict future use. For example, a developer may agree to restrict any other similar restaurants in a larger development as an inducement to a restaurant owner to locate in his or her development. Although such a restriction may appear appropriate at the time, it may prove an unwise restriction ten, twenty, or thirty years in the future. If a portion of the restriction is violated and is not challenged and remains so for a period of time, the restriction may be ruled invalid.

RESUBDIVISION

If a previously filed plat of a subdivision is replatted to include further division of the lots, this becomes a resubdivision of the original plat. This resubdivision is usually the result of a changing use of the property. For example, if the original subdivision was for two-acre lots and the developer decides that half-acre lots are more in demand, he or she may resubdivide the plat into the smaller half-acre lots.

When resubdividing, a developer must be concerned with any restrictions that may have been filed with the original plat, requiring, for instance, that all lots in the development be at least two acres. If such is the case, then resubdivision may be prohibited by the restrictive covenant.

Resubdivision may also be done for an older development when the lot divisions were, for instance, 50-feet wide. With newer homes often requiring larger lot sizes, a resubdivision may be useful to accommodate them.

RETAIL MAP

A retail map shows the location of existing buildings, their use, and their ownership. It will also show the physical characteristics of the land, such as streets, highways, driveways, and type of parking surface. The map is designed to detail the land use of a relatively small area and is used by retailers and related service operations to determine proximity of other stores and services. Such a map is especially useful in the marketing of a limited area. It is also used by retailers and service operations to determine the viability of a new location.

REVERSE MORTGAGE

A homeowner whose mortgage is paid off or who has a low remaining balance and needs additional income may initiate a reverse mortgage with a lender. Typically, this type of mortgage is for retirees or fixed-income homeowners. In a reverse mortgage, the homeowner receives a monthly payment while retaining ownership of the home. The owner is borrowing against the equity he or she has in the home. The longer the reverse mortgage is in effect, the less equity is retained in the home. This type of mortgage provides a continuing income to the owner for a period of time.

A reverse mortgage becomes due and payable on a specified date agreed to in the mortgage or upon the occurrence of a specific event. Such an event is usually the death of the borrower or the sale of the home. Reverse mortgages provide the homeowner a method of securing equity from the home during his or her lifetime without selling the home. At the specified date or upon the death of the owner or sale of the home, the mortgage must be paid off by the owner or heirs. If the heirs are unable to pay off the mortgage in the event of death, the home must be sold to satisfy the mortgage or repossessed by the lender to satisfy the debt.

As the population ages, reverse mortgages have become a popular method for retirees to subsidize their income. With the increased value of homes in recent years, creating in many cases large equities in homes, more and more retirees are providing additional income during retirement years through the use of the reverse mortgage.

REVPAR

Revpar is a method of measuring the performance of a motel or other lodging property with similar properties for investment purposes. Revpar is an acronym for *revenue per available room.* This unit of comparison is calculated by multiplying a property's percentage of occupancy by the average room rent. For example, if the percentage of occupancy is 70 percent and the average room rent is $60, the revpar would be $42.

In recent years, other methods of calculating the performance of lodging facilities have come into use, but revpar remains an industry standard for evaluating lodging performance.

RIGHT OF FIRST REFUSAL

Right of first refusal is often granted to a lessee as part of the lease agreement in the event the property owner decides to sell the property. If the owner places the property for sale, the owner will wait until a buyer is ready to purchase and then provide the lessee a period of time to match the buyer's offer, or the owner may also contact the lessee and inform him or her of the decision to sell and specify a period of time in which to complete the purchase.

Although the owner is legally obligated through the right of first refusal to offer the property to the lessee, the lessee is under no obligation to purchase. If the lessee does not complete the purchase in the time agreed, the owner may sell to any other buyer.

The right of first refusal may also be used when a property owner desires to purchase an adjacent property. The two owners may enter into a binding right of first refusal. Occasionally, this right may be granted by the owner to any person who wishes to purchase the property at such time as the owner is ready to sell.

RIGHT-OF-WAY

When a property is purchased it will be subject to any right-of-way previously existing. It may be in the form of a privilege to pass through property by a designated pathway or an easement for present or future use. Most common rights-of-way agreements are used for railroad or highway passages or for pipelines, pole lines, or utility lines. They may include surface, underground, or overhead rights-of-way.

Generally, a right-of-way, if underground or overhead, will prohibit building construction on or over the right-of-way. However, it may allow for parking lots or driveways to be built over the right-of-way. In such instances the owner of the right-of-way will retain the right to service or expand the use of the right-of-way. This will often require the right to disrupt the existing parking lot, driveway, or landscaping placed over the right-of-way.

In the case of a road or street right-of-way, the extent of the right-of-way may extend several feet beyond the existing street or road and allow for utilities to be placed on the extended portion of the right-of-way or even allow for the widening of the street or road.

RIPARIAN RIGHTS

Riparian rights are the rights of use and enjoyment held by owners of property adjacent to a lake, stream, or river. This right entitles owners to the use of the water that flows across their land or that is adjacent to it. Riparian rights are limited to use or enjoyment that does not materially interfere with the quality of use by or quantity of water for other owners. These rights are not limited by the location or the time when the property was purchased.

Riparian rights provide the owner with the right to the water for adding piers or boathouses, for fishing or boating or for other such uses provided it does not impede or otherwise obstruct the use by other owners. The interpretation of such rights may at times need to be made by the courts. For example, if an owner decides to create a dam that prevents the normal flow of water and hinders the use of other property owners downstream, the courts may rule that the rights of other owners have been violated.

Riparian rights may be applied to the use of water for irrigation purposes as well. If an owner's use of the available water is such that it impairs the rights of other owners, the doctrine of beneficial use may supersede the doctrine of riparian rights. This has become an ongoing battle in states where water from public waterways is scarce and upstream owners use water in amounts that reduce the available supply for other owners downstream.

RISK ANALYSIS

A lender may use a risk analysis in the process of determining whether to loan money for an investment property. Risk analysis is a quantitative method used by a lender to assess the risk of failure by measuring the probability of various occurrences that can influence the investment performance.

A risk analysis attempts to measure the potential for change in market conditions, property performance, and any other factors that may affect the net operating income (NOI) projections and ultimately the value of the investment. A risk analysis is a subjective approach to investment performance but is nevertheless used in the lending and investment analysis process. Although the risks considered may or may not occur, they still enter into the analysis of an investment's probability of future return. For example, if a shopping center is located in an area where population and traffic patterns are changing, an analysis of the risk may determine that, even though the investment is sound today with an adequate NOI, the NOI may change in the future. A lender will want to consider this changing demographic as he or she looks into the future impact of these changes and how they will effect the investment during the term of the loan.

ROYALTY

In addition to land and buildings, an owner may also possess as part of the property the minerals, such as oil, gas, sand, gravel, or coal. The property owner can sell the mineral rights and receive royalty payments for the minerals as they are depleted. Mineral rights, according to state law, can be retained by a former owner even if the property is sold. In some states, there is a term limit on the holding of mineral rights by a former property owner if there is no production on the property. If, for example, ten years pass during which no production occurs, the mineral rights revert to the current property owner. In other states, the mineral rights by law pass to the next owner without any right of the current owner to retain ownership.

If the minerals by law are allowed to be retained by a former owner, this right of ownership can extend for as long as there is any production or, in some states, for ten years beyond the last production. In states that allow retained ownership, mineral rights are treated as a separate entity from the property itself. In other states the minerals may be an integral part of the land and not separate from the land.

Mineral rights may be sold to another party, such as an oil or gas company, for a specified term. Even if no viable amount of minerals are found after drilling, the company can retain these rights for the specified period by making payments to the property owner.

Royalty is considered a payment to the holder of mineral rights for the right to deplete the minerals. Such payments are calculated as a price per unit of the amount extracted or a combination of rent and depletion of minerals.

RULE OF 72

When a sum of money is deposited in a fixed-interest-bearing account, the rule of 72 can be used to calculate the number of years for the amount deposited to double in value. The number of years is calculated by dividing the fixed interest rate by 72.

For example, if an interest rate is fixed at 10 percent, the investor divides the rate by 72 and discovers that it will take 7.2 years to double the investment. If the interest rate is 6 percent, it will take 12 years to double. If the interest rate is 4 percent, it will take 18 years to double.

S CORPORATION

S corporation, sometimes called a Subchapter S corporation, is a corporation that has elected to be taxed similar to a partnership. In an S corporation, the owners are treated for tax purposes in a manner such that profits or losses flow through the corporation to the individual or the individuals in proportion to their percentages of ownership. S corporations are treated as a normal corporation, with deductions for qualified expenses and depreciation deducted from the income stream. However, any profits or losses, unlike a regular corporation, pass through to the individual owner or owners. The profits or losses are then applied to the individual tax returns. The provisions of the S corporation are defined in Subchapter S of the Internal Revenue Code.

An S corporation is unlike a regular corporation, which retains the profits or losses within the corporation. The advantage of the S corporation is that the profits and losses are dispensed each year to the individual owners. The S corporation is treated as any other corporation in which the corporation is a separate entity from its owners. This protects the owner from any legal action that may be filed against the corporation.

SALE LEASEBACK

A sale leaseback is a contract between a buyer and seller in which the seller agrees to lease the property after the sale from the buyer. The advantages of the sale leaseback are that it provides the seller with capital, the buyer with a guaranteed tenant to service any mortgage payment and other expenses, and a fixed return to the buyer on the investment.

The seller simultaneously with the sale executes a standard lease contract with rental payments, security deposit, term of years, and re-

Concise Encyclopedia of Real Estate Business Terms
© 2006 by The Haworth Press, Inc. All rights reserved.
doi:10.1300/5637_16

newal options. The seller assumes any and all obligations of a lessee, which is generally a triple net lease with the lessee responsible for utilities, taxes, insurance, maintenance and replacement of systems or component parts, and all other expenses associated with the property.

In some cases, the seller may be given an option at some future date to repurchase the property or even provide the buyer with a guarantee to repurchase at a specified date. The repurchase price is normally based on the appraised value at the time of repurchase. With a guarantee to repurchase, the buyer is assured of a lease income during the term of ownership and a guaranteed sale in the future.

Sale leaseback arrangements are popular with property owners who want to raise capital for a business expansion without having to create a mortgage. Such an arrangement is also used by older owners who want to sell the business without the encumbrance of real estate. If the business is sold, the new owner assumes responsibility for the lease; however, the seller lessee usually remains responsible for the lease.

SECONDARY EASEMENT

An easement that is granted with the right to enter at will to maintain the easement is a secondary easement. Such an easement grants the holder the right to keep the easement in a state of good repair and to provide essential construction, such as roads and bridges, to keep the easement in usable condition.

The granting of a secondary easement for the use and enjoyment of the holder is distinguished from the right to another's property to carry off profits, such as timber, sand, or gravel, which is referred to as an *ancillary easement*. In the secondary easement, the property owner, called the *servient estate*, has granted to the easement holder, known as the *dominant estate*, a specific right to enter the property to repair, construct, or perform any other action required to use, enjoy, and repair the easement for as long as the easement right is held.

SECTION 8 HOUSING

Section 8 is a U.S. Department program administered by the Housing and Urban Development (HUD) to provide rent assistance to lower income families. A standard of rent subsidy is established according to federal guidelines for properties based on a formula of income and family size. Under these guidelines, the government will pay an allowable rent for each unit in the program. The difference in the rent paid by Section 8 and the rent charged by the property owner is paid by the tenant.

For example, if a family of four qualifies under income guidelines for a rent subsidy of $400 per month and the property owner charges $450, HUD will pay the property owner $400 per month and the renter is responsible for paying $50 per month. If the renter fails to pay his or her $50 per month share of the rent, the owner may evict for non-payment of rent.

Under HUD guidelines, properties must meet certain criteria in order to be rented to a Section 8–subsidized renter. HUD has recently adopted a voucher program for the renter who may rent any property that meets minimum Section 8 requirements. These guidelines require, in addition to standard property conditions, the correct number of bedrooms based on family size. HUD allocates a number of Section 8 vouchers for a geographic area based on the average income of households for the area and on the number of those that fall below the HUD income guidelines. In most areas, there is a waiting list for vouchers. Some applicants must wait 12 to 24 months or more before they receive a voucher providing them with Section 8 subsidy.

SECTOR THEORY

Sector theory is a theory of land use development that proposes that retail, commercial, and industrial development proceed outward from a central economic core. The theory projects the development of distinct districts differentiated by the social and economic status of the households. The districts are connected by the highways and thoroughfares that lead from a central business core.

The development of the districts depends on the economic needs of the residents. For example, low-income residential areas will attract the retail and commercial development that best meet their needs. High-income residential areas will develop more upscale retail and commercial development. These distinct districts are always connected by traffic arteries back to the central business core from which they originally developed. A beltway around a large metropolitan area will often become the axis that connects the districts. The time-cost factor of transportation promotes the development out from the central business core.

In many areas the central core from which these districts develop may be a concentrated office area where many people work. As they travel to and from their workplace, the individuals have their retail and commercial needs met by these distinct districts or sectors according to economic and social needs. The sector theory is sometimes referred to as the *wedge theory*. This theory was developed by Homer Hoyt after observing how areas of retail and commercial clusters developed over a number of years.

SECURED LENDER

A secured lender is one whose mortgage is secured by the borrower, the real estate, or some other form of collateral. Generally a mortgage is secured by the real estate purchased by the borrower and by the personal guarantee of the borrower. However, the lender may require additional security in the form of other real estate owned by the borrower or other assets such as stocks or mutual funds or even savings accounts. In rem loans are secured only by the real estate purchased and do not carry any other form of security for the lender. These loans are often called *nonrecourse loans.*

A loan secured by the personal guarantee of the borrower, in addition to the real estate purchased, is further secured by all the assets of the borrower, including the equity in other real estate holdings. With a personal guarantee a lender has the security interest in all the assets of the borrower in the event of default. Although a borrower does not pledge other assets to the lender, he or she grants to the lender a claim against all of his or her assets in the event of default.

SECURITY DEPOSIT

Contracts to sell real estate usually require a deposit by the buyer, which is made upon acceptance of the contract by buyer and seller. The amount of the deposit is negotiated along with the price and other terms and conditions of the contract. A deposit may be cash, a promissory note, or sometimes other forms of value. A deposit is usually placed with the seller's broker when there is a real estate agent. However, it may be agreed that the deposit be placed with another party, such as an attorney or title company, who acts as the escrow agent. The deposit is almost always applied to the purchase price at closing as part of the down payment by the buyer. When the buyer agrees to place a deposit but does not do so, it is considered a breach of the contract by the buyer.

A deposit given by a buyer is considered earnest money unless specified otherwise with such language as "not to be considered earnest money" or in a specific performance clause. Absent such language in the contract, the buyer may negate the contract by forfeiting the deposit.

SELLER IN BAD FAITH

A seller is considered to be in bad faith if he or she knew of a defect but failed to disclose it to the buyer. The establishment of bad faith is important in determining the extent of recovery by the buyer. Bad faith also will determine the prescriptive period that governs any action of redhibition by the buyer.

A seller is not considered to have acted in bad faith if he or she hired a vendor who installed a faulty product. For example, if a seller hired a roofer to install a new roof and the roofer, an independent contractor, completed the installation in a faulty manner, the seller cannot be held to have acted in bad faith.

However, a builder who sells a house or a developer who sells a lot can be held to have acted in bad faith based on an irrefutable presumption of knowledge if the house or lot is found to be defective.

SETBACK

Zoning and/or building restrictions may require that a building constructed on a property be a certain number of feet from the property lines. Such regulations or restrictions may designate setback lines from the front property line or may designate such setback distances from all sides of the property. For example, construction of a building may be required to be twenty-five feet from the front property line, ten feet from the back property line, and only five feet from each side property line.

In commercially zoned areas, the setback line may be designated as so many feet from the front and back property lines but permit zero setback from the side lines. In residential construction, there may be areas of small lot development that are designated as zero side lot setback on one side and, for instance, ten feet setback from at least one side line.

If a property owner determines that the proposed construction will require invading the setback lines, he can request a variance from the appropriate governmental entity charged with enforcing setback requirements. If such a variance is granted, it will only apply to the particular property to which it is granted and not apply to any other property owners.

SETTLEMENT STATEMENT

As required by law under the Real Estate Settlement Procedures Act (RESPA) of 1974, a listing of all costs related to the closing of a real estate sale, including the net to the seller and the amount required to close for the buyer, is shown on the settlement statement. The statement will list the borrower's (buyer's) cost and the seller's cost, such as the following:

Borrower's (Buyer's) Cost	Seller's Cost
loan origination fee	broker's commission
loan discount	document preparation
appraisal fee	recording fees
credit report	pest inspection
interest from closing	survey
mortgage insurance	prorated taxes
property insurance	
closing fee	
title search	
title examination	
title policy	
document preparation	
recording fees	

Additional charges can include cancellation or preparation of a second mortgage, notary fees, and assignment of lease. The borrower (buyer) and seller are required to sign the statement acknowledging their acceptance of the charges.

SHARED APPRECIATION MORTGAGE

A mortgage that grants the lender, in addition to the mortgage on the property, a percentage of the future appreciation of the property value is called a *shared appreciation mortgage.* The borrower in return receives capital from the lender. An appraisal of the property establishes the value at the time the mortgage is made that serves as the benchmark for future appreciation of the property value.

For example, if the appraised value at the time of the mortgage is $500,000 and the property is sold for $800,000 with the lender participation at 10 percent of the appreciated value, the lender receives $30,000 as its 10 percent share of the $300,000 appreciated value.

The incentive for the borrower, in addition to capital provided from the lender, may be the ability to secure the mortgage. The risk for the lender is that the property, due to poor management, lack of adequate maintenance, or perhaps a deterioration of the surrounding area of the property, may have little or no appreciation or even a decrease in value. The lender must determine that these issues are appropriately evaluated and addressed prior to making the mortgage.

A SAM is a highly specialized mortgage and relatively rare in the funding of real estate loans. Depending on the lender, the mortgage may provide input by the lender in factors that may adversely affect the property value and future appreciation.

SHOPPING CENTER

Land that has been developed into a group of connected retail stores for the purpose of offering a variety of goods for sale is a shopping center. Identified as developments for the sale of retail products, they may vary in size from a few thousand square feet to several hundred thousand square feet. Shopping centers have free parking and separate stores with individual entrances. They generally do not have interior corridors.

Shopping centers are characterized also by easy access to shoppers from main traffic corridors or intersections. They represent the retail establishment of cluster shops or anchor stores designed to provide one-stop shopping convenience. They may be categorized by anchor tenants, fashion centers, neighborhood centers, outlet centers, regional centers, specialty centers, or super regional centers.

Shopping centers are distinguished from shopping malls by the lack of air-conditioned corridors, fewer anchor stores, and generally smaller size. Retail areas began as a cluster of individual free-standing stores in close proximity to a small group of stores within a common structure. They evolved into shopping centers with a planned variety of stores to meet the needs of most shoppers to larger regional and super regional centers and then into very large shopping malls with several large anchor stores and a mixture of smaller stores all designed for one-stop interior comfort shopping convenience.

SHORT-TERM LEASE

An office or retail lease with a term of less than ten years is a short-term lease. These leases are designed to fit the requirements of small-use tenants. Tenants with short-term leases generally provide little or no initial investment in the leased space. Short-term leases are designed for the new business or a growing business that anticipates out-growing the space in a few years or upgrading to a better location.

Landlords generally provide a vanilla space (a space that is finished for the occupancy of a tenant but is not customized per the requirements of a particular tenant) that the short-term tenant can easily adapt to his requirements. Short terms are not suited to build-to-suit leases or leases in which the tenant provides a great deal of the improvements, which will become a lost investment when the tenant moves. Short-term leases may carry a higher rent per square foot than long-term leases because the landlord may be required to do additional work when the tenant vacates the space.

SOFT COSTS

When calculating the total cost of new construction or extensive renovation of an existing building, the individual costs are divided into categories. The costs of construction materials and labor are called the *hard costs,* and the other costs associated with the project are called *soft costs* or *indirect costs.* To calculate the total cost of a project, it is necessary to determine both hard and soft costs.

Soft costs include the following:

> architect fees
> construction loan interest
> soil sampling
> blueprint reproduction
> engineering fees
> loan closing costs
> marketing costs
> insurance
> environmental testing
> administrative costs

The soft costs can be a substantial percentage of the total cost of the project. Soft costs are incurred not only during the construction phase but also after construction is complete for such items as marketing and leasing/sales commissions.

Many projects that appear to provide a good return on investment according to the calculated hard costs can develop a serious negative cash flow when the soft costs are included and the subsequent debt service calculated. The construction bid price generally will not include all the soft costs associated with the project, especially the marketing and leasing/sales commissions.

SPECIAL-PURPOSE PROPERTY

Construction that is designed for a special and limited market use can be classified as a special-purpose property. Many buildings are designed for a special use and have limited or no appeal to the broader commercial market. Because they are suited to a specific use, the cost to retrofit them for an alternative use can approach or exceed new construction cost. In such instances the seller of a special-use property must almost always find a buyer with a similar or same use for it. Such a requirement may significantly affect the price for which the property can be sold.

These are many types of special-purpose properties, including churches, health clubs or facilities especially with interior pools, recreational facilities, stadiums, and motels. There are others that, although designed and built for a special use, can be redesigned for an alternative use at a cost somewhat less than the cost of new construction.

SPECIALTY SHOPPING CENTER

A specialty shopping center is a retail center that is designed and leased to shops along a specified product line or developed around a theme. These nontraditional centers are characterized by the absence of an anchor tenant and appeal to a special but limited market. The stores are designed to attract a shopper interested in a wide selection of specific products. For example, a sporting center may have stores that all sell products for only recreational purposes. Stores may specialize in fishing, hunting, and team sports and sell such products as boats, guns, baseball equipment, and football, basketball, and hockey merchandise. They may sell soft goods for the runner, hiker, and walker, such as shoes and clothes.

Other specialty centers may feature only women's clothing of all types or clothing and shoes only for children. A home furnishing center may have furniture stores, appliance stores, and home accessory stores.

Specialty centers are usually found only in larger metropolitan markets, where there is a customer base sufficient to support a wide variety of products with limited shopper appeal.

SPECIFIC PERFORMANCE

Specific performance is a clause contained in most real estate purchase contracts that can be used to force a buyer or a seller to take action to uphold his or her obligation in the contract. This is most commonly used when monetary damages will not satisfy both parties. A standard specific performance clause in a real estate purchase agreement might state: "Both parties reserve the right to demand and receive specific performance." This clause gives both the buyer and the seller the right to sue the other party if the other party does not fulfill his or her part of the contract. Many times lawsuits can be more expensive than the judgments received, so more commonly buyers and sellers agree on some level of monetary damages when the contract terms are not lived up to. Without a specific performance clause in a contract, total damages for not carrying out the contract terms may be limited to the amount of deposit placed by the buyer.

An example showing the benefits of specific performance clauses is a situation in which the buyer has placed a $1,000 deposit on one acre of land on the outskirts of town. The contract states that the buyer has ninety days to close the transaction. After sixty days, the local newspaper announces that Wal-Mart Corporation has placed a large parcel of land adjacent to the acre under contract. Suddenly, the value of this land could go up as much as ten times, and the seller decides not to sell at the original contract price. If the buyer has written a specific performance clause into the contract, he or she may force the seller to sell the land at the original contract price. If the buyer neglected to include a specific performance clause in the contract, it is possible that the seller could refuse to sell the land at the contract price and simply refund the deposit put up by the buyer as damages, therefore declaring the contract void.

SPECIFICATIONS

The plans for new construction will contain the architect's set of specifications detailing all the material and finish to be used. The specifications will include the type and quality of lumber, the roof material, the exterior facade covering, the interior doors, walls, and moldings, and all other materials the contractor will use.

Very detailed specifications are an integral part of the plans for any new construction as well as renovation projects. Without such specifications, the contractor may use materials that are not satisfactory to the owner and do not meet the owner's expectations. Specifications are an integral part of the construction process as they determine the quality and cost of the finished project.

The more detailed the specifications are, the less room there is for disputes between the contractor and owner. For example, if the specifications do not detail the quality and type of flooring to be used, a lesser grade may be installed by the contractor that does not meet the expectations of the owner. When contractors bid on a project, they must estimate the cost of construction based not only on the plans but more importantly on the specifications.

SQUARE FOOT COST

A developer will calculate the construction cost based on a weighted average of the square foot cost. These square foot costs will include the land, the parking area, the building, and the soft costs such as design, architecture, engineering, and site preparation. When all the costs are considered, the result can be expressed as a cost per square foot.

A further calculation of office and retail construction can be expressed as cost per square foot of leasable or usable square feet. By knowing the cost of the entire project based on leasable square feet, the developer can then calculate the return on investment based on the projected income when the project is finished and leased to, say, 90 percent occupancy.

Sometimes in residential construction a homeowner will express the total cost based on price per square foot of heated or living area. For example, if a home cost $300,000 to complete and has 3,000 square feet of heated or living area, the cost will be expressed as $100 per square foot.

STABILIZED OCCUPANCY

A project that has reached a projected occupancy rate at competitive market rents and is expected to retain the rate for the life of the project has stabilized occupancy. When a project, such as a retail center, office building, or apartment complex, is built, developers will want to calculate the time required to reach stabilized occupancy. This will indicate the time they will be required to support the project with additional infusions of cash. A lender will want to know this time frame and the ability of the developer to fund the project until it reaches stabilized occupancy.

Stabilized occupancy assumes that, absent unforeseen events, the project will continue at this level of income throughout its economic life. Stabilized occupancy assumes competent management, sufficient promotion, reasonable maintenance, and stable economic conditions.

Once a project has achieved stabilized occupancy, the income may increase based on reasonable inflationary factors. However, the income base can be expected to remain relatively stable throughout the useful life of the project.

STABILIZED VALUE

An appraisal of value is based on the stabilized income during the life of the project. This value assumes that the project will be unaffected by unusual swings in supply and demand created by abnormal economic times, such as high inflation, boom economics, or depression. The stabilized value further assumes that the long-term costs and the sale price do not exceed the long-term value based on boom economic conditions or depressed value during economic downturns, when cost and value may depress long term value.

A stabilized value approach provides a weighted value of the project based on long-term assumptions. Because projections for the economic life of the project are based on assumptions of long-term value, they are not used to predict what short-term impact economic conditions may have on the value placed on the project. For example, if the economic life of the project is fifty years, short-term economic conditions may be significant in the short term but insignificant in the long term.

STRAIGHT LINE DEPRECIATION

One method of depreciating assets, such as real estate improvements, through capital recapture is called *straight line depreciation.* The asset is assigned a number of years and depreciated in equal increments over the number of years assigned. This assumes that the capital improvement is recaptured equally in each period. For example, if the capital improvement is assigned a life of thirty-nine years, the depreciation is calculated as 2.5 percent each year.

Other assets are assigned a useful life and depreciated equally each year. Assets such as appliances may be assigned a life of five years and depreciated in equal amounts each year. For instance, in an apartment complex, the assigned life of the stoves and refrigerators may be five years. In such case they can be depreciated each year 20 percent of the actual cost of purchase. In some cases, a straight line change per period may be assigned that increases by a fixed amount per year.

Depreciation of the investment assets are allowed under Internal Revenue Service guidelines as set forth in published documents. These guidelines change from time to time. For example, in 1986 the IRS disallowed the double declining balance method (whereby the depreciable amount was calculated as twice the amount allowed under the straight line method). New tables were established for depreciation at that time based on the straight line method.

STRIP DEVELOPMENT

A strip development is a type of commercial development, generally retail stores, along the main traffic arteries that are laid out in a continuous row of buildings. There may also be complementing service stores in addition to retail stores. This type of development can consist of free-standing buildings on individual contiguous lots or buildings that contain several retail stores each with separate customer entrances.

A strip development, especially under a common roof, is designed primarily for the small retailer and generally contains less than 2,000 square feet per store. It is primarily designed to meet the needs of a limited geographic market. This type of retail and service development combines customer convenience with ease of access. Parking space is usually adequate but limited and accommodates only a few customers at a time. Strip developments are especially popular in areas with a limited population base but a relatively high traffic count.

SUBDIVISION

Subdivision is the division of open land into segments for development for a variety of uses or for only one type of use. The tract will be divided into lots with streets, alleys, and open or park areas as appropriate for the specific development, such as residential, office, retail, industrial, or commercial.

A subdivision will most often be regulated as to lot sizes, alley requirements, and green or park areas by the governing entity and zoned for the intended use accordingly. A developer will designate certain areas for the intended type of development in a mixed-use environment. For example, certain areas may be designated for commercial use fronting the main street or highway, with other areas designated for multifamily and perhaps single family. Each area may have special requirements for alleys, fencing, lighting, access routes, and type of construction to ensure the integrity of the development and the aesthetic quality of the entire project.

SUBJECT TO THE MORTGAGE

Property that is purchased in whole or in part may include a subject to the mortgage clause that excludes the purchaser from liability to the lender for an existing debt. This is sometimes used when a property owner sells a percentage of ownership of a project to one or more additional owners. The original borrower will remain solely responsible for the mortgage without the new percentage owners assuming any personal liability. However, the property may be foreclosed on by the lender if the mortgage is in default.

This legal clause in its simplest interpretation means "without mortgage liability." Therefore, although there is ownership or a percentage of ownership with participation in the profit or loss of the project as well as the profit upon sale, there is no personal liability for the existing mortgage.

SUBLEASE

When a tenant wishes to vacate the leased space prior to expiration of the term of the lease, the tenant or lessor may sublet the space subject to certain conditions of the lease. A lease will most often require the approval of the lessor of any sublet tenant. In a sublease the original tenant may or may not be required to retain liability for the payment of the rent. However, if the lessor determines that the sublet tenant is of sufficient financial strength, he or she may decide to release the original tenant from this obligation.

The sublet tenant will assume all the obligations and responsibilities of the original tenant per the lease agreement. The original tenant remains obligated for rent payments to the lessor, even if he or she vacates the space, until a sublet tenant can be found for the duration of the lease term.

Sublease agreements are primarily used when the original tenant has outgrown the space or become unable to continue the lease payments.

SUBORDINATION

A lender who has a mortgage on a property may under certain circumstances agree to subordinate his or her first mortgage to another mortgage. A subordinate or junior mortgage then comes behind a first or superior mortgage as to its claim to the asset. For example, if a lender has only a small remaining principal and the property owner wishes to acquire additional capital for improvements, a lender may be willing to subordinate his or her first mortgage provided the total mortgages do not amount to more than an agreed upon loan to value ratio. In such case the property owner will have more capital available by not being required to pay off the original first mortgage.

In the event of a foreclosure, the first mortgage holder will be paid first, with any surplus over the first mortgage applied to the payment of any junior or subordinate mortgages. Priority of mortgage payoffs in foreclosure is usually determined by the chronological sequence in which the mortgages were initiated as established by the recorded date of the mortgages.

SUBROGATION

A person may subrogate the collection of his or her debts or damages to another party. This right may be assigned to a third party granting the right to file a claim or institute a lawsuit against another party if the primary party does not do so. An insurer may require a right of subrogation as part of the insurance policy to sue for collection of damages on the part of the insured. With the exercise of the right of subrogation the insurance company may step into the place of the insured and issue a claim for damages or enter a lawsuit against a third party as if the third party were the insured. Legally, subrogation places another party or person in the place of the original party with all the legal rights afforded under the law.

For example, if party A has been injured by party B and files a claim for damages against his or her own insurance company, the insurance company may pay the insured and then sue party B or the party's insurance company if the party is insured under its right of subrogation to collect any monies paid to the insured.

SUBSURFACE RIGHTS

A subsurface rights agreement grants one party the right to use of that which lies under the property without owning the property. Subsurface rights, sometimes referred to as mineral rights, include the legal right to oil, gas, gravel, minerals, coal, and any other subsurface substances. Also included is the right to construct and maintain underground pipelines, water lines, sewers, or tunnels. If surface area is disturbed when the subsurface rights are exercised, the holder is required to return the surface to its original condition after extraction.

The holder may be allowed a set time in which to determine underground value and began extraction. If no action is taken during this time the subsurface or mineral rights may revert to the property owner and the subsurface rights expire. However, if exploration is begun, the right may extend until all exploration is concluded.

The buying of mineral rights is a popular method for exploration companies to purchase oil, gas, and coal without having to purchase the property. This allows companies to control the existing minerals under large land masses.

SUCCESSION

The legal process of passing through a will the title to property owned by a person who has died is succession. The property passed in such a manner can be done so in whole as 100 percent ownership or in part as percentages of ownership to related persons, other persons not related, or an entity such as a charitable institution or church, all in accordance with a legally recognized will. If no valid will is available, a court of law will decide the succession of the estate.

A probate court is a court of law charged with validating a will and settling an estate of the deceased person. Probate courts are responsible for the proving of a will as genuine and/or otherwise settling the estate of the deceased. A probate court will issue a certificate verifying the validity of the will.

Succession is the orderly and legal process of passing ownership of a deceased person's property.

SUCCESSORS

Some contracts include an obligation on the part of not only the parties to the contract but also the parties' heirs, assigns, and successors. This assures the other party to the contract that if the primary party is incapacitated or dies that his or her heirs or successors are obligated to fulfill the terms of the contract. The successors are then given the full rights and obligations of the primary party to conclude any and all obligations of the primary party.

For example, if the seller executes a buy/sell agreement for the sale of his or her home and is incapacitated or dies before the sale is concluded, the buyer has the right to force the sale by the seller's successors under the same price, terms, and conditions as the original seller agreed to. The successors by law inherit all the obligations of the seller. The same is true of a mortgage in which the lender has obligated not only the borrower but also the borrower's heirs and successors to repay the debt.

SUPERFUND

Superfund is a program established by congress through the Comprehensive Environmental Response, Compensation, and Liability Act in 1980 to clean up soil, subsurface, and water contamination by hazardous materials. This act recognized the immensity of the problem of hazardous material contamination and the corresponding threat to public health. It further recognized that the cleanup cost exceeded the ability of many property owners to absorb.

If the property owner made a prudent effort to determine the site was clean at the time of purchase and used the property in a prudent manner so as not to intentionally create contamination and the site was later determined to be contaminated, the Superfund would pay the cost of cleanup.

When property is determined to be contaminated, an application is made to the Superfund program to pay the cost of cleanup and to certify that the site is free of contamination. The Superfund is funded by fees from oil companies, etc., paid in accordance with the congressional act.

SURVEY

The establishment of boundary lines for a property is accomplished by a survey. A survey is completed by a registered surveyor, who establishes a point of reference traced to a point of beginning for the subject property. Using survey equipment, a surveyor will describe the property lines in measurements in feet in each direction. Angles and curves are described in minutes and degrees.

A survey is important in the purchase of any property to determine the legal description of the exact lines of the property the buyer is purchasing. A survey will also note any encroachments on the property by adjoining structures, sidewalks, etc.

SURVIVAL

Survival is a condition of a real estate contract that continues to exist after the closing. Such a condition may apply to a warranty of the seller regarding the land or improvements and their environmental or other unknown or undiscovered problems that become known after the closing. Warranties that survive the closing provide the buyer with a continuing warranty and the seller with continuing liability. A seller on occasion will grant the buyer a survival warranty as a condition of closing the sale.

For example, a buyer may have a period of due diligence in which to test for environmental problems. However, the buyer may in addition ask the seller for a warranty clause, which survives the closing, that the property has never been used as a waste material dump. If the buyer discovers after the closing that, even unknown to the seller and prior to the seller's purchase, the property is contaminated by hazardous materials deposited at the site the buyer will have recourse against the seller. A seller may also warrant that there are no asbestos-containing materials used in the construction. If the seller warrants this with a "shall survive the closing" clause in the purchase agreement and asbestos materials are discovered by the buyer even years later, the buyer will have recourse against the seller because the seller's warranty survived the closing.

SUSCIPIENT BUSINESS

A retail business that depends on the customer draw of another business to survive is a suscipient business. The term is generally limited to small retail stores that could not survive without the volume of customers drawn to the area by another business. The suscipient business depends on a generative business to draw customers. A generative business is defined as an anchor store, supermarket, or other retail business that through advertising or other sources generates a large customer base. The suscipient business survives off the proximity of the customer volume. By locating in the same mall or shopping center as a generative business, the smaller business is able to expose its products to more customers. In some cases the suscipient business may have the right to cancel the lease if the larger anchor store closes or moves to another location.

SYNDICATION

When a group pools funds to purchase or develop a real estate project and participate in the future profits and/or losses, it is referred to as a *syndication*. To syndicate a project is to sell ownership interest in the project under a legal arrangement that provides for participation in profits and losses. In certain syndications, losses are limited to some partners.

A general partnership is one in which each partner contributes funds and receives a percentage of ownership. Each partner participates in the profits and losses in accordance with his or her percentage of ownership. For example, if a partner purchases 20 percent of the project and the profits or losses are $100,000, he or she will be responsible for $20,000 of the losses or receive $20,000 of the profits.

A limited partnership is an ownership arrangement in which there are a number of limited partners and one or more general partners. The limited partners are passive owners and limit their liability to the loss of their initial capital investment. The general partners are responsible for managing the project and assume full liability for the project indebtedness. However, both limited and general partners share in the profits in accordance with their percentage of ownership.

Syndication is a general term that indicates the ownership by more than one person whether the project is purchased or developed under terms of a general partnership or a limited partnership.

TARGET MARKET

Identifying the most likely group of potential buyers or tenants can be essential in the sale of commercial or industrial real estate. A target market is the group of potential buyers or tenants for a given property. To identify a target market, it is necessary to first identify the highest and best use of the property. Although most often the highest and best use of a property is a continuation of its current use, occasionally that use may be changed, in which case the target market will also change.

By way of example, if a free-standing commercial building has a past history of use as a retail store, the target market will include primarily retail users, beginning with similar users to the most recent retailer to vacate the building. However, the target market will also include other retailers that use a similar size and type of building. If the traffic pattern has changed and the area has become more industrial, the target market may reach out to light industrial users as well.

Identifying a target market is an essential part of the marketing plan prepared for the property owner or the marketing entity. Without identifying the target market, any marketing plan will adopt a hit and miss approach that more often will fail than succeed.

TAX-DEFERRED EXCHANGE

Based on the Internal Revenue Code, Section 1031, tax-deferred exchange allows owners to sell their property, place the funds in an escrow account, and defer any tax on their gain. Even though it is sometimes known as the "like kind exchange," the IRS has broadened the definition of "like kind" to include almost any type of investment real estate. It does, however, exclude the residence of the investor.

A seller may defer the capital gains on the sale by identifying at the time of the sale or within forty-five days after the sale a property that

Concise Encyclopedia of Real Estate Business Terms
© 2006 by The Haworth Press, Inc. All rights reserved.
doi:10.1300/5637_17

qualifies for an exchange. Once the exchange property is identified, the seller will have a specified number of days to close the exchange sale. A seller may identify up to 200 percent in exchange properties of the capital gains he receives at closing and then choose which property he or she wishes to close as the exchange property. The seller may also identify a property that is more expensive than the capital gains, in which case only that portion that equals the capital gains qualifies for the exchange portion.

For example, if the seller's capital gain is $100,000 and the exchange property price is $250,000, only the $100,000 in capital gain will qualify as tax deferred.

The seller is allowed to continue this process over a series of purchases and sales continuing to use the 1031 tax-deferred rule.

TAX SALE

State law permits property to be sold at a tax sale for nonpayment of real estate taxes. If sold at a tax sale, the property may be redeemed within three years after the sale is recorded, by the owner of record, another party such as the owner's heirs, a mortgagee, or a purchaser of the property from the former owner. To redeem the property the person redeeming must pay a penalty and interest specified by law. If any improvements have been made to the property by the buyer at the tax sale, the redeeming party must also pay for the cost of the improvements.

A tax sale can only be annulled based on an irregularity in the tax sale, such as proof that the debtor had paid the taxes due. Any action to annul the sale must be made within five years of the recorded tax deed. However, if the tax debtor continued, for example, to live in the home the five-year period would be interrupted.

The usual defense to a tax sale is proof of payment of the taxes prior to the sale. However, proper notice of delinquency is mandatory and is not given can constitute grounds for annulment of the sale. A notice of the delinquent taxes must be sent to the owner by certified mail, informing the owner of the amount of taxes due and that the property will be sold at a tax sale if not paid. In addition the property to be sold, the owner of record, and the amount of taxes owed must also be advertised in a public publication such as the local newspaper.

A tax title even after the three-year redemptive period is generally not considered merchantable because of the defenses a tax debtor can assert, such as lack of proper notice. The purchaser of property at a tax sale may file a lawsuit, called an *action to quiet title,* against the former owner after three years from the date of recording the tax deed.

A tax sale cancels all mortgages against the property with the exception of some federal liens.

TENANCY AT WILL

An arrangement in which a tenant and landlord agree that the term of the lease will be indefinite and may be cancelled by either the landlord or the tenant. In such case the tenant occupies only as long as he or she wants to, and the landlord retains the right to repossess the space or building at any time.

This arrangement can be useful for temporary occupancy by the tenant or if the tenant determines the space or building is not suitable and wants to occupy only until a more suitable space is found. The landlord may have plans for an alternate use of the space or building and allow the tenant to occupy only until the new plan is implemented.

In either case, the tenancy is only for a duration until either the tenant decides to vacate or the landlord to repossess.

TENANCY IN COMMON

Tenancy in common occurs when a property is owned by two or more persons each of whom has an undivided interest. Although each person owns a percentage of the property, it is possessed as a portion of the whole property and not identified as a specific portion of the property. The person who desires to sell his or her interest may sell to the existing partners or another person. However, the person purchasing the percentage of ownership buys a percentage of the entire property without division of the property.

Because division of the property is not possible, each person owns a percentage of the whole property.

TENANT

A person who inhabits the property of another, usually through a legal document called a *lease,* is a tenant. Although not possessing ownership, a tenant does hold certain rights. Possession is generally granted upon the payment of a specified amount either annually or monthly. The tenant's right of possession will cease if payments are not made as agreed, and the property owner retakes possession of the property.

The legal document that grants a tenant possession under certain terms is called a *lease* and supercedes the sale of the property. For example, if a tenant holds a written lease to property for a five-year term and the property owner sells the property during the term of the lease, the property must be sold subject to the terms of the lease. The new owner is required to honor the lease under the same terms of possession as the original owner. This also applies to any options to renew the lease that may have been granted to the tenant and that he or she exercises.

Tenant rights are recognized by a court of law and are required to be honored by the original owner or any subsequent owners provided that the tenant fulfills his or her obligations under the terms of the lease.

A tenant is also referred to as a *lessee,* and the property owner is called a *lessor.*

TENANT IMPROVEMENTS

Improvements that the lessor agrees to make in the leased space in accordance with the tenant's requirements is called *tenant improvements.* The cost of the tenant improvements may be the sole responsibility of the lessor or may be shared by the tenant. When the space leased is unimproved or unfinished space, the lessor may grant the tenant a dollar amount per square foot leased by the tenant to finish out the space. If the cost to finish the space exceeds the cost allowance, the tenant will be responsible for the additional cost. In retail leases, the lessor may agree to finish the space with the standard finish, which generally includes wall finish, lighting, rest room(s), heat, and air-conditioning. The tenant will then be responsible for customizing the space to his or her particular requirements. For existing offices, the lessor and tenant may agree on a scope of work for the lessor to provide. Additional improvements the tenant requires will then be at the tenant's expense.

For example, if the lessor agrees to spend $25 per square foot and the tenant submits completion specifications that cost $30 per square foot, the tenant will be responsible for $5 per square foot in improvement costs.

Tenant improvements either through lessor performance or tenant improvement allowance are always negotiated as part of the lease agreement. Generally, the lessor will be granted a period of time in which to complete the tenant improvements with or without penalties for failure to complete on time.

TENANT WORK LETTER

If tenant improvements are required prior to or during the occupancy by the tenant, an agreement generally incorporated into the lease or added as an addendum to the lease will specify who is responsible for performing the work and who will pay the cost of the work. A tenant work letter, sometimes called a *scope of work* letter is a method to prevent misunderstanding between tenant or lessee and landlord or lessor.

For example, if the lease space is to be painted and the carpet replaced, the tenant work letter may specify what type of paint to be used and the color and quality of carpet to be installed as well as who pays the cost. It may also specify whether lighting is to be upgraded, the type of lighting, and who will pay for the expense.

Generally if the tenant requires special items, such as built-in cabinets, the tenant will pay for the expense either at the time of occupancy or as an additional cost in the monthly rent paid over the initial term of the lease.

A tenant work letter can prevent problems between tenant and landlord as to the cost and scope of work that either agrees to perform. The tenant work letter will usually also state the time during which such work is to be competed.

TENDER

If an offer is made in writing and signed by the buyer, the buyer is said to tender an offer. To tender an offer, there are terms and price to which the buyer is bound. A seller may tender a contract by offering to sell under specific terms and at a specified price. To tender a formal offer to buy or sell, one must specify certain terms, conditions, and price.

For example, a buyer may offer $100,000 for a property, subject to financing, and agree to close on or before a certain date. A seller may tender a counteroffer at $110,000 and accept all other terms and conditions of the buyer's offer. Both buyer and seller tendered formal contracts that bind each to a specified price and terms if accepted by the other.

When a contract is tendered, it binds the buyer or seller to the price and terms agreed upon.

TERMITE CERTIFICATE

Some states where termites are prevalent require a termite certificate to ensure that the property is free of active termite infestation and to note any previous damage caused by such infestations. The inspection is limited to a visual inspection of the structure, and, if damage is found, a general description of the location and extent of the damage is provided.

Especially in southern states, where warm temperatures create a climate for active termite and wood-destroying beetles, extensive damage can occur to any wood structure. Generally, the requirement for a certificate is limited to residential properties but may include commercial structures also. Because many commercial structures are not constructed with wood materials, they may be excluded from this requirement.

TERTIARY TRADE AREA

A tertiary trade area is an area identified as being outside the normal trade area but that is expected to contribute at least 10 percent of the customer base for a retail store. The tertiary trade area reaches beyond the primary and secondary trade areas. By identifying the tertiary trade area, a retailer may decide that the primary and secondary trade areas are too small for a particular market.

For example, if a location has an inadequate market size but can be expected to draw at least 10 percent of its customers from another town in close proximity, it may then qualify under market size guidelines set forth by the retailer. Tertiary trade areas are important in smaller markets, especially where the product to be sold has appeal to only a limited segment of the market. A tertiary trade area is identified from data from other retailers whose customer base is known.

TESTATE

A person who dies and leaves a valid will is said to have died testate, or with a will, as opposed to intestate, meaning without a will. A probate court is charged with the responsibility to determine the validity of the will. By leaving a valid will a person can determine who inherits his or her estate or some portion of the estate. If a person dies intestate or without a will, the appropriate court of law is required to determine who are rightful heirs and what portion of the estate each will inherit.

Testate is the legal process of passing an estate upon death to the heirs or others in accordance with the wishes of the deceased.

TIME OF ESSENCE

A time of essence clause is used in real estate agreements to emphasize the importance of completing conditions of the agreement or proceeding to close the sale. Although there are no specific time requirements to the steps, it is incumbent on all parties to the agreement to proceed with diligence to complete the terms of the agreement and to close the sale. The time is of essence clause can also be used in a lease when tenant finish out or improvements are required.

For example, a purchase agreement for real estate in which the seller agrees to complete repairs may state that "time is of the essence" in completing agreed upon repairs.

TIMESHARE

Timeshare is a popular method of granting limited ownership or rights of use and occupancy to condominiums, apartments, or hotel rooms to a large number of individuals. Timeshares are often sold in one-week increments and identified as a specific week of each year. This permits the owner to sell up to fifty-two weeks each year to as many timeshare holders.

For example, a single structure may be divided into fifty-two units, and the use and occupancy of each unit is sold. A timeshare owner may, for instance, purchase a unit for the third week of October, which then becomes his designated time of occupancy each year. Timeshares are usually sold with an up-front price and a yearly maintenance fee to be used to maintain the property. Timeshare deeds are similar to fee simple ownership and may be passed on as part of the estate of a deceased owner.

There are two types of timeshares—fee timeshares and nonfee timeshares. Fee timeshares are based on timeshare ownership or interval ownership.

There is also nonfee ownership through a prepaid lease agreement, a vacation license, or a club membership.

TITLE

The document that proves ownership of property is a title. Being vested in the public records is the proof of ownership for any property. An abstract of a title is a summary of facts related to the chain of title for a property, including conveyances and transfers of title as evidence of ownership as well as other public records that may show impairment to the title.

When a dispute occurs as to ownership, the final determination of ownership rests in a search of public records to reveal possessions of title. Legally executed documents must be filed in appropriate jurisdictions to establish a clear and authoritative title to any property, especially when a dispute as to ownership occurs.

Proof of title can be made with a combination of documents that certify ownership, primarily including a properly executed deed. For example, if a husband and wife own property and the deed is not signed by both, the legal title may be clouded and the passing of legal title to a buyer could be disputed. Even though the deed is properly recorded, a court of law could set aside the sale if challenged.

TITLE INSURANCE POLICY

To avoid the expense of a title problem discovered years after the purchase, a policy of title insurance may be purchased to cover the expense. This policy will cover the buyer from a title problem discovered at the time the owner decides to sell.

A buyer is advised to read the policy carefully for any exclusions to the coverage that it may contain. Often a title insurance company will write a policy for a title with minor problems but exclude certain parts from coverage that it deems to be at risk.

Many states regulate the cost of title insurance policies. The cost of the policy is based on a percentage of the purchase price that represents the company's exposure to loss.

TORRENS SYSTEM

The Torrens system is a system for registering real estate titles designed to simplify the transfer of land. It was introduced by Sir Robert Torrens in the 1850s in South Australia. Under the Torrens system, the governmental authority issues title certificates for the transfer of land ownership. This certificate sometimes is used as title insurance.

TORT

Tort is a French term. Its Latin root is *tortum,* meaning injustice. Tort is a legal term indicating a harm or injury, excluding breach of contract, for which the injured party has the right to sue for damages in a civil court.

The attorney of a person who thinks he or she has been harmed and seeks recourse in a civil court will file a tort asking for relief or damages. For example, if someone continually trespasses on property and will not stop after being asked, the property owner can file a tort or suit in a civil court asking the tresspasser to cease. If the property has been damaged, the owner can also seek restitution through a monetary award. If the court agrees that harm has been done, it will issue an order requiring the party to cease trespassing. It may also award the owner a sum of money to restore the property or compensate for the damages.

TOTAL NET LEASE

When the tenant assumes the total cost associated with a leased property, the lease is called a *total net lease.* Under a normal lease, the landlord assumes some of the costs or potential costs associated with the leased property. With a gross lease, the landlord assumes all costs associated with the leased property. With a triple net lease, the tenant assumes the cost of property taxes, property insurance, and repair or maintenance of all systems (i.e., heat, air-conditioning, plumbing, electrical, etc.), with the landlord retaining responsibility for the roof and exterior structure of the building.

In a total net lease, the tenant assumes the total responsibility and all the cost associated with the property—taxes, property insurance, operating systems, roof, structure, and all other costs of the leased premises. Generally, a total net lease is associated with a long-term lease of ten, twenty, or even forty years or longer. It is also often entered into with a build-to-suit lease in which the structure is customized for the tenant.

Total net leases are more common with major national or regional tenants that have a history of absorbing costs related to this type of lease. A small local tenant will seldom agree to enter into a total net lease because of concern over long-term building maintenance and all related costs.

TOWNSHIP

Township is a term used in the U.S. survey system to describe a region of land between two township lines and two range lines containing thirty-six sections. Each section consists of approximately 640 acres (6 square miles). This method provides land locations and descriptions. It is used with the land description of ranges that describes a row of townships each six miles square between two meridians each six miles apart.

TRADE AREA

A trade area is defined as the geographic area that provides the customer base for a shopping center, retail store, or restaurant. The specific trade area may be dependent on other centers or on stores within the defined area. For instance, if the center or store is the only one of its kind in a wide geographic area, its trade area will be greater than if there is another like one within close proximity. Other influencing factors include accessibility, major traffic patterns, household count, and median household income. If a store sells only upper scale, higher priced products, the trade area may exceed the normal geographic area because its appeal is limited to upper income households.

A primary trade area is defined as the geographic area from which 70 percent or more of the customers are drawn. This area can vary significantly depending on the types of products sold. It also depends on the drive time required to reach the center or store and on the competition for the same or like products. If this is the only center or store servicing a large population, the primary trade area is greatly increased.

A tertiary trade area is defined as an area outside the normal trade area that contributes at least 10 percent of the customer base perhaps from a surrounding area or town that does not offer a similar product line. This often occurs in small towns that may not have a shopping center or similar retail store.

The measurement of a trade area with its customer potential is important to a shopping center developer or retail store when determining the potential for a new development or store location.

Demographic studies provide important data to help determine the trade area. A careful evaluation of these data many times determines the difference between a successful shopping center or retail store and a failed one.

TRIPLE NET

A lease that requires the lessee to pay, in addition to the rent, three other charges associated with the property is a triple net lease. Triple net charges are property taxes, property insurance, and common area maintenance. However, under terms of specific leases other expenses can be charged to the lessee, including maintenance of all equipment and systems (i.e., plumbing, heating, ventilation, air-conditioning, and electricity). The lessor will generally retain responsibility for the exterior of the building and the roof.

A triple net lease is different from a total net lease in which the lessee assumes any and all costs associated with the property including all triple net charges plus the exterior of the building and the roof.

If a tenant assumes responsibility for the cost associated with the property, particularly taxes, insurance, and maintenance/repairs, it is considered a triple net lease. In this lease the tenant assumes all responsibility for repairs, replacement, and maintenance of the operating systems, specifically the heating, air-conditioning, electricity, and plumbing associated with the space the tenant occupies. However, if a problem occurs outside of the tenant's space, such as a sewer line stoppage, the landlord remains responsible.

With the tenant paying property taxes and property insurance, any increases in cost are passed through to the tenant. Should the property costs increase due to the tenant's use of the space for something considered to be a higher risk the tenant also assumes this increased cost.

Many smaller tenants are reluctant to enter into a triple net lease because of the possibility of having to replace expensive heat and air-conditioning equipment, especially when they have short-term leases under five years. Tenants generally determine the condition of the operating systems through inspection by a contractor prior to occupancy or lease execution and require the landlord to repair any existing problems prior to assuming responsibility.

The triple net expenses for taxes and insurance are determined on a monthly basis and added to the rent payment. Any increases may be passed through as a one-time payment, or the monthly charge may be adjusted to cover the increase.

In a multitenant property the triple net charges include common area maintenance (CAM) and are based on the percentage of the tenant's occupancy of the total space. For example, if the total space is

50,000 square feet and the tenant occupies 5,000 square feet, then the tenant's share of taxes, insurance, and CAM is 10 percent of the combined expenses.

TRUSTEE

A trustee is a person appointed or selected to have control over the assets of another person, including legal title to real estate. Trustees are provided for children, heirs, the mentally incompetent, and any others considered incapable of handling their own assets. A trust deed transfers legal title of property to a trustee and sets forth the trustee's authority and the conditions that govern that authority and bind the trustee.

A trustee is generally given specific legal authority. For example, upon the death of the property owner, the property deed may be transferred to a trustee with instructions that the heirs or others receive the rental income until they reach a certain age. The trustee may then be instructed to sell the property and pass the proceeds to the heirs or deed the property to the heirs. Trustees of property or other assets have legally recognized authority in all states.

UNDIVIDED INTEREST

When more than one person has ownership of a property, it is considered ownership in common with an undivided interest. Although each owner may own a specified percentage of the whole, each owner's interest is an undivided interest in the entire property. The part owner may sell his or her undivided percentage of ownership to the other partners or to another person. However, he or she cannot sell a specific piece or section of the whole property because ownership lies in a percentage of the whole.

If a dispute arises among the partners and no agreement can be reached to divide the property into parcels of whole ownership, a partner may go to court to seek a partition of the property. If granted by the court, an equitable division of the property may be granted according to the percentage of ownership.

For example, if five partners own 100 acres of land and one partner seeks and is granted a partition of the property, he or she may receive 20 acres as a deeded portion of which he or she has 100 percent ownership. The remaining eighty acres may remain as an undivided ownership of the four remaining partners or the entire property divided into twenty-acre parcels with each former partner then possessing 100 percent ownership.

UNIT VALUE

The value of a property can be expressed as a value per unit that when added together make up the value as a whole. Property that is composed of a number of units, such as apartment complexes, retail centers, or hotel/motel properties, can have their value calculated as a unit value. The unit value can differ based on the square footage of each unit, such as a shopping center with a variety of unit sizes. In motel or apartment properties, where all sizes are similar, the unit value can be expressed equally for all units.

Concise Encyclopedia of Real Estate Business Terms
© 2006 by The Haworth Press, Inc. All rights reserved.
doi:10.1300/5637_18

For example, if an apartment complex is composed of forty two-bedroom units and the value of the complex is $800,000, the unit value could be $20,000 per unit. If the forty units are twenty one-bedroom apartments and twenty two-bedroom apartments, the unit value could be $15,000 per one-bedroom apartment and $25,000 per two-bedroom unit for a total property value of $800,000.

Establishing unit values is especially important when calculating the value of the whole based on an income approach. By expressing a unit value of the whole, a buyer can determine the revenue stream expected from the property.

UNSECURED MORTGAGE

A mortgage for which the lender does not require the security of real estate, stocks, bonds, etc., as collateral to make the loan is unsecured. A lender may determine that the assets and net worth of the borrower are sufficient that a security mortgage against real estate is not required. In an unsecured mortgage the only security the lender has is the guarantee of the borrower to repay the loan.

Generally a mortgage is a pledge against property. However, a loan that is not secured by the property is often referred to as an *unsecured mortgage*. Even though this term is literally incorrect, it has come to be the accepted term when property is purchased without requiring property as security. An *unsecured line of credit* or *loan* more accurately describes this type of loan. Although the proceeds may be used to purchase a property, a mortgage is not recorded against the property as security for repayment. Should the borrower default on repayment of the loan, the lender does not have a mortgage on the property to secure the loan. However, with the personal guarantee of the borrower, the lender has recourse against the equity in all property owned by the borrower.

UPSIDE/DOWNSIDE

Upside/downside is a method to calculate the risk and/or profit potential of a project. In this calculation, a projection is made as to the best and worst outcome for the project. A potential buyer may then determine what the project will return if the worst situation occurs and what it will return if the best situation occurs. Such projections are useful to determine what income the project must return in order to reach the break-even point. A prudent investor will always determine the upside potential as well as the downside potential when analyzing of a projected investment.

For example, if an 100-unit apartment complex is projected to rent at least 40 units in the worse situation and at most rent 90 units, an investor using minimum and maximum rents can readily determine what the risk and profit potentials are for the investment. With this method, the investor can avoid surprises if the project yields a minimum or a maximum return.

USABLE AREA

Usable area is the rentable area of a building or a specified floor in a multilevel building. The accepted standard unit of measurement is defined by the national Building Owners and Managers Association. Usable square feet is calculated by measuring from the inside wall to the centerline of partitions that separate the space from other usable areas. No deductions are made for columns or projections necessary to the building.

The usable area may differ from the rentable area of a building or floor when the calculation is made on rent charged a tenant excluding stairways, mechanical rooms, etc. This calculation is sometimes used in multifloor office buildings where only the actual occupied space is used for rent calculation.

For example, if a tenant occupies a space measured as 50' × 50', or 2,500 square feet, the tenant may be charged for only the space occupied. However, the tenant may also be charged at the same rent per square foot for his or her proportionate share of the common area. If the common area equals 20 percent of the total building space, the tenant would be charged for 2,500 square feet plus an additional 20 percent for a total of 3,000 square feet.

USE VALUE

If property is valued based on its current use and not on its true market value, then the value is said to be its use value. Market value can sometimes far exceed use value. When alternate use value is placed on property for tax purposes, it can result in property taxes that exceed the ability of the owner to pay based on current use. Sometimes legislation is enacted to require value based on current use as a means of preserving farmland, timberland, or open spaces that are located in close proximity to city or town expansion.

For example, if a property is located in an area of urban expansion that is currently used as farmland but whose true market value is use as a retail or industrial site, the value difference can be significant. If the current value as farmland is $3,500 per acre, the true market value may be closer to $50,000 per acre.

USE VARIANCE

A city can grant on a property by property basis a use variance that violates the existing zoning laws. This variance is granted by the appropriate zoning authority or board of adjustments, which obtains its authority from the city or town governing body. It is generally granted when the zoning authority perceives such a variance will not adversely affect the use or value of other properties in proximity and governed by existing zoning laws. This variance is seldom granted when other properties in the area may be negatively impacted. For example, an application for an industrial use in a residential area that would affect the homeowners and the values of their property is never approved. If the variance will only minimally affect the homeowners and their properties, the zoning authority may grant such a variance. For example, if an open land area lies within an area zoned for single-family homes, the authority may grant a variance to permit construction of multifamily units limited to a maximum of four residence units, commonly known as fourplex units with four apartments per structure, or based on a set number of units per acre.

USUFRUCT

Usufruct is a Latin word that means "to have the use and fruit of without ownership." In this context, there are two types of ownership, naked ownership and usufruct, which components may be separated by law. The most common use of usufruct is a parent who wishes to avoid a succession and donates or sells the property to an heir but retains usufruct until death. In such case, the parent retains the use of the property for as long as he or she lives after which the property automatically transfers from the usufructory to the naked owner of the property. To have a usufruct of a property gives the usufructory owner the right to any gain produced by the property, such as a rental house or farmland that produces an income.

Although a usufruct can be granted only for a specified time period, say, twenty-five years, or upon the occurrence of a certain event, it is most often granted for the life of the usufruct owner. For example, if John deeds his son a property but retains a usufruct for life, the son has naked ownership, and John retains the use of or income from the property until he dies. Upon John's death, the usufruct will expire. If the son decides to sell the property before John's death, he may do so subject to the existing and continuing usufruct John possesses.

USURY

Regardless of the type of mortgage, whether fixed, adjustable, wrap-around, or graduated, the amount of interest cannot exceed the lawful rate. The amount of interest charged must be stated in writing. If the interest charged is usurious, greater than that allowed by law, it will result in the forfeiture of the entire amount of interest charged, not just the amount of interest in excess of the lawful amount. Different states set different levels of interest that can lawfully be charged.

Many states exempt from usury all loans for commercial or business purposes. Laws also govern the amount of interest a lender may charge for default of a mortgage. Mortgages may also be exempt from ordinary usury when guaranteed by the Veterans Administration or the Federal Housing Administration except as federal laws apply. Consumer loans secured by a mortgage on real estate may exceed the allowed limit subject only to consumer credit laws.

VACANCY RATE

The vacancy rate is the rate of current occupancy compared with the total rentable space or units in a development. A vacancy rate is usually expressed as a percentage of the total rentable space or units. A developer of a project will often calculate the break-even point of occupancy based on a percentage of vacancy. This will determine the level of vacancy permitted before the project can pay all related expenses. It is also a means of determining the future profit potential for a development when the vacancy rate decreases and the occupancy rate increases based on projected rental rates.

For example, if a developer of an apartment complex determines that the break-even point in a 100-unit complex is 70 units, then a vacancy rate in excess of 30 percent will result in a negative cash flow position. The developer may also determine the return on investment by reducing the vacancy rate.

VENDOR'S PRIVILEGE

A seller possesses a vendor's privilege against the real estate sold for any part of the purchase price that is not paid. A vendor's privilege must be recorded to affect any third persons. The recording of the "credit sale" or "act of vendor's lien" showing that the full purchase price has not been paid is the method used to preserve this privilege.

Generally in the credit sale document the purchaser grants a special mortgage in favor of the seller as security for payment of the balance of the sale price.

Concise Encyclopedia of Real Estate Business Terms
© 2006 by The Haworth Press, Inc. All rights reserved.
doi:10.1300/5637_19

WARRANTY DEED

A warranty deed is a deed that possesses the warranty or guarantee of the seller that the deed given to a buyer is free and clear of all encumbrances except those that are revealed. It is the seller's guarantee that a buyer of the property is receiving the property without liens or encumbrances, such as leases, except those specifically noted in the deed. Such a warranty passes from the seller to the seller's heirs and assigns should a problem be discovered in the future.

A warranty deed also warrants that the seller has good, clear, and merchantable title with the right to sell the property.

WETLANDS

Section 404 of the Clean Water Act defines wetlands as "areas that are inundated or saturated by surface or ground water at a frequency and duration sufficient to support and that under normal circumstances do support a prevalence of vegetation typically adapted for life in saturated soil conditions." This type of land is often referred to as marshes, bogs, swamps, bottomland, or lowlands and is most easily identified by the type of plants growing on the property. Property that is in a wetlands but has potential for development may be reclaimed through a process of mitigation in which property located in the same drainage district may be excavated to retain both its original water-holding capacity plus an amount equal to the reclaimed property. For example, if the property to be reclaimed for development is determined to hold two acre-feet of water, the mitigation property may be excavated to the depth of at least two feet per acre to equal its current holding capacity plus two acre-feet for the reclaimed property. By using this formula, it is determined that the drainage area does not lose any water-holding capacity.

Concise Encyclopedia of Real Estate Business Terms
© 2006 by The Haworth Press, Inc. All rights reserved.
doi:10.1300/5637_20

WRAP MORTGAGE

A wrap mortgage is a mortgage that wraps around an existing mortgage and includes additional funding. The wrap mortgage includes the current mortgage, which is not paid off, and new funding at a rate generally equal to or greater than the existing mortgage rate. The advantage is that the first mortgage is not paid off, and the wrap mortgage provides new funds for purchase by a new owner.

For example, if the remaining balance of the existing mortgage is $50,000 with an interest rate of 7 percent and only five years remaining on the term, a wrap mortgage may be made for $150,000 at an interest rate of 8 percent for a fifteen-year term. The first mortgage remains in place with the payments the responsibility of the seller. The buyer pays the payments of the wrap mortgage to the seller, who retains the difference between the wrap mortgage payment and the first mortgage payment. The deed remains in the seller's name but is held in escrow by an attorney who will file in the buyer's name when the first mortgage is paid in full.

ZONING

A governmental agency may establish areas within its jurisdiction for residential, business, multifamily, and commercial construction. The public regulation of the type of construction permitted in a designated area has its origin in protection of the public good. The resulting effect is to provide like occupancy in part for the protection of property values. Such a regulation supercedes property owners' rights.

The governing agency can exercise the zoning right only within its area of jurisdiction. A city can only regulate within the city limits. A county governing body can only regulate within the county geographical area not to include any incorporated city limits.

When the governing agency determines at its sole discretion that the public good is served by permitting a nonconforming structure, it may grant a one time variance. Such variances can be granted, for example, to allow duplex and fourplex construction in a single-family residential zoned area.

Within each of the zoning designations there can be subareas of zoning. For example, B-1 may allow only neighborhood business development, and B-3 may allow large shopping center development. R-1 may allow only single-family housing, and R-2 may allow multifamily development.

Structures that are built prior to the zoning law are grandfathered in. However, if they are destroyed, the new structure must generally comply with the prevailing zoning requirement.

Concise Encyclopedia of Real Estate Business Terms
© 2006 by The Haworth Press, Inc. All rights reserved.
doi:10.1300/5637_21

Appendix A

Sample Forms and Contracts

AGENCY DISCLOSURE FORM

This document describes the various types of agency relationships that can exist in real estate transactions.

An **Agency** relationship exists when a real estate licensee represents a client in an immovable property transaction. A client is anyone who engages a licensee for professional advice and service as his or her agent. Agency relationships can be formed with buyers/lessees or sellers/lessors or both.

Designated Agency results from a contractual relationship between a broker and a client when a licensee affiliated with a broker is designated by the broker to represent the client. The licensee appointed by the broker to represent the client is the Designated Agent. There is a presumption that the licensee with whom a client works is his or her Designated Agent unless there is a written agreement to the contrary. Other licensees employed by the broker do not work for the client, so the client should confine his or her discussions to his or her Designated Agent. Designated Agents must

1. obey all lawful requests of the client,
2. promote the client's best interest,
3. exercise reasonable care and skill in representing the client,
4. maintain the confidentiality of all information that could materially harm the client's negotiation position,
5. present all offers in a timely manner,
6. seek a tansaction at the price and on terms acceptable to the client, and
7. account for all money and property received from the client in a timely manner.

A Designated Agent may show alternate properties to buyers, show properties the client is interested in to other buyer clients, or receive compensation based on a percentage of the sale price without breaching the duty he or she owes to a client.

Dual Agency exists when a licensee is working with both the buyer and seller or both the landlord and tenant in the same transaction. For example, if the Designated Agent is also the listing agent, Dual Agency exists. Dual Agency is allowed only with the informed consent of all clients. Informed consent is presumed if a client signs the separate Dual Agency Disclosure form prescribed by the Louisiana Real Estate Commission. Dual Agents owe the following duties to both the buyer/seller and the lessor/lessee:

1. treat all clients honestly,
2. provide information about the property to buyers/tenants,
3. disclose all latent material defects in the property known to the licensee,
4. disclose financial qualifications of buyers/tenants to sellers/landlords,
5. explain real estate terms,
6. help buyers/tenants arrange for property inspections,
7. explain closing costs and procedures,
8. help buyers compare financing options, and
9. provide information about comparable properties that have been sold so that both clients can make educated buying/selling decisions.

Dual Agents are not permitted to disclose

1. confidential information of one client to the other,
2. the price the seller/landlord will take other than the listing price without the permission of the seller/landlord, and
3. the price the buyer/tenant is willing to pay without the permission of the buyer/tenant.

Confidential Information is information that could materially harm the position of a client if disclosed. Confidential Informaton does not include material information about the physical condition of the property. Thus, a licensee may disclose material information about the condition of the property and in fact has a duty to disclose known material defects regarding the condition of property. It is permissible for Confidential Information to be disclosed by a Designated Agent to his or her broker for the purpose of seeking advice or assistance for the benefit of the client. Information that would otherwise be confidential will no longer be confidential if

1. the client permits disclosure of such information by word or conduct,
2. disclosure of such information is required by law or would reveal serious defect, or
3. the information becomes public from a source other than the licensee.

By signing below you acknowledge that you have read and understand this form and that you are authorized to sign this form in the capacity in which you have signed.

Seller/Lessor: Buyer/Lessee:

_____   _____

By: _____   By: _____

Title: _____   Title: _____

Date: _____   Date: _____

Licensee: _____   Licensee: _____

Date: _____   Date: _____

Agency Form 12/02

BUSINESS DISCLOSURE
OF CONFIDENTIAL INFORMATION

CONFIDENTIALITY AGREEMENT

This Agreement is made as of this _____ day of _____, 2006, between _____ and _____, its agents and assigns (hereinafter referred to as "the Recipient") who will be receiving certain Confidential Information from _____ (hereinafter referred to as "Business").

Recipient has expressed interest as a qualified, interested buyer that is interested in acquiring Business, and has, therefore, requested certain Confidential Information for the purpose of review and evaluation as part of the valuation process for possible acquisition.

Business is willing to provide certain Confidential Information for the sole purpose listed above and upon the following terms and conditions.

NOW THEREFORE, in consideration of the foregoing and the covenants and agreements contained herein, the parties hereto agree as follows:

Confidential Information. The term "Confidential Information," as used in this Agreement, shall mean any and all discoveries, ideas, facts, or other information of whatever type and in whatever form, concerning Business, its employees or associates, obtained by or provided, directly or indirectly, to the Recipient.

Nondisclosure of Confidential Information. Recipient will use Confidential Information only to the extent necessary for the sole purpose described above. The Recipient agrees that it will not provide, communicate, or transmit any of the Confidential Information, except for the purpose described above, to any third party. The Recipient will hold in confidence, including from employees of Business, and not cause, permit, or enable, directly or indirectly, the disclosure, publication, transfer, misappropriation, or revelation to any person or entity of the Confidential Information without prior written consent of Business' President. In the event Recipient is required by valid legal process to disclose the Confidential Information, it is agreed that Recipient will provide Business with prompt notice of such requirement and that compliance with such valid legal process shall not be regarded as a breach of the provisions of the Agreement.

Recipient will not disclose to any third party, including Business employees, and not cause, permit, or enable, directly or indirectly, the disclosure, publication, transfer, misappropriation, or revelation to any person or entity that the Recipient has expressed an interest in acquiring Business.

Return or Destruction of Confidential Information. If discussions in connection with the proposed transaction cease for any reason, other than completion of the transaction, Recipient's obligations of confidentiality under this Agreement, except for all corporate information rights to which shall have been acquired through said transaction completion, shall continue permanently, and Recipient shall (a) within five days, return to an officer of Business all copies of all Confidential Information received, (b) destroy all notes with respect to such Confidential Information, (c) not make any other use of Confidential Information, and (d) not provide such Confidential Information to any other person or entity for any purpose.

Enforcement. Recipient and Business both understand and agree that, because of the unique nature of the Confidential Information, the Recipient, Business, or third parties will suffer immediate, irreparable harm if either party fails to comply with its obligations under this Agreement, and both parties will pay monetary damages as established in a court of law to compensate the other for such breach. Further, the damaged party shall be entitled to recover from the other all costs of enforcing this Agreement, including reasonable attorney's fees.

Entire Agreement Governing Law and Amendment. This Agreement sets forth the entire understanding and agreement of the parties with respect to the written matter hereof and supersedes all other oral and written representations and understandings. If any provision hereof or any of the parties' obligations hereunder is found invalid or unenforceable pursuant to judicial decrees or decision, any such provision or obligation shall be deemed and construed only to the extent permitted by law, and the remainder of this Agreement shall remain valid. The laws of the State of _____ shall govern the interpretation and performance of this Agreement. This Agreement may be amended or modified only in writing signed in advance by an officer of Business and Recipient to be bound by such amendment.

Agreed:

Recipient: _____

By: _____

Title: _____

Date: _____

Business: _____

By: _____

Title: _____

Date: _____

BUSINESS LISTING REQUIREMENTS

_____ Signed agreement

_____ Two years tax return (one year minimum)

_____ List of furniture, fixtures, and equipment

_____ Two years profit and loss statements (one year + YTD minimum)

_____ Price to purchase with explanation as to how structured (with inventory, with partial inventory, etc.)

_____ If real estate included—Need plat

_____ Estimated level of inventory

_____ Pictures

_____ If location leased—Term, rent, years/months remaining on lease, renewal options, other conditions

_____ Any leases of equipment, etc.

_____ Will owner sell business and lease real estate of owned?— If so, price for each

_____ Prepare complete package

CHECK-OFF LIST FOR CLOSING

MLS#:   _____

BUYER: _____

SELLER: _____

AGENT: _____

PROPERTY LOCATION: _____

COMMISSION STATEMENT
PREPARED: _____

SEND COMMISSION
STATEMENT TO: _____

                                   _____

                                   _____

ESCROW CHECK: _____

MADE PAYABLE TO: _____

KEYS: _____

HEALTH INSPECTION: _____

TERMITE INSPECTION: _____

INSURANCE: _____

OTHER INSPECTIONS (LIST):

      _____   _____

      _____   _____

      _____   _____

BUYER'S ATTORNEY
REVIEWED: _____

SELLER'S ATTORNEY
REVIEWED: _____

DEED: _____

RECEIVED SETTLEMENT
STATEMENT: _____

OTHER (LIST):

_____   _____

_____   _____

COMMERCIAL BUILDING LEASE

This lease, made this _____ day of _____, **2006,** between: _____, as "Lessor," and _____, as "Lessee."

1.1 In consideration of the rents to be paid and the obligations to be performed by Lessee, Lessor leases to and Lessee rents from Lessor, the premises described below situated upon the property described in Exhibit "A" on the terms and conditions set forth below:

1.2 A. LOCATION:
B. LEASED PREMISES:
C. APPROXIMATE SQUARE FEET OF LEASED PREMISES:
D. LEASE TERM:
E. COMMENCEMENT OF LEASE TERM:
F. FIXED MINIMUM RENT:
(Rent is due on the 1st day of the month—it is late after the 10th day of the month. On the 11th day there is an automatic additional $25.00 Late Fee due PLUS an additional $10.00 charge for each day after the 10th day until the monthly amount is paid in full.)
G. PERCENTAGE RENT:
H. TENANT'S ADDRESS:
I. TENANT'S TRADE NAME:
J. PERMITTED USES:
K. CONDITIONS ON ACCEPTANCE:
L. SECURITY DEPOSIT:
M. RENEWAL OPTIONS:

1.3 The exhibits listed below and attached to this lease are incorporated by reference:
Exhibit A. Legal Description.
Exhibit B. Security Deposit.

1.4 The riders described below and attached to this lease are incorporated by reference:

1.5 Each reference in the lease to a fundamental lease provision contained in paragraph 1.2 above shall be construed to incorporate all the terms provided under each such fundamental lease provision.

2.1 Lessor covenants that it has the full power and capacity to make this lease with Lessee.

2.2 The leased premises are described in paragraphs 1.2 A, B, and C above and attached as Exhibit A and include only the above-described building space and the land.

2.3 All buildings shown on Exhibit A as Guaranteed Initial Construction and being in existence at the date of commencement of this lease shall be and remain in existence at all times during the term of this lease or any extension of it (except deletions or changes resulting from fires, casualties, or exercise of eminent domain as set forth below).

3.1 To have and to hold the leased premises for the full term set forth in paragraph 1.2D, unless earlier terminated as provided in this lease, the term to commence on the date set forth in paragraph 1.2E or riders, if applicable.

4.1 Lessee, its employees and customers are granted the nonexclusive right to use the common facilities of the Building. "Common facilities" means all areas, space, equipment, and special services provided by Lessor for common or joint use and benefit of Lessor and the occupants of the Building, their employees and customers, including if such are provided, but not limited to, parking areas, service roads, loading facilities, employee parking areas, exits, entrances, approaches, access roads, driveways, court, stairs, ramps, sidewalks. Lessor shall have the right from time to time to change the size, area, grade, location, and arrangement of parking areas, service roads, entrances, exits, approaches, and other common areas and facilities; to police the parking areas; to restrict parking by tenants, their officers, agents, and employees, to employee parking areas; periodically to close a portion of the parking areas, service roads, exits, entrances, approaches, or sidewalks, for purposes of repair, construction, and reconstruction and to such extent may be sufficient legally to prevent a dedication of them, and Lessor shall have the right to do any other acts in and to the common facilities which Lessor shall determine to be advisable with a view to the improvement of the convenience and use of them by tenants, their employees and customers.

5.1 Lessee agrees to pay without set-off, deduction, or demand whatsoever, the fixed minimum annual rent set forth in paragraph 1.2F above during the term of this lease in equal monthly installments on or before the first day of each calendar month in advance at the office of Lessor or at any other place designated by Lessor in writing. Per this agreement, forward monthly rent to: _____. For any fractional month at the beginning or end of the term, one-thirtieth of such monthly payment shall be paid for each day of such fractional month, on the first day of such month. Rent is due on the 1st day of the month—it is late after the 10th day of the month. On the 11th day there is an automatic additional $25.00 late fee due PLUS an additional $10.00 per day charge for each day after the 10th day until the monthly rental amount is paid in full. All rent, whether fixed minimum rent, percentage rent, or additional rent shall be paid at the office of Lessor or other place designated by Lessor in writing without any set-off or deduction whatsoever.

6.1 Lessor will retain responsibility for the roof, less and except any leaks caused by Lessee's renovation work. Lessor will maintain the roof and exterior structure of the leased premises **not** including all glass, entrances, show windows, doors. Lessee agrees to begin such repairs as soon as practicable after written notice from Lessor of the need for such repairs. The provisions of this paragraph shall not apply to damage or destruction by fire, other casualty, or eminent domain. Lessee accepts the leased premises in their present condition except for the exceptions set forth in paragraph 1.2K. After delivery and acceptance of the leased premises, no repairs shall be due Lessee except those expressly noted herein.

7.1 Upon payment by lessee of all rent due and upon the observance of all its obligations under this lease, Lessee shall peaceably and quietly hold and enjoy the leased premises for the term of this lease, without hindrance or interruption by Lessor or any other person or persons lawfully or equitably claiming by, through, or under Lessor, subject, nevertheless, to the terms and conditions of this lease.

8.1 Lessee shall use the leased premises solely for the permitted use or uses set forth in paragraph 1.2J above and no other purposes and shall conduct its business so as to produce the maximum volume of sales and to help establish and maintain the high reputation of the Building.

8.2 Lessee shall occupy the leased premises and open for business therein within **SIXTY (60) DAYS** after the commencement of the lease term, and shall conduct the business stated above within the leased premises during the term of this lease. The leased premises shall not be used for any other business without the written consent of the Lessor which shall not be unreasonably withheld.

8.3 During the entire term of this lease Lessee shall

(a) furnish, install new or reconditioned trade fixtures, and maintain them;
(b) carry a complete and full stock of seasonable merchandise;
(c) maintain adequate trained personnel for efficient service;
(d) conduct actively the business described above in the leased premises and utilize 100 percent of the leased premises with due diligence and efficiency so as to produce the maximum amount

of gross sales consistent with efficient operation, unless prevented from doing so by causes beyond Lessee's control;

(e) conduct its business in the leased premises during the regular customary days and hours for business during the same days, nights, and hours as the majority of the chain stores located in the Building, or during the days, nights, and hours agreed upon by a majority of the members in the Merchants' Association as provided below; and

(f) keep the display windows and signs in the leased premises well lighted during the hours from sundown to nine o'clock p.m., or to the hour agreed upon by a majority of the Merchants' Association, unless prevented by causes beyond its control.

9.1 Lessee at its sole cost shall at all times maintain the leased premises and every part of them in good condition and neat appearance. Lessee's obligation for maintenance and repair of the leased premises includes, but is not limited to: maintenance of exterior entrances, glass, show windows, moldings, partitions, doors, fixtures, ceilings, floors, walls, and all equipment, including plumbing, sprinkler, and sewage system, electrical, mechanical, lighting, heating, escalators, air-conditioning and heat systems. "Repairs" means repairs, replacements, renewals, alterations, additions, and betterments.

9.2 Lessee may at its own cost and expense alter or remodel the interior of the leased premises in any manner that it elects, provided that the work does not make any modification to the structure of the building and is done in a good and first-class workmanlike manner. No work which will result in structural modification to the building will be commenced without the prior written approval of Lessor of the plans and specifications submitted by Lessee. Lessor's approval will not be withheld unreasonably. Lessee shall pay promptly all contractors and material men so as to minimize the possibility of lien attaching to the leased premises; should any such lien be made or filed, Lessee shall bond or discharge it within ten days after written request by Lessor. Where the cost of the work is in excess of **$1,000**, Lessee will secure workmen's compensation and public liability insurance and payment and performance bonds, which will run in favor of Lessor as well as Lessee and will guarantee the payment of all bills, wages, and obligations incurred in the work and the discharge of all liens or claims. The requirements of paragraph 15.1 shall be met by Lessee also. Lessee's work shall not interfere with Lessor's work and shall be subject to rules promulgated by Lessor or Lessor's architect. Lessee and its contractor shall employ labor compatible with labor employed by Lessor or its contractor.

9.3 If Lessee fails to make the repairs required by his or her lease or to maintain the leased premises in the condition required by this lease within **THIRTY (30) DAYS** after written notice by Lessor or such additional time as is required reasonably to perform such work, Lessor may have the necessary work done and Lessee agrees to repay Lessor the expense incurred on demand together with interest thereon from the date of demand until paid. Any sums thus by Lessor together with interest shall be secured as if they were rentals due under the terms of this lease. Lessor may do any such work without liability to Lessee for any loss or damage that may accrue to Lessee's merchandise, fixtures, or other property of Lessee or its business.

9.4 Upon the expiration or termination of this lease, Lessee shall return the leased premises in as good repair as they were when received, ordinary wear and tear excepted. Lessor shall have the option to require that the leased premises be restored to their original condition at Lessee's expense or to require Lessee to leave in the leased premises, without molestation, disturbance, or injury, any part of or all of the alteration, additions, or improvements which Lessee has made or affixed to the leased premises. These shall become the property of the Lessor, and Lessee waives all rights to compensation.

10.1 Lessee further agrees as follows:

(a) All delivery, loading, and unloading of goods shall be done at such times, in the areas, and through the routes, exits, and entrances designated for such purposes by Lessor.

(b) All garbage and refuse shall be kept in a completely enclosed container of fireproof construction, and shall be placed outside the premises prepared for collection in the manner and at the times, and places specified by that authority and by Lessor. Lessee shall cause and pay the cost of removal of all of Lessee's refuse or rubbish at such intervals as specified by Lessor.

(c) No loud-speaker, television, phonograph, radio, or other device shall be used in a manner so as to be heard or seen outside of the leased premises without the prior written consent of Lessor.

(d) The leased premises will be kept continuously at a temperature sufficiently high to prevent freezing of water in pipes and fixtures.

(e) The plumbing facilities and drains shall be kept open; the expense of any stoppage or damage resulting from violation of this provision shall be borne by Lessee.

(f) Lessee shall employ a pest extermination contractor, at such intervals as Lessor may require, at Lessee's expense.

(g) Lessee shall not burn anything or operate an incinerator on or about the leased premises of the Building, or within one mile of the outside property lines of the Building, without the written consent of Lessor.

(h) No auction, fire, removal, going out of business, or bankruptcy sale will be conducted within the leased premises, nor will the premises be used as a "second hand store," a "surplus store," or a "discount house."

(i) All windows, doors, glass, and plate glass will be kept neat and clean, and Lessee will promptly replace such when cracked or broken. No signs shall be placed on doors or windows, inside or out, nor shall the painting, placing of advertising media, banners, pennants, awnings, or the like be permitted without obtaining prior written consent of Lessor.

(j) No offensive odors or continuous loud noise will be caused on the leased premises.

(k) No catalog sales or orders shall be made or received in or from the leased premises except orders for merchandise which Lessee is permitted by this lease to sell.

(l) Lessor will warrant all systems to be in working condition at time Lessee opens for business, to include HVAC, Plumbing, and Electrical Systems.

(m) If Lessee shall violate any provision of paragraph 10.1(a) through 10.1(m), then Lessor (in addition to any other remedy provided in this lease) may, at its option charge Lessee $25.00 per day for each day that such violation shall continue, as liquidated damages.

11.1 Lessee shall pay before delinquency all municipal, county, parochial, state, or federal taxes assessed during the term of this lease against any leasehold interest or personal property of any kind on the leased premises.

12.1 Lessee with Lessor's approval may erect at its own expense a sign upon the exterior of the leased building in accordance with the terms of any applicable ordinance of any governmental authority in force and effect at the time. The sign shall be within the height and width of the parapet-facade of the leased premises and shall not be composed of neon or flashing lights nor painted on the facade. Lessee may further furnish and install a sign under the canopy or covered sidewalk in front of the leased premises.

13.1 At the termination or expiration of this lease, Lessee, at its own expense, shall remove all signs painted or placed in or upon any part of the leased premises to Lessor's satisfaction. Any damage to the leased premises as a result of the removal will be repaired by Lessee at its own expense. If Lessee fails to do so, Lessee shall reimburse Lessor for all costs of removal.

14.1 Lessor shall not be liable for any damage from any cause whatsoever to Lessee, the property of Lessee, or to others on the leased premises or to their property. By way of illustration only and without limitation, Lessor shall not be liable for any injury or damage to Lessee, its property, others located on or near the leased premises, or their property, resulting from

(a) theft, fire, explosion, falling plaster, stucco or fixture, steam, gas, electricity, water, wind, rain, or snow;

(b) the bursting, stopping, or leaking of water, gas, sewer, downspouts or steam pipes, boilers, unit heaters, fixtures, transformers, condensers, towers, or air-conditioning equipment;

(c) leaks from any part of the leased premises or from the pipes, appliances, sprinkler system, or plumbing works, or from the roof, street, parking lot, subsurface, or from any other place;

(d) dampness;

(e) any equipment or appliances becoming out of repair;

(f) any defect in or failures of plumbing, sewage, heating, or air-conditioning or other equipment including but not limited to elevators, escalators, conveyors, or installation of such;

(g) broken glass;

(h) any injury or damage caused by persons on the leased premises, persons occupying adjoining leased premises or any portion of the Building, persons occupying property adjacent to the Building, the public, or for any injury or damage caused by operations in construction of any private, public, or quasi-public work.

All property kept or stored on the leased premises by Lessee or any other persons shall be kept or stored at the risk of Lessee only, and Lessee shall hold Lessor harmless from any claims arising out of damages to such property, including subrogation claims by insurance carriers of Lessee or others. These agreements do not apply if the damage is caused by the willful act of Lessor or by failure to take action toward remedying defects which Lessor is required by the lease to repair within a reasonable time after receipt of written notice of such defects.

14.2 Lessee's assuming possession of the leased premises constitutes an admission that it has examined the leased premises and found them in good and safe condition. Lessee will indemnify Lessor and agrees to defend and hold Lessor harmless from any and all loss, expense, and responsibility whatsoever for damages to any person whomsoever or to any property of the Lessee or others arising from the occupancy, use, condition, upkeep, and maintenance of the leased premises or occasioned wholly or in part by any act or omission of Lessee, its agents, contractors, employees, servants, lessees, or concessionaires. Lessee expressly relieves Lessor of any and all liability for injuries or damages caused by any vice or defect of the leased premises to any occupant or to anyone in or on the premises or in or on the sidewalks or curbs or walks or parking lot adjacent to the leased premises. Lessor shall not be liable for any latent defect in the leased premises or in the building of which they form a part. The above agreement applies even to those damages arising from defects which Lessor is required by this lease to repair, except in the case of positive neglect or failure to take action toward the remedying of such defects within a reasonable time after receipt of written notice of such defects. Should Lessee fail promptly to notify Lessor in writing of any such defects, Lessee shall be responsible for any damage resulting to Lessor or others.

14.3 If Lessor should be made a party to any litigation commenced by or against Lessee, Lessee shall protect and hold Lessor harmless from all loss and expense of any kind, including attorneys fees, which Lessor may sustain or which may be asserted against Lessor.

15.1 For the mutual protection of Lessor and Lessee, Lessee agrees to at all times

- (a) maintain in full force a policy of public liability and property damage insurance with respect to the leased premises, and where applicable, the air-conditioned walk or the sidewalks in front of and business operated in the leased premises in the minimum amounts **of $500,000 per person, $1,000,000 per accident, and $200,000 for property damage.**
- (b) Further Lessee shall, at its expense, maintain fire and extended insurance coverage **of the replacement cost of the leased space together with an amount** adequate to cover the cost of replacement of all fixtures, contents, decorations, and improvements installed by Lessee or which Lessee is obligated to maintain and replace.
- (c) All policies of insurance will name Lessor, any mortgagee, person, firm, or corporation designated by Lessor, and Lessee as

insured, and shall contain a clause that the insurer will not cancel or change the insurance without first giving Lessor thirty days' written notice.

(d) Lessee waives and each policy shall also contain a waiver of subrogation by the insurer against Lessor for any reason whatsoever. The insurance shall be approved by Lessor, and a copy of the policy or certificate of insurance shall be delivered to Lessor or Agent for Lessor.

(e) Lessee shall, at Lessee's expense, maintain a workmen's compensation policy in the minimum amount necessary to meet the requirements of any applicable workmen's compensation act, and a copy of the policy or a certificate of insurance shall be delivered to Lessor or Agent for Lessor.

(f) _____, **as well as the leasing company, shall be named as additional insureds.**

(g) **These items must be furnished to the Lessor and the leasing company, before Lessee begins business operations.**

15.2 Lessee will not carry on any activity or have or use any article in the leased premises which would forfeit the Lessor's fire and extended coverage insurance or increase the rate charge for such insurance. Should any action be taken by Lessee, whether authorized under this lease or not, which results in an increase in the rate of the premiums on insurance on the building or its contents, then Lessee shall pay the additional premiums caused by the increased rate. If Lessee's occupancy or business prevents securing proper insurance, then Lessee hereby grants to Lessor the option of either

(a) requiring the immediate termination of such use;

(b) considering such use a default entitling Lessor to all of the rights given by this lease in the event of default by Lessee; or

(c) canceling this lease, waiving all delays and requiring Lessee to surrender possession at once.

Lessee shall notify Lessor or Lessor's agent, in writing, any time the leased premises will be unoccupied, so that necessary vacancy permits may be obtained from Lessor's insurer. Failure to comply with this condition will make Lessee liable for any loss sustained by Lessor.

15.3 Lessee shall give immediate notice to Lessor of (a) fire, other casualty, or accidents to the leased premises or in the building of which the premises are a part; and (b) defects or malfunction in the leased premises.

15.4 If Lessee fails to obtain or maintain any insurance required by this lease, Lessor shall have the option, after fifteen days' written notice to Lessee, to obtain such insurance. Any sums thus advanced by Lessor for Lessee's account shall be secured as if they were rentals due under the terms of this lease and shall bear interest at the highest legal rate from the date of such expenditures.

16.1 Lessee shall be responsible solely for and pay promptly all charges for heat, water, gas, electricity, sewer charges, or any other utility used in the leased premises. In no event shall Lessor be liable for an interruption or failure in the supply of any such utilities to the leased premises.

17.1 Lessee shall be responsible for all Real Estate Taxes associated with the leased premises. Lessor shall initially pay all real estate taxes assessed by lawful authority against the real property upon which the Building is situated. If the sum of real estate taxes levied against the land and the Building shall exceed in any lease year the amount of such taxes for the first full tax year, Lessee shall pay as additional rent that portion of the excess equal to the product derived by multiplying such tax excess by a fraction, the numerator of which is the square footage of the leased premises and the denominator of which shall be the total square footage of the completed building area of the Building, exclusive of common facilities. The term "first full tax year" shall mean the lease year in which the building of which the lease premises form a part shall have been first assessed by governing authorities as a completed building. This additional rent shall be accrued and paid in monthly installments on or before the first day of each month.

18.1 Lessor reserves the right to subordinate this lease or any part of it at any time from time to time to the lien of any mortgage or mortgages presently existing or hereafter placed upon the Lessor's interest in the leased premises, or upon the land or premises of which the leased premises are a part, or upon any building hereafter placed upon land of which the leased premises form a part. Lessee agrees to execute and deliver, upon Lessor's demand, any further instruments subordinating this lease or any part of it which Lessor may require. Any such mortgage shall, however, recognize the validity and continuance of this lease in the event of foreclosure on the Lessor's interest or in the event of conveyance in lieu of foreclosure, as long as the Lessee shall not be in default under the terms of this lease.

18.2 If any mortgage on the leased premises is foreclosed, all of Lessor's rights shall pass to the purchaser at any such foreclosure.

18.3 Within ten days after any request by Lessor for any reason Lessee will deliver in recordable form a certificate to Lessor or to any proposed mortgagee or purchaser certifying (if such be the case) that this lease is in full force and effect and that there are no defenses or offsets to it or, if so, stating those claimed by Lessee, and the dates to which the fixed minimum rent, percentage rent, and other charges have been paid. Lessee irrevocably appoints Lessor as agent and attorney in fact with full power to execute and deliver in the name of Lessee any such instruments or certificates should Lessee fail to respond, execute, and deliver such timely.

18.4 Lessee shall not be entitled to enforce the provisions of this lease by offset of rental against a mortgagee without the prior consent of the mortgagee, its successors, or assigns. However, nothing herein shall prevent or restrain Lessee from seeking any and all remedies or damages at law against Lessor for Lessor's failure or default.

19.1 Lessee will not assign this lease in whole or in part, nor sublet all or any part of the leased premises, without the prior written consent of Lessor in each instance, **and Lessor's approval for sublet will not be unreasonably withheld.** Notwithstanding any assignment or sublease, Lessee and Guarantor, if any, shall remain liable fully on this lease.

19.2 If Lessee is a corporation and if at any time during the term of the lease the person or persons who own a majority of its voting shares at the time of execution of this lease cease to own a majority of such shares except by transfers by gift, bequest, or inheritance to their spouses or children, Lessee shall notify Lessor in writing, and Lessor may terminate this lease by written notice to Lessee within ninety days thereafter. This paragraph shall not apply if Tenant or its 80 percent voting stockholder is a corporation the stock of which is traded actively on a securities exchange or in the national over-the-counter market. In the latter event the purchaser, surviving corporation, or reorganized entity which has assumed control of Lessee shall automatically be obligated jointly and severally (in Louisiana in solido) with Lessee under this lease and shall execute such instruments as may be required to confirm such guarantee.

20.1 Lessee shall, at Lessee's sole cost and expense, comply with and observe all of the requirements of all county, parochial, municipal, federal, and other applicable governmental authorities, now in force, or which may hereafter be in force, pertaining to the leased premises.

21.1 Lessee will join a Merchants' Association if one is formed among the tenants of the Building; cooperate and assist in its programs; and pay regular monthly dues to the Merchants' Association in such an amount as shall be fixed by the percentage of the members of the association set forth in paragraph 1.2I, the dues to cover the cost of joint advertising, trade promotion, and other programs approved and established by majority vote of the association. These regular monthly dues shall not, in any event, exceed the sum set forth in paragraph 1.2G above.

22.1 If the leased premises are damaged by fire, the elements, unavoidable accident, or other casualty, but are not thereby rendered untenantable in whole or in part, Lessor shall, **out of insurance proceeds**, at its own expense cause the damage to be repaired, and the rent shall not be abated. If by reason of such occurrence and without fault or negligence of Lessee, or Lessee's agents or employees, the premises are rendered untenantable only in part, Lessor shall, if such casualty is covered by Lessor's insurance, out of insurance proceeds at its own expense, up to the insurance proceeds received as a result of such damage, cause the damage to be repaired and the fixed minimum rent meanwhile shall be abated proportionately to the portion of the premises rendered untenantable. If the premises are rendered wholly untenantable by reason of such occurrence, Lessor shall at its own expense cause such damage to be repaired, and the fixed minimum rent shall be abated in whole until the leased premises have been put in substantial repair, but this lease shall continue in full force and effect and shall be extended as to term for a time equal to that during which the premises remain untenantable, provided, however, that if the leased premises are rendered wholly untenantable or if 50 percent or more of the leased premises are damaged or destroyed by fire or other causes during the last twenty-four month period of the term of this lease or any extension thereof, or if the casualty is not **fully** covered by Lessor's insurance, Lessor shall have the right to cancel and terminate this lease if it gives Lessee written notice to that effect within sixty days after it first receives written notice from Lessee of such damage or destruction. In such event, this lease shall terminate upon the third day after notice is given by Lessor, and Lessee shall vacate the leased premises immediately. Nothing herein shall be construed to abate or reduce percentage rent.

22.2 If 50 percent or more of the existing rentable area of the Building shown on Exhibit A is damaged or destroyed by fire or other cause, then, unless Lessor shall within **SIXTY (60) DAYS** after the date of such destruction begin restoration, and unless Lessor shall have repaired substantially such damage within nine months from the date of such destruction, Lessee at its option may cancel this lease by written notification to Lessor within sixty days after the expiration of the six-month period or within sixty days after the expiration of the **NINE (9) MONTH** period. Upon giving of such notice to Lessor, the term of this lease shall expire by lapse of time upon the third day after notice is given, and Lessee shall vacate the leased premises immediately.

23.1 If any part of the leased premises is taken under the power of condemnation or eminent domain, then this lease shall cease upon the part taken from the day that the actual possession of that part shall be taken by the expropriating party. Rent shall be paid up to that day, and from that day the fixed minimum rental shall be reduced in proportion to the amount of the leased premises taken. If 25 percent or more of the leased building space is taken, Lessor shall give Lessee notice and Lessee and Lessor each shall have the option to cancel this lease, to be exercised by written notice thirty days after notice by Lessor of taking. If neither Lessee nor Lessor elects to cancel this lease, then Lessor shall at its cost, but not to exceed the proceeds of the taking allocable to the leased premises, build on the new building line a wall, or front, similar to the one removed. The terms "condemnation or eminent domain" shall include conveyances and grants made in anticipation or in lieu of such proceedings.

23.2 If 20 percent or more of the parking area is taken, and, if Lessor does not at its option commence within ninety days and thereafter pursue diligently the furnishing of additional parking space to bring the reduction in parking area to less than 20 percent, Lessor shall give Lessee written notice and Lessee shall have the option to cancel this lease to be exercised by written notice within thirty days after receipt of the notice from Lessor.

23.3 All compensation awarded for any taking under the power of eminent domain, whether for the whole or a part of the leased premises or for part of the common facilities, shall be the property of Lessor, whether such damages are awarded as compensation for loss of value of the leasehold of fee of the leased premises or otherwise; and Lessee assigns to Lessor all of its right to such compensation; provided, however, Lessor shall not be entitled to any award made to Lessee for diminution in value of Lessee's interest, such as furniture, stock, equipment, and fixtures which were paid for by Lessee.

24.1 Any of the following shall constitute a default by Lessee:

    (a) failure to pay any rental or additional rental, provide the insurance required by this lease, pay the premiums for such insurance, or pay utility bills and other expenses or obligations assumed under this lease within ten days after the due date;

(b) any violation at any time of any other condition of this lease if such violation continues for fifteen days after written notice of such violation is mailed by Lessor to Lessee, including, but not by way of limitation, the following violations:

  (1) the discontinuance of the use of the premises for the purposes for which they are rented or failure actively to conduct that business in the leased premises **without the written permission of the Lessor;**

  (2) Lessee's using the leased premises or any portion of them at any time for any illegal or unlawful purpose; or

  (3) Lessee's committing or tolerating the commission on the leased premises of any nuisance or of any act of waste, or of any act made punishable by fine or imprisonment under the laws of the United States or the state in which this lease is effective, or of any ordinance of the city, parish, or county;

(c) Lessee's bankruptcy or insolvency;

(d) the filing in any court of a petition in bankruptcy, receivership, reorganization, for respite, or for any other debtor's proceedings by or against Lessee;

(e) the adjudication of any sublessee or assignee of Lessee then occupying more than 50 percent in area of the leased premises as bankrupt or insolvent; or the appointment of a receiver or trustee to take charge of the property or of any part of it, or the cession to creditors or assignment for benefit of creditors by Lessee or any sublessee or assignee of Lessee occupying more than 50 percent in area of the leased premises; or

(f) any seizure of this lease under any writ of seizure or execution.

24.2 If any such default shall occur, then, in addition to any other rights which Lessor may have under law or under the provisions of this lease, Lessor shall have the following options:

  (a) Immediately to re-enter and remove all persons and property from the leased premises. Such property may be removed and stored in a public warehouse or elsewhere at the cost of, and for the account of, Lessee, all without service of notice or resort to legal process and without being deemed guilty of trespass, or becoming liable for any loss or damage which may be occasioned thereby. Such re-entering and removal of persons and property from the leased premises shall not be deemed to preclude Lessor from exercising any other options granted by this lease;

(b) To proceed for past due installments only, reserving its rights to proceed later for the remaining installments and to exercise any other option granted by this lease;

(c) Immediately to cancel this lease and to proceed for past due installments;

(d) To re-enter the leased premises and let them in the manner set forth below. Subsequent to such re-entering and re-letting under this clause, however, Lessor shall have the option at any time thereafter to terminate the lease for such previous breach; or

(e) To accelerate the rental for the unexpired term of the lease.

If Lessor elects to accelerate the rental, then, at Lessor's option, Lessor shall have the further option to re-enter the premises and to re-let them in the manner set forth below.

24.3 Should Lessor elect to re-enter, under any provision of this lease, or should it take possession pursuant to legal proceedings or pursuant to any notice provided for by law, it may, without terminating this lease, make such alterations and repairs as may be necessary in order to re-let the premises and may re-let the premises or any part thereof. This re-letting shall be for such rental and on such terms as Lessor in its sole discretion may deem advisable, including a lease on a monthly basis or for a term extending beyond the term of this lease. All payments received by Lessor from such re-letting shall be applied:

(a) If Lessor has not elected to accelerate the rent for the whole unexpired term of the lease, first, to the payment of any indebtedness other than rent due from Lessee to Lessor; second, to the payment of any costs and expenses of such re-letting, including brokerage fees and attorney's fees, and the cost of such alterations and repairs; third, to the payment of rent due and unpaid hereunder, and the residue, if any, shall be held by Lessor and applied in payment of future rent as it may become due and payable hereunder. If such monthly rentals received from the re-letting are insufficient to pay the amount owed by Lessee, then the deficiency shall be paid during that month by Lessee hereunder to Lessor. Such deficiency shall be calculated and paid monthly in the manner provided below;

(b) If Lessor has elected to accelerate the rent for the whole unexpired term of the lease, first, to the payment of any indebtedness other than rent due thereunder from Lessee to Lessor; second, to the payment of any costs and expenses of such re-letting, including brokerage fees and attorney's fees, and of costs of such alterations and repairs; third, to the payment of the rental due for the full unexpired term of the lease, reserving the right to sue thereafter for any balance remaining due after credit for the rental actually received or estimated to be received. Any balance thus due shall be considered rental due under this lease and shall be secured by the Lessor's privilege and right of detention.

24.4 Exercise of the right of re-entry and privilege to re-let shall not in any way prejudice Lessor's right to hold Lessee liable for any amount due under this lease in excess of the amount for which the property is re-let. Any sum due Lessor for future rental, or any sum which may be due Lessor subsequent to Lessor's re-entry under the terms of this lease, shall be considered rental due under this lease and shall be secured by the Lessor's lien, privilege, pledge, and right of detention. If Lessor exercises its option to accelerate the rent for the unexpired term of the lease or if Lessor exercises its option to re-enter the premises, the amount of annual rent which would be payable by Lessee subsequent to such option shall be equal to the average annual minimum and percentage rents paid by Lessee from the commencement of the term to the time of default or during the preceding three full calendar years, whichever period is shorter. If the period for which rent would be payable is not an annual period, then the amount payable shall be the proportion of the annual payment which the period to be calculated bears to one year. If the Lessee fails or refuses to permit Lessor to re-enter the premises, Lessor shall have the right to evict Lessee in accordance with the provisions of law without forfeiting any of Lessor's other rights under this lease or under the Law, and Lessor may at the same time or subsequently sue for any money due or to enforce any other rights which Lessor may have. No such re-entry or taking possession of the premises shall be construed as an election on its part to terminate this lease unless a written notice of such intention be given to Lessee or unless its termination be decreed by a court of competent jurisdiction. Re-entry or taking possession of the premises shall not be construed as an election to accelerate the rent for the unexpired portion of the lease unless a written notice of such intention is given to Lessee.

24.5 In the event of any default, Lessee shall remain responsible for all damages or losses suffered by Lessor. Lessee waives any putting in default for any such breach, except for any expressly required by this lease.

24.6 Should Lessor at any time terminate this lease for any breach, in addition to other remedies it may have, it may recover from Lessee all damages it may incur by reason of such breach, including the cost of recovering the leased premises and reasonable attorney's fees.

24.7 Failure strictly and promptly to enforce the conditions set forth above shall not operate as a waiver of Lessor's rights. Lessor expressly reserves the right always to enforce prompt payment of rent and to treat the failure to pay rent in accordance with this lease as a default, regardless of any indulgences or extensions previously granted. The acceptance of rent by Lessor shall not waive any preceding breach by Lessee of any term or condition of this lease, other than the failure of Lessee to pay the particular rental so accepted, regardless of Lessor's knowledge of the preceding breach at the time of the acceptance of such rent. Lessor's acceptance of any rent in arrears, or after notice of institution of any suit for possession or for cancellation of this lease, will not be considered as a waiver of such notice or of the suit, or of any of the other rights of Lessor. The waiver by Lessor or Lessee of any breach of this lease shall not be deemed a waiver of any subsequent breach of the same or any other term or condition of this lease. No term or condition of this lease shall be deemed to have been waived by Lessor or Lessee unless such waiver is in writing and signed by Lessor or Lessee.

24.8 Lessee hereby expressly waives any and all rights of redemption granted by or under present or future laws in the event of Lessee's being evicted or dispossessed for any cause, or in the event of Lessor's obtaining possession of the leased premises by reason of the violation by Lessee of any of the covenants or conditions of this lease, or otherwise.

25.1 Lessor or its agents shall have the right to enter the leased premises at all times to examine them, to show them to prospective purchasers or lessees, and to make any repairs, alterations, improvements, or additions which Lessor may desire. No such act shall constitute an eviction of Lessee in whole or in any part, and the rent shall not be reduced in any manner while such repairs, alterations, improvements, or additions are being made because of loss or interruption of business of Lessee, or otherwise. Nothing contained in this paragraph shall be construed to require Lessor to make any repairs whatsoever, unless elsewhere provided in this lease.

25.2 During the **SIXTY (60) DAYS** prior to the expiration of the term of this lease or any renewal term, Lessor may place upon the premises the usual notices of "For Lease " or "For Sale." If Lessee shall not be present personally to open and permit access to the premises, at any time, when for any reason of emergency an entry therein shall be necessary, Lessor or Lessor's agents may enter them by master key, or may forcibly enter them without rendering Lessor or its agents liable for, and without in any manner affecting the obligations, whatsoever, for the maintenance or repair of the leased premises except as otherwise specifically provided above.

26.1 At the expiration of this lease, or its termination for other causes, Lessee shall surrender possession immediately. Should Lessee fail to do so, Lessee shall pay any and all damages suffered by Lessor, but in no case less than twice the rent per day, plus attorney's fees and costs. Lessee also expressly waives any notice to vacate at the expiration or termination of this lease and all legal delays, and hereby confess judgment with costs placing Lessor in possession to be executed at once. Should Lessor allow or permit Lessee to remain in the leased premises after the expiration or termination of this lease, this shall not be construed as a recondition of this lease, but shall be a tenancy on a month-to-month basis.

26.2 The terms and conditions of this lease and all rights and liabilities herein given to or imposed upon the Lessor and Lessee, including the prohibition against assignment or sublease, shall inure to the benefit of and extend to and bind the respective heirs, executors, administrators, successors, trustees, or assigns of the parties. If there is more than one lessee, they shall be bound jointly and severally (jointly and in solido in Louisiana) by this lease. No rights, however, shall inure to the benefit of any assignee or subtenant or Lessee unless such assignment or such sublease has been approved by Lessor in writing. The Lessor's obligations shall bind it only with respect to breaches occurring during its ownership.

27.1 All monetary sums due Lessor shall bear interest from the date due at the rate of 8 percent per annum or such lesser rate as in the highest legal rate of interest permitted by the state where the leased premises are located.

27.2 If an attorney is employed to enforce or protect any claim of Lessor arising from this lease, Lessee shall pay, as the fee of that attorney, an additional sum amounting to 25 percent of the first $2,500 of the amount of the claim and 15 percent of the amount of the claim in excess of $2,500, or if the claim is not for money, then such as will constitute a reasonable fee, together with all costs, charges, and expenses, the minimum fee in any event to be $50.00.

28.1 If either party shall be delayed or hindered in or prevented from the performance of any act required hereunder (other than payment of rental) by reason of strikes, lockouts, labor troubles, inability to procure labor or materials, failure of power, restrictive governmental laws or regulations, riots, civil commotion, insurrection, enemy action, acts of God, fire or other casualty, war, or other reason of a like nature not the fault of the party delayed in performing work or doing acts required under the terms of this lease, then performance of such act shall be excused for the period of the delay and the period for performance of any such act shall be extended for a period equivalent to the period of such delay.

29.1 Any notice from Lessee to Lessor must be sent by certified or registered mail, postage prepaid, addressed to Lessor or such other addresses as Lessor may designate by written notice.

29.2 Any notice by Lessor to Lessee must be sent by certified or registered mail, postage prepaid, addressed to Lessee at the address set forth in paragraph 1.2H or at such other address as Lessee may designate by written notice.

29.3 If any part of the Building is mortgaged by Lessor, Lessee shall send a copy of all notices sent to the Lessor to the mortgagee by registered or certified mail addressed to the address that the mortgagee shall designate in writing to Lessee. Upon notification to Lessee of any such mortgagee, no notice shall be effective upon Lessor while the mortgage is in effect unless the copy is also served upon the mortgagee, so that the mortgagee shall have the opportunity to foreclose and perform such act for Lessor as may be called for by the notice.

30.1 This lease and the Exhibits and Riders, if any, attached to it and forming a part of it, set forth all of the covenants and agreements between Lessor and Lessee concerning the leased premises, and there are no agreements, conditions, or understandings either oral or written, between them other than those set forth herein. No subsequent alteration, amendment, change, or addition to this lease shall be binding upon Lessor or Lessee unless reduced to writing and signed by them.

30.2 Lessee agrees that it shall look solely to the property of Lessor in the land and buildings of which the leased premises are a part, subject to the rights of any mortgagee, for the collection of any judgment in the event of default in performance of this lease by Lessor, and no personal judgment shall attach to or be rendered against Lessor, its successor and assigns, and their other assets.

30.3 The captions, paragraph numbers, and article numbers appearing in this lease are inserted only as a matter of convenience and in no way define, explain, modify, amplify, limit, construe, or describe the scope, purposes, or intent of such paragraphs or articles or in any way affect this lease.

30.4 If any term, provision, or condition of this lease or the application of it to any person or circumstance shall to any extent be invalid or unenforceable, the remainder of this lease, or the application of such term, provision, or condition to persons or circumstances other than those as to which it is held invalid or unenforceable, shall not be affected thereby, and each term, provision, covenant, or condition of this lease shall be valid and be forced to the fullest extent permitted by law.

30.5 Submission of this lease to Lessee shall not constitute an offer to Lessee. This lease shall not be final and binding upon Lessor until it is executed and delivered fully by Lessee and accepted in writing by an officer of Lessor.

31.1 Lessee shall not record this lease without the written consent of Lessor. The Lessor agrees that upon the request of Lessee it will execute and deliver a short form lease for the purpose of recording.

32.2 Lessee warrants that it has dealt with the leasing company and _____ as agent for this lease and covenants to defend with counsel approved by Lessor, hold harmless and indemnify Lessor from and against any and all cost, expense, or liability for any compensation, commissions and charges claimed by any broker or agent with respect to Lessee's dealings in connection with the lease or the negotiation thereof. Broker's commission to be paid according to Commission Agreement by and between the leasing company and _____.

Signed by Lessor and Lessee on the day and year first above written in the presence of the undersigned competent witnesses. This instrument may be executed in counterpart copies, each of which shall be deemed an original for all purposes.

WITNESS: LESSOR:

_____   _____
                                                        DATE

_____   _____
                                                        DATE

WITNESS: LESSEE:

_____ _____

BY: DATE

           Tax ID# or SS# _____

WITNESS: LESSEE:

_____ _____

BY: DATE

           Tax ID# or SS# _____

LESSOR _____

LESSEE _____

- -

EXHIBIT "A"

Legal Description

EXHIBIT "B"

Security Deposit

Exhibit "B," dated _____, 2006, between
_____, LESSOR, and
_____, LESSEE.

A security deposit in the amount of $_____ shall be due and payable together with the first month's rent at the time of lease execution.

Security Deposit:	$_____
1st Month's Rent:	$_____
Total:	$_____

The Security Deposit shall be forfeited in the event of default by Lessee as set forth in article 24.1.

COMMERCIAL LISTING AGREEMENT

PROPERTY ADDRESS:

LEGAL DESCRIPTION: See Exhibit "A" attached.

FOR THE SUM OF:

TERMS OF: Cash or as acceptable to Seller.

LISTING BROKER:

For and in consideration of service to be performed by above-named BROKER, hereafter called "AGENT." SELLER/LESSOR hereafter called "OWNER" employ said AGENT as my/our sole and exclusive AGENT to sell the above-described real property at the price as above outlined and hereby grant said AGENT the exclusive right to sell the same and to accept a deposit thereon.

OWNER agrees to pay said AGENT a commission of _____ (_____) percent of the sales price, or in the event of a lease execution commission will be the same percentage of the lease amount for the initial lease term and all renewal options. The fee for Brokerage Services shall be paid by OWNER to AGENT at the time of closing or lease execution or as collected. This agency and authority shall continue for a term of _____ (____) months from the date of signed listing agreement.

OWNER also agrees to refer all prospects to AGENT.

OWNER further agrees to pay commission as above stipulated in event of sale, lease, or option that leads to a sale of said property during the term of the agreement or within one hundred twenty (120) days, after the expiration of this agreement, provided purchaser has become interested in said property as a result of the efforts or advertising of said AGENT during the active term of this listing.

OWNER agrees to furnish a good and merchantable title to the purchaser. Should title not be valid, a reasonable time shall be allowed OWNER to clear title and at his or her expense. Should title prove not merchantable or should the sale fail to be consummated for any cause due to OWNER's fault, AGENT's commission shall nevertheless be earned and shall be paid by OWNER to AGENT in cash. Should OWNER fail to pay the agreed upon commission and it is necessary for _____ to turn this matter over to an attorney at law for collection, then OWNER agrees to pay the commission owed, as well as reasonable attorney fees and all court costs.

Of said property, the OWNER represents that property has no known latent structural defects or any other defects to his or her knowledge unless listed in this agreement. That all written information relating to the property provided to AGENT by OWNER is true and correct.

OWNER shall agree to be bound by the terms and conditions of the State Licensing Law and Rules and Regulations of the State Real Estate Commission. It is understood that AGENT is a member of the _____ Multiple Listing Services ("MLS"). OWNER agrees that this agreement will be filed in MLS and processed in accordance with the rules and regulations of MLS, unless otherwise requested by OWNER.

I acknowledge that I have read and understand the reverse side of this form regarding Disclosure and Consent to Dual Agency. By my signature below I authorize that the undersigned AGENT may act as a disclosed Dual Agent in securing a buyer or lessee for the above-listed property.

Other Conditions: _____

You may place a "For Sale" sign on the property.
Occupancy will be granted on date of passing of title.

RECEIPT OF COPY OF THIS LISTING AGREEMENT IS HEREBY ACKNOWLEDGED

SELLER/LESSOR:

SIGNED: _____   DATE: _____

SIGNED: _____   DATE: _____

ACCEPTED BY:
AGENT: _____   DATE: _____

The parties hereto may rely on a facsimile transmission as to their acceptance of this agreement.

EXHIBIT "A"

Legal Description

COMMERCIAL REAL ESTATE PURCHASE AGREEMENT

THIS AGREEMENT FOR THE PURCHASE AND SALE OF REAL ESTATE is made as of the days and dates indicated hereinafter by and between _____, with a mailing address of _____ _____, hereinafter referred to as "Seller," and _____, with a mailing address of ____ _____, hereinafter referred to as "Buyer," according to the following terms and conditions.

1. Seller agrees to sell to Buyer and Buyer agrees to purchase from Seller that certain real estate located in the city of _____, Parish of _____, State of **Louisiana**, containing _____ **SF or Acres**, more or less as shown on **Exhibit "A"** attached hereto, together with all building improvements, all the rights, privileges, easements, and appurtenances, if any, along with the title and interest of Seller.

2. The purchase price to be paid by Buyer to Seller for the property shall be _____, payable as follows:

    (a) Buyer shall have deposited with the leasing company the sum of $_____. Said deposit shall constitute a portion of the sales price.

    (b) The balance of the sales price, namely, $_____, shall be paid at closing.

3. The sale shall be made with full warranty of title and complete subrogation of any and all rights and actions in warranty against all former proprietors of the property to be conveyed, together with all rights of prescription, whether acquisitive or liberative, to which the Seller may be entitled. Title to the subject property must be approved by Buyer's attorney. Seller agrees to pay for any curative work reasonably required in order to deliver marketable title. In absence of the approval of title by Buyer's attorney, Buyer may terminate this agreement and receive the return of its deposit.

    (a) Buyer shall deliver at closing the sum of $_____ subject to the prorations specified herein.

    (b) If a Title Insurance Policy or Title Opinion is required, it shall be at the _____ expense.

    (c) Buyer and Seller shall each pay its own attorney's fees incurred in connection with the sale, execution, and negotiation of this agreement.

(d) Real estate taxes shall be prorated (based on the most current tax bill) except that Seller shall be responsible for any taxes from previous years, penalties incurred, or settlement of previous years' tax liens.

(e) If Buyer requires a Site Assessment Study, it shall be at Buyer's expense.

(f) Seller shall deliver possession of the property to the Buyer at the date of closing free and clear of all leases, if any are in effect.

(g) Buyer shall have _____ days from acceptance of this agreement by Seller to complete an inspection ("inspection period"). Should "inspection period" show property reveals problems that prevent Buyer from using property for its intended purpose, this agreement shall become null and void and Buyer shall so notify Seller in writing and receive a full refund of all monies held as deposit. Buyer shall have _____ days from notification of its acceptance of the property to close sale.

4. A property survey shall be furnished by _____.

5. The property shall be zoned appropriately for Buyer's intended use. If rezoning is required, it shall be the Buyer's responsibility and at Buyers's expense.

6. Both parties reserve the right to demand and receive specific performance.

7. Any notices which shall be required under the terms of this agreement, shall be in writing and sent certified mail addressed to the parties as follows:

Buyer: _____

_____

_____

Seller: _____

_____

_____

8. Buyer shall have the right to assign or transfer its interest in this agreement without the prior written consent of Seller.

9. A Real Estate Brokerage Fee shall be paid at closing in accordance with a separate document between Seller and the leasing company.

Buyer and Seller agree to hold each other harmless of any other claims for any commissions or other compensation for Brokerage Fees committed by them to another party.

10. Buyer and Seller agree to execute and deliver any other instruments or documents, as may be required to consummate this sale, as called for in this agreement.

11. Buyer and Seller mutually agree that time is of the essence in consummating the closing of this sale. Should performance of any of the terms and conditions called for in this agreement fall on a Saturday, Sunday, or legal holiday, it is understood that the time shall be extended to the next business day thereafter.

12. This agreement shall be enforced in accordance with the laws of the State of Louisiana and shall be binding upon the respective heirs, successors, and assigns. Should any of the terms and conditions of this agreement conflict with the laws of the State of Louisiana, the laws of Louisiana shall take precedence over the terms and conditions of this agreement.

13. In the event either party shall be required to enforce the terms of this agreement through litigation, in addition to other damages which may be awarded, it shall be entitled to recover court costs and attorneys' fees from the losing party.

14. Both parties acknowledge and agree that this agreement in its final form, which has been executed and delivered by Buyer and Seller, contains the entirety of their agreement. Both Buyer and Seller acknowledge that oral agreements between them shall have no force and effect whatsoever.

15. Offer to purchase is contingent upon the following:

    (a) All utilities shall be available to the site, i.e., water, sewage, electric, telephone.

    (b) _____

         _____

    (c) _____

         _____

16. Buyer shall take possession of said property at closing date or such other date as agreed to by Buyer and Seller. Buyer specifically acknowledges that it has not relied on any representations or warranties made by or on behalf of Seller or Seller's agents as to the conditions of any improvements located on property or the condition of the surface or subsurface, soil conditions, or any matter pertaining to hazardous materials or toxic waste.

17. Seller specifically grants to Buyer the right to enter the property for purposes of determining the condition of the surface or subsurface soil, of the existence of any hazardous materials or toxic waste. In the event Buyer discovers a problem with the soil condition or the existence of hazardous or toxic materials, Buyer may at its option cancel this agreement by written notice to Seller and receive a full refund of its deposit or take the property in "as is" condition and proceed to close. Buyer shall be furnished by Seller any and all information, studies, or prior knowledge relating to hazardous or toxic materials, including but not limited to soil contamination or conditions.

18. This agreement remains binding upon Buyer until 5:00 p.m., Central Standard Time, _____, 2____. If not accepted by Seller on or before 5:00 p.m., Central Standard Time, _____, 2____, this agreement shall become null and void, and the Broker shall return the Buyer's deposit to Buyer.

19. Should the Act of Sale fail to take place by virtue of any of the resolutory conditions contained hereinabove, then Buyer shall receive the return of its deposit.

Acceptance: The parties hereto may rely on a facsimile transmission as to their acceptance of this agreement.

I acknowledge that I have read and understand the reverse side of this form regarding Disclosure and Consent to Dual Agency. By my signature below, I authorize this real estate company to act as a disclosed Dual Agent representing both Buyer/Lessee and Seller/Lessor for the above-described property.

IN WITNESS WHEREOF, the parties have executed this Agreement as of the days and dates indicated herein.

BUYER: _____   SELLER: _____

_____   _____
by: Date   by: Date

_____   _____
Witness   Date   Witness   Date

BUYER: _____   SELLER: _____

_____   _____
by: Date   by: Date

_____   _____
Witness   Date   Witness   Date

- -

EXHIBIT "A"

Legal Description

CONSTRUCTION DEVELOPMENT BUDGET

_____
(Date)

Developer: _____

_____

Concept: _____

Location: _____

City/State: _____

LAND COST:

   Acreage: _____ Sq. Ft. @ $_____/Sq. Ft.Total $_____

HARD COSTS:

   Bldg. Costs: _____ Sq. Ft. @ $_____/Sq. Ft. $_____

   Site Work (approximate $2.50/Sq. Ft. based on land size)

      Grading, Compaction & Stabilization $_____

      Parking, Curbing/Sidewalks $_____

      Landscape, Irrigation & Dumpster Enclosure $_____

      Exterior Plumbing $_____

      Exterior Lighting (if applicable) $_____

      Tl Allowance $_____

      Other (explain) _____ $_____

      _____ $_____

TOTAL HARD COSTS: $_____

SOFT COSTS:

   Architectural & Engineering $_____

   Soil & Survey Reports $_____

   Environmental Study $_____

   Building Permit $_____

   Appraisal Report $_____

   Utility Fees $_____

   Title/Closing Costs $_____

Insurance $_____

Legal Fees $_____

Property Taxes (during construction) $_____

Leasing Commission $_____

Interim Interest Expense

     $_____ % int. / _____ mos. /_____ %

Outstanding Loan Balance $_____

Expense: Construction loan cost of project
@___ % × __ months × .75 %
(construction loan staged so average 75 percent
outstanding balance) $_____

Financing costs ($ ____ %) Explain _____

_____ $_____

TOTAL SOFT COSTS: $_____

TOTAL PROJECT COSTS: $_____

EXCLUSIVE RIGHT TO SELL AGREEMENT

FIRM: _____ AGENT: _____ DATE: _____

PROPERTY ADDRESS: _____

LEGAL DESCRIPTION: _____

_____ CITY: _____ PARISH: _____ STATE: ____

The undersigned seller/lessor(s) hereby exclusively lists and places with the undersigned real estate broker (hereinafter referred to as Broker) for sale, lease, or exchange the above-described real property for the sum of ($_____) _____ cash, new loan, or the following terms: _____ or for any other price, or upon any other terms, as may hereafter be agreed upon. The property to be sold/leased/exchanged includes all buildings, components, and other permanently installed or attached improvements thereon, including but not limited to fences, outside TV antenna, built-in appliances, fixtures, heating, air-conditioning, window units, ceiling fans, bathroom mirrors, window treatments, light bulbs, and fixtures which are in place at the time this agreement is executed, unless otherwise stated herein.

Other Conditions: _____

Convey with sale Mineral rights __ Yes __ No   Timber rights __ Yes __ No (Initials)

FOR AND IN CONSIDERATION of services to be performed by the above-named Broker, I/We hereby employ Broker as my/our sole and exclusive agent to sell, lease, or exchange the above-described real property at a price acceptable to me/us and accept a deposit thereon. **I/WE ALSO AGREE TO REFER ALL PROSPECTS TO THE BROKER DURING THE TERM OF THIS LISTING.** This agreement shall expire at 11:59 PM on _____, _____.

AGENT'S FEE: The seller/lessor (s) agree to pay Broker a negotiated professional fee, irrespective of agency relationships, as follows:

(a) _____ percent of the selling price or $_____, if the Agent presents to seller/lessor an offer and acceptance in an amount equal to or greater than the offering price, or such lesser price or terms as seller/lessor may accept, or if the property is otherwise sold, exchanged, leased, rented, or disposed by Agent or any other person, including seller/lessor, during the listing period.

(b) The compensation provided for in subparagraph (a) above if property is sold, conveyed, or otherwise transferred within _____ calendar days after the termination of this authority or any extension thereof to anyone with whom Broker was procuring cause and/or has had negotiations prior to final termination. However, seller/lessor(s) shall not be obligated to pay the compensation provided for in subparagraph (a) if a valid listing agreement is entered into during the term of said protection period with another licensed real estate broker.

(c) Seller/lessor(s) authorize Broker to cooperate with other brokers and may pay a portion of the professional fee stated above to such other broker in any manner Broker sees fit.

(d) In the event of an exchange or trade, permission is hereby given Broker to represent all parties and collect compensation or service fees from them, provided there is full disclosure to all principals of such agency. Broker is authorized to share with other brokers such compensation in any manner acceptable to brokers.

(e) Seller/lessor(s) has been informed of the possibility of dual agency should a buyer/client become interested in this property.

TITLE: Seller/lessor(s) agree to furnish a good and merchantable title to the purchaser. Should title not prove merchantable or should the sale fail to be consummated for any cause due to owner(s) fault, the professional fee shall nevertheless be earned and shall be paid by the seller/lessor(s) to Broker in cash.

DEPOSIT: Broker is authorized to accept from prospective purchaser, or his/her representative, a deposit represented by cash or check and to place said cash deposit in a noninterest-bearing account in a federally insured banking or savings institution selected by the Broker pending settlement. Agent shall have no responsibility in case of failure or suspension of said banking or saving institution. Seller/lessor(s) shall further agree that seller/lessor shall be bound by, and the terms and conditions would be controlled by, the provisions of the state licensing law and rules and regulations of the state real estate commission. A "For Sale"/ "For Lease " sign [ ] **may**

[ ] **may not** be placed on the property. A lock box [ ] **may** [ ] **may not** be placed on the property. Seller/lessor declare that I hold said company, its associates, and _____ harmless from any responsibility or liability in connection herewith.

HOME PROTECTION PLAN: Seller/lessor is informed that home protection plans are available. Such plans may provide additional protection and benefit to a seller/lessor and buyer. Cost and coverage may vary.

DISCLOSURE: Seller/lessor shall provide a Property Disclosure Statement concerning the condition of the property. Seller/lessor(s) agree to save and hold Broker harmless from all claims, disputes, litigation, and/or judgements arising from any incorrect information supplied by seller/lessor(s), or from any material fact known by seller/lessor(s), which is not disclosed. Seller/lessor(s) exceptions are: (If "as is" sale, see addendum.) Seller/lessor(s) shall indemnify Broker against all liability, loss, and expense, including reasonable attorney's fees and court costs that Broker may incur as a result of any claim or suit against Broker by any person for personal injury or property damage sustained by such person while on or about the herein described premises, due to the condition of said premises or seller/lessor(s) negligence.

THIS PROPERTY WILL BE OFFERED, SHOWN, AND MADE AVAILABLE TO ALL PERSONS WITHOUT REGARD TO RACE, COLOR, RELIGION, NATIONAL ORIGIN, HANDICAP, FAMILIAL STATUS, OR SEX.

MULTIPLE LISTING SERVICE: It is understood that Broker is a member of the _____ multiple listing service (MLS). Seller/lessor agrees that this agreement will be filed in MLS and processed in accordance with the rules and regulations of MLS. If the seller/lessor(s) do not want his/her property placed in said MLS system, then see the addendum attached to and made a part of this contract. _____ *Please initial.* **SELLER/LESSOR(S)** understand and agree that their property may be advertised on the Internet, including but not limited to Realtor.com and Internet Data Exchange (IDX). Nothing contained herein is intended to nor shall it be construed as making _____ multiple listing service a party to this listing agreement. Seller/lessor(s) authorize Broker to disclose to any prospective purchaser or agent whether or not there are any outstanding offers at any given time to purchase the property, but Broker is not to disclose the price or other details of the offer. This form is provided as a service and sole use to its members by the _____ Board of

Realtors. Use of this form is not mandatory. **ANY LEGAL QUESTIONS SHOULD BE REFERRRED TO YOUR ATTORNEY.**

APPOINTMENT OF DESIGNATED SELLER/LESSOR'S AGENT:
Broker designates and seller/lessor accepts _____ (seller/lessor's Designated Agent) as the only legal agent of seller/lessor. Broker reserves the right to name additional designated agents when, in Broker's discretion, it is necessary. If additional designated agents are named, seller/lessor shall be informed in writing within a reasonable time. Seller/lessor acknowledges that seller/lessor's Designated Agent may from time to time have another sales associate who is not an agent of the seller/lessor sit an open house of seller/lessor's property or provide similar support in the marketing of seller/lessor's property. Seller/lessor understands and agrees that this agreement is a contract for Broker to market seller/lessor's property and the seller/lessor's Designated Agent is the only legal agent of seller/lessor and that neither Broker nor any other sales associates affiliated with Broker will be acting as legal agent of the seller/lessor. Seller/lessor's Designated Agent will be primarily responsible for the direct marketing and sale of the seller/lessor's property.

BREACH OF AGREEMENT: If the seller/lessor fails to comply with this agreement for any reason within the time specified, Broker may recover costs and/or fees, including reasonable attorney's fees, incurred as a result of breach of this agreement.

I/WE HAVE READ, UNDERSTAND AND ACKNOWLEDGE RECEIPT OF A COPY OF THIS LISTING. I/WE WARRANT THAT I/WE OWN THE PROPERTY AND/OR HAVE FULL AUTHORITY TO EXECUTE THIS AGREEMENT.

SELLER/LESSOR(S): _____ SIGNED _____ DATE: _____
             (Please Print)

ADDRESS:_____ SIGNED _____ DATE: _____

CITY: _____ STATE: _____ ZIP: _____

PHONE: Home: _____Work: _____

ACCEPTED BY: _____ AGENT: _____
          (Broker)

GROUND LEASE

This Ground Lease made and entered into as of _____, 2006 by and between _____ **and** _____ (hereinafter referred to as Landlord), and _____ (hereinafter referred to as Tenant). The parties hereto agree that this Ground Lease sets forth all agreements, covenants, and conditions, expressed or implied, between the parties and supersedes any prior oral or written agreements between the parties with respect to the premises hereinafter described. The following exhibits are attached to this Ground Lease and made a part hereof:

> Exhibit "A"—Plot Plan
> Exhibit "B"—Subordination, Nondisturbance, and Attornment Agreement
> Exhibit "C"—Title Exceptions

1. **DEMISED PREMISES:** (A) The Landlord hereby leases to Tenant and Tenant hereby leases from the Landlord the premises located on _____, _____, _____, with not less than _____ feet of frontage on _____ and not less than _____ feet of usable depth, in the City of _____, Parish or County of _____, State of _____, containing approximately _____ square feet of vacant land (the Demised Premises, hereinafter) that is identified as Demised Premises and shown outlined in Exhibit "A," together with all improvements now and hereafter erected thereon which will include but not be limited to parking, lighting, and any other improvements deemed necessary by Tenant, and all rights and appurtenances thereunto belonging.

(B) Landlord further grants to Tenant, easements of access across the areas identified as Drive Easement and outlined in Red on attached Exhibit "A," to provide continuous, uninterrupted access to, from, and among the driveways of the Demised Premises and all streets adjacent to the Demised Premises as long as this Ground Lease is in effect. These easements shall be nonexclusive access easements, and the easement areas shall be maintained in good order and repair by Landlord, at no cost to Tenant.

The legal description of Demised Premises and the Drive Easement areas mentioned above shall be prepared as part of the survey described herein, **and the parties shall execute an amendment to this lease and a Short Form Lease for recording, acknowledging, and agreeing to the said legal descriptions.**

2. TERM OF LEASE: The term of this Ground Lease (The Term) shall be for a period of _____ ( ) years, which shall commence on _____ and shall end on _____ unless sooner terminated as herein provided.

3. RENTAL PAYMENTS: Tenant shall pay to the Landlord as a minimum rent during the original _____ years of The Term of this Ground Lease, the monthly sum of as follows: Years 1-5 _____ Dollars and _____ Cents ($_____) per month in advance, on the first day of each and every month, beginning _____ days from the execution of this Ground Lease or the opening for business which-ever occurs first. The rent and other sums payable hereunder shall abate un-til such date. All rents and other sums payable to Landlord hereunder shall be paid to the order of _____ and _____ whose social security numbers are _____ and _____ re-spectively, unless written notice to some other entity or to another address within the United States of America shall be given to Tenant by Landlord at least ten (10) days prior to the date when the next rent payment is due.

Tenant shall pay all real estate and personal property taxes assessed solely against the Demised Premises during The Term prior to delinquency. All taxes for any partial tax years within The Term shall be prorated. If the Demised Premises areas are assessed as part of a larger parcel, Landlord shall pay all taxes on the larger tax parcel prior to delinquency, and Tenant shall reimburse Landlord for Tenant's equitable share of such taxes within _____ ( ) days of receipt of billing therefore together with copies of the paid tax receipts and a copy of the tax map showing the tax parcel in which Demised Premises is included. Tenant's said equitable share shall in-clude all taxes based upon assessed value of the improvements to Demised Premises, and an equitable percentage of the taxes due based on the value of the land.

Tenant shall pay for all utilities furnished to the Demised Premises dur-ing The Term, and all other fees, charges, and government impositions which arise out of or in connection with the rental, operation, possession, occupancy, or use of Demised Premises during The Term, and all other fees, charges, and government impositions which arise out of or in connection with the rental, operation, possession, occupancy, or use of Demised Pre-mises thereto by Tenant during The Term.

4. TITLE AND QUIET POSSESSION: Landlord covenants that Land-lord has fee simple title to the premises described herein and has full right and authority to make this Ground Lease; that the Demised Premises and Drive Easement are free and clear of and from all liens, restrictions, leases, and encumbrances, except as designated in Exhibit "C"; and that there are no laws, ordinances, governmental rules or regulations, or title restrictions or zoning or other matters which will restrict, limit, or prevent Tenant's use of the Demised Premises; and that so long as Tenant is not in default hereunder Tenant shall have quiet and peaceful possession and enjoyment of the Demised Premises, the Drive Easement, and all other easements, rights, and appurtenances thereunto belonging.

5. TITLE EXAMINATION: As soon as reasonably possible following the execution of this Ground Lease, Landlord shall pay up to $_____ for an examination of title of the Demised Premises and Drive Easement and furnish Purchaser a Commitment for Title Insurance on Tenant's leasehold estate in the Demised Premises, and rights in the Drive Easement, together with full copies of all documents which create exceptions to title set forth therein, including but not limited to covenants, conditions, restrictions, reservations, easements, rights, and rights of way of record. Tenant shall have _____ ( ) days after receipt of said Commitment and the survey described herein, together with full copies of all documents creating such exceptions, within which to notify the Landlord, of Tenant's objections to title thus disclosed to Tenant. Landlord shall remove all encroachments disclosed by the survey or title search prior to the commencement of The Term at Landlord's cost. If such exceeds $2,500 and Landlord is not willing to pay the additional money above $2,500, Tenant shall then have the option to pay the additional money or cancel the Lease by written notice to Landlord. Landlord shall have until _____ ( ) days following the date of Landlord's receipt of Tenant's said notice of objection to title exceptions, whichever is longer, to attempt to eliminate the exceptions to title that are objected in Tenant's said notice. Tenant shall promptly notify Landlord of any other objections by Tenant to exceptions to title discovered by Tenant other than by the procedure aforesaid. If any of the exceptions to title objected to by Tenant other than encroachments (all of which shall be removed as aforesaid) are not eliminated within the time limits stated above, then Tenant may elect to terminate this Ground Lease or may withdraw its objections and continue this Ground Lease without modification. The Policy of Title Insurance shall be an ALTA Owner's Policy Form B revised 1987 or 1990 or other form approved by Tenant insuring Tenant's leasehold estate in Demised Premises and rights in the Drive Easement granted herein with standard exceptions deleted and with a liability not exceeding $500,000 and shall specifically insure the boundary lines of the Demised Premise and the Drive Easement and shall be paid for by Landlord. Tenant shall pay all additional premiums for any additional title insurance coverage desired by Tenant.

Landlord shall execute and deliver to the Escrow Agent or person designated to hold documents, i.e., attorneys, title company, at or prior to closing a customary Landlord's Affidavit and such other documents as may be reasonably requested by the Escrow Agent and the title insurance company insuring Tenant's Title to the Property in order to close the purchase and sale and issue the title insurance policy as required in this Ground Lease.

6. SUBORDINATION AND NONDISTURBANCE: Landlord shall also furnish an agreement in form satisfactory to Tenant executed by any Mortgagee holding a mortgage or holder of a lien executed prior to this Ground Lease subordinating any such mortgage or lien affecting the Demised Premises or Drive Easement to the provisions of this Ground Lease unless such Mortgage or the holder of any such lien executes a nondisturbance agreement as set forth hereinafter within _____ (   ) days following the execution of this Ground Lease. Otherwise Tenant may terminate this Ground Lease.

As used in this Ground Lease, the term, "Mortgage" shall include a Deed of Trust, and the term "Mortgagee" shall include the holder of a Deed of Trust. The Landlord has the right to Mortgage its fee interest in the Demised Premises, and if any Mortgagee so requests, this Ground Lease shall be subject and subordinate to any Mortgage covering the Demised Premises and to all renewals, modifications, consolidations, replacements, and extensions thereof, provided the Landlord's Mortgagee and Landlord execute and deliver to Tenant, acknowledged and in recordable form, three (3) original counterparts of a Subordination, Nondisturbance and Attornment Agreement in the form attached hereto as Exibit "B" and, as a part hereof. Upon receipt of the said executed and acknowledged counterpart agreements, Tenant agrees promptly to execute, acknowledge, and return two of the counterpart agreements to Landlord.

7. UTILITIES: It is a condition of this Ground Lease that adequate utilities, including water, sewage disposal, telephone service, and energy sources, to service the Demised Premises for Tenant's intended use shall be available to the satisfaction of the Tenant. If adequate utilities are unavailable to the satisfaction of Tenant, Tenant shall have the option to pay for the cost to bring utilities to property line, or Tenant may cancel the Lease by written notice to Landlord. Landlord shall grant to or secure for Tenant all easements that are necessary in order for Tenant and/or utility companies, as applicable, to be able to use, maintain, repair, and replace said utility lines as necessary for Tenant's purpose throughout The Term.

8. REPAIRS AND MAINTENANCE: Tenant shall keep and maintain the Demised Premises and all improvements thereto, including but not limited to the building and paving located on Demised Premises, in good order and repair, at Tenant's cost, and at no cost to Landlord. Tenant shall also maintain lighting to the extent Tenant deems necessary at Tenant's costs, and at no cost to Landlord.

9. **INSURANCE:** Tenant shall, at Tenant's sole cost and expense, maintain general public liability insurance against claims occurring upon or within the Demised Premises, such insurance to afford single limit protection of not less than $1,000,000.00 Dollars in respect to bodily injury, death, or property damage. Said insurance may be in the form of a general coverage or floater policy covering these and other premises, provided that Landlord and the leasing company are named as additional insureds in said policy.

10. **CONDEMNATION:** If the whole of the Demised Premises shall be taken or appropriated under any right of eminent domain or under any other legal right whereby the taking authority is obligated to compensate Landlord therefore, then Tenant may terminate and cancel this Ground Lease as of the date on which the condemning authority takes physical possession upon giving to Landlord written notice of such election to terminate and cancel. Landlord agrees that immediately after any notice of intended or actual taking or appropriation is received, to give Tenant written notice thereof, providing to Tenant full details of such taking or appropriation, including, without limitation, copies of all condemnation plans or surveys submitted by the condemning authority and such other information as might be necessary to enable Tenant to determine its future course of conduct. If this Ground Lease shall be terminated and canceled as a result of any taking or appropriation, Tenant shall be released from any further liability, and the rent and other sums for the last month of Tenant's occupancy shall be prorated and Landlord shall refund to Tenant the sums paid in advance. At the time of such taking or appropriation the amount of the award attributable to Tenant's improvements to the Demised Premises shall be payable to Tenant out of any award, **subject and subordinate to the rights of any Tenant Mortgagee.** The Tenant's right to receive compensation for loss of business or damages for its fixtures and its personal property shall not be affected in any manner by this provision of this Ground Lease.

If part of the Demised Premises or Tenant's rights in any Drive Easement shall be acquired or condemned by use of the power of eminent domain for any public or quasipublic purpose and if such partial taking shall render the Demised Premises unusable for the business of Tenant in the opinion of Tenant, then Tenant at its option may terminate this Ground Lease as of the date title is vested in the public body, and the rights of Landlord and Tenant shall be as set forth above for the taking of the whole.

If such partial taking is not sufficiently extensive to render the Demised Premises unusable for the business of Tenant in the opinion of Tenant, the rentals shall be prorated and adjusted based on the percentage of such partial taking relative to the original size of the Demised Premises.

11. **DEFAULT BY TENANT:** If Tenant shall default in the payment when due of the rents and other payments designated in this Ground Lease or if Tenant fails to maintain the insurance Tenant is required to maintain by this Ground Lease, Landlord shall forward written notice of such default to Tenant and the failure of Tenant to cure such default within _____ ( ) days after the date of receipt of such notice shall at the option of Landlord be deemed a forfeiture of this Ground Lease.

If Tenant shall default in the performance of any other of the terms or provisions of this Ground Lease, and if Tenant shall fail to cure default within _____ ( ) days after notice of such default, or if the default is of such a character as to require more than _____ ( ) days to cure and if Tenant shall fail to use reasonable diligence during such default, Landlord may cure such default for the account of and at the cost and expense of Tenant and the sums so expended by Landlord shall be deemed to be additional rent and on demand shall be paid by Tenant on the day when rent shall next become due and payable. In no event, however, shall any default under the terms of this paragraph be the basis of a forfeiture of this Ground Lease or otherwise result in the eviction of the Tenant or the termination of this Ground Lease.

12. **INDEMNITY FOR LANDLORD AND THE LEASING COMPANY:** Tenant agrees to indemnify and hold harmless the Landlord and The Leasing Company from:

A. Any penalty or damages or charges imposed for any violation of Federal, State, or Municipal laws or ordinances caused by the acts of the Tenant; or

B. Any cost, loss, damage, or expense arising out of any accident or other occurrence causing injury or damage to any person or property whomsoever or whatsoever due to the negligence of the Tenant.

During the term of this Ground Lease the demised premises and Tenant's improvements thereto shall be kept by the Tenant in a clean, safe condition and the Tenant will keep the Landlord and The Leasing Company harmless and indemnified at all times against any loss, damage, penalty, cost, expense, judgments, and decrees by reason of violation of any law, ordinance, or regulation above referred to by Tenant, or by reason of any use which may be made of the Demised Premises, or improvements thereon during The Term of this Ground Lease; provided, however, Tenant shall only be obligated with respect to HAZARDOUS SUBSTANCES as stated hereinafter.

13. **BROKERAGE:** Landlord covenants and warrants to pay any sums due to any real estate agent or broker with which Landlord has dealt in connection with this Ground Lease, and Landlord agrees that it will indemnify and save harmless Tenant from any liability, claims of, or demands by any real estate agents or brokers who claim or contend that this Ground Lease was negotiated for or by such agents or brokers for Landlord or with the knowledge, permission, or consent of Landlord.

14. **LIENS:** Tenant will promptly remove and discharge, at its cost and expense, all liens, encumbrances, and charges upon the Entire Premises, Demised Premises, or Tenant's interest therein which arise out of the Tenant's use or occupancy of the Demised Premises or by reason of the furnishing of labor or materials with respect to the Demised Premises by or for Tenant.

15. **HAZARDOUS SUBSTANCES:** (A) As used in this Section "HAZARDOUS SUBSTANCES" shall be defined as any hazardous, toxic, or dangerous waste, substance (including, but not limited to, petroleum derivative substances), or material defined as such in (or in purposes of) any state, federal, or local environmental laws, regulations, decrees, or ordinances or in the Comprehensive Environmental Response, Compensation and Liability Act, as amended, or in any of the so-called state or local "Superfund," "Super Lien " or "Cleanup Lien" laws or any of their federal, state, or local regulation, order, or decree relating to or imposing liability or standards of conduct concerning any such substances or materials or any amendments or successor statutes thereto.

(B) Tenant represents and warrants that, during The Term of this Ground Lease no HAZARDOUS SUBSTANCES will be stored on the Demised Premises and further that no HAZARDOUS SUBSTANCES will be discharged on the Demised Premises by Tenant or anyone under its direction or control. Tenant agrees that such representations and warranties shall survive any termination of this Ground Lease, and Tenant agrees to indemnify and hold harmless the Landlord from any and all costs, expense, claims, and damages arising from Tenant's breach of any of the foregoing representations and warranties.

(C) Landlord shall indemnify and hold Tenant harmless from and against all costs, expenses, and damages arising out of any claim for loss or damage to property, injuries to, or death of persons, any contamination of or adverse effects on the environment or any violation of any environmental or other law, caused by or resulting from any hazardous waste or HAZARDOUS SUBSTANCE or any leakage or contamination from underground tanks on or under the Demised Premises that do not result from Tenant's operations. This indemnification proceeds, is concurrent with, and survives this Ground Lease.

(D) Furthermore, Landlord represents and warrants to Tenant that Landlord has no actual knowledge

(1) of the presence of any HAZARDOUS SUBSTANCES on, under, or within the Demised Premises or Entire Premises;

(2) of any spills, releases, discharges, or disposals of HAZARDOUS SUBSTANCES that have occurred or are presently occurring on or onto the Demised Premises or Entire Premises;

(3) of any spills or disposal of HAZARDOUS SUBSTANCES that have occurred or are occurring adjacent to the Demised Premises or Entire Premises as a result of any construction on or operation and use of the Demised Premises, or any property located adjacent thereto;

(4) of any failure to comply with any or all applicable local, state, and federal environmental laws, regulations, reuse, sale, storage, handling, transport, and disposal of any HAZARDOUS SUBSTANCES on the Demised Premises, Entire Premises, or any property located adjacent thereto; or

(5) the presence of any underground storage tanks now or in the past on the Demised Premises or Entire Premises.

Tenant may, at Tenant's expense, obtain a Phase I Environmental Audit of the Demised Premises.

If the results of the Phase I Environmental Audit or any other tests for Hazardous Materials are unacceptable to Tenant, then Tenant may terminate this agreement by furnishing written notice of termination to Landlord.

16. **NOTICES:** All notices and demands required or permitted to be given or served pursuant to this Ground Lease shall be deemed to have been given or served only if in writing forwarded by Certified U.S. Mail or Federal Express with all postage and other applicable shipping charges prepaid and addressed as follows:

LANDLORD: TENANT:

_____   _____

_____   _____

_____   _____

Landlord and Tenant and any other person to whom any such notice, instrument, or communication may be given, shall each have the right to specify, from time to time, as its address for purposes of this lease, and address in the United States upon giving 15 days' notice thereof to each other person then entitled to receive notices, instruments, or communications hereunder.

17. **ESTOPPEL CERTIFICATES:** Landlord and Tenant shall, from time to time upon 10 days' request by the other, execute, acknowledge, and deliver a statement, dated currently, certifying that this Ground Lease is unmodified and in full effect (or, if there have been modifications, that this Ground Lease is in full effect as modified, and identifying such modifications) and the dates to which the rents and other amounts payable hereunder have been paid, and that no default exists in the observance of this Ground Lease and no event of default has occurred and is continuing, or specifying each such default or event of default of which the signer may have knowledge, it being intended that any such statement may be relied upon by the Landlord's or Tenant's Mortgagees or by any prospective purchaser of the interest of Landlord or Tenant in their respective premises described herein or any assignee or sublessee of Tenant or any Mortgagee or its assigns.

18. **GENERAL PROVISIONS:** If any provision or section of this Ground Lease shall be construed as though such provision or section had not been included in it, and if any provision or section of this Ground Lease shall be subject to two (2) constructions one of which would render such provision or section invalid, then such provision or section shall be given that construction which would render it valid.

All provisions of this Ground Lease shall be construed as covenants and agreements where used in each separate provision hereof and shall bind and endure to the benefit of the parties hereto their respective heirs, legal representatives, successors, and assigns.

No amendment or modification of this Ground Lease shall be effective unless in writing executed by Landlord and Tenant and consented to by the Mortgagees.

19. **LAW GOVERNING:** This Ground Lease shall be governed by and construed and enforced in accordance with the laws of the State in which the Demised Premises are located.

20. **USE:** For the purpose of this Ground Lease, Tenant's intended use of the Demised Premises is defined as: storage and vehicle parking area.

21. **PROTECTIVE COVENANT:** In order to induce Tenant to enter into this Ground Lease, Landlord agrees for itself, its successors and assigns, and any party affiliated with it, that none of the foregoing shall use, suffer, permit, or consent to the use or occupancy of any part of the Entire Premises

except for the Demised Premise as a storage and vehicle parking area as long as this Ground Lease is in effect.

22. **REZONING, CONDEMNATION, AND OTHER GOVERNMENTAL ACTION:** Landlord and Tenant agree that if any City, County, State, Federal, or Municipal Body or any other authority having such powers shall initiate a rezoning and/or condemnation of the Demised Premises or Drive Easement described herein or any part thereof, Tenant may terminate this Ground Lease by written notice to Landlord. Landlord warrants that Landlord is not aware nor has Landlord received any notification of any such proposed rezoning or condemnation, and that Landlord will promptly furnish Tenant copies of all such notices received by Landlord. If Tenant shall discover any other proposed governmental action (such as but not limited to any proposed changes to the street right-of-ways located adjacent to the Demised Premises or to the road network in the vicinity of the Demised Premises) which would, in Tenant's opinion, impair Tenant's use of the Demised Premises for the purposes described in this Ground Lease, then Tenant may terminate this Ground Lease by written notice to Landlord.

23. **RESPONSIBILITY OF LANDLORD:** If Landlord fails to apply any installment of taxes or assessments or any interest, principal, costs, or other charges upon any Landlord Mortgage or other liens and encumbrances affecting Demised Premises or the Drive Easement when any of the same become due, or if Landlord fails to make any repairs or do or complete any work required of it under any of the provisions of this Ground Lease, or if Landlord fails to perform any covenant or agreement in this Ground Lease contained on the part of Landlord to be performed, Tenant, after the continuance of any such failure or default for _____ (   ) days after written notice thereof is given by Tenant to Landlord, may elect to pay said taxes, assessments, interest, principal, costs, and other charges or cure such defaults on behalf of and at the expense of Landlord and do all necessary work and make all necessary payments in connection therewith. This shall include, without limitation, the payment of any attorney's fees, and costs and charges of or in connection with any legal action which may be brought by Tenant, and Tenant may further take such other proceedings at law or in equity as Tenant deems necessary, notwithstanding any other remedy herein provided. In the event of such election by Tenant, Landlord agrees to pay Tenant any amount so paid by Tenant, and agrees that Tenant may withhold any and all rental payments and other sums due and becoming due after the expiration of the aforesaid notice period to the Landlord pursuant to the provisions of this Ground Lease and may apply the same to the payment of such indebtedness of the Landlord until such indebtedness is fully paid. In addition to the foregoing, Tenant may proceed in equity to enjoin any

breach by Landlord or by any other party of any provision of this Ground Lease. Nothing herein contained shall preclude the Tenant from proceeding to collect the amount so paid by it, as aforesaid, without waiting for rental offsets to accrue. If at the expiration The Term of this Ground Lease there shall be any sums owing by Landlord to Tenant, then this Ground Lease may at the election of Tenant be extended and continued in full force and effect until the last day of the month following the date when the indebtedness of Landlord shall have been fully paid. If any alleged nonmonetary default by Landlord is of such a nature that it cannot be completely remedied or cured within the   (   ) day period above provided, then notwithstanding the provisions of this Section to the contrary, Tenant shall not have a right to enforce any of the remedies herein set forth if Landlord shall commence curing such default within such   (   ) day period and shall proceed with diligence in good faith to complete the curing thereof.

24. **ACCEPTANCE:** In the event this agreement is not accepted by Landlord on or before _____, 2____, Tenant's within offer to Ground Lease shall be void.

IN WITNESS WHEREOF the parties hereto have executed this Ground Lease the day and year first above written.

LANDLORD: TENANT:

BY: _____   By: _____

By: _____

STATE OF _____

PARISH OR COUNTY OF _____

     BE IT KNOWN, that on this _____ day of _____,
2____, before me, the undersigned authority, duly commissioned, qualified, and sworn within and for the State and Parish or County aforesaid, personally came and appeared _____ in its ca-
pacity as **Tenant** to me personally known to be the identical person whose
name is subscribed to the foregoing instrument as Tenant and declared to
me, Notary, in the presence of the undersigned competent witnesses, that it
executed the same on its behalf and that the said instrument is the free act
and deed its, and was executed for the uses, purposes, and benefits therein
expressed.

WITNESSES: _____   _____

                                     (Tenant)

                                     _____

                                     NOTARY PUBLIC

STATE OF _____

PARISH OR COUNTY OF _____

     BE IT KNOWN, that on this _____ day of _____, 2____,
before me, the undersigned authority, duly commissioned, qualified, and
sworn within and for the State and Parish or County aforesaid, personally
came and appeared _____, appearing in their capacity as
Landlord, to me personally known to be the identical persons whose names
are subscribed to the foregoing instrument as Landlord, and declared and
acknowledged to me, Notary, in the presence of the undersigned competent
witnesses, that they executed the same on behalf of themselves, and that the
said instrument is the free act and deed of the theirs, and was executed for
the uses, purposes and benefits therein expressed.

WITNESSES: _____   _____

                                     (Landlord)

_____   _____

                                     (Landlord)

                                     _____

                                     NOTARY PUBLIC

INVESTMENT QUESTIONNAIRE

Date _____

1. Name _____

2. Address _____

3. Age: _____25 - 35   _____45 - 55
                 _____35 - 45   _____55 - 65

4. Current Investments: Type   Approximate Value
   (Stocks, Mutual Funds,   _____   _____
   Bonds, Real Estate, etc)   _____   _____
                               _____   _____
                               _____   _____

5. Retirement Portfolio: Type   Approximate Value
   (IRA, 401k, etc.)   _____   _____
                               _____   _____
                               _____   _____
                               _____   _____

6. Do you own your home?
   _____Yes   _____No
   If yes: How long? _____
   Approximate Value _____
   Approximate Equity _____

7. Have you previously owned rental property?
   _____Yes   _____No
   If yes: Type_____
   Number
   Approximate Value _____

8. If you owned investment property would you
   _____Do the maintenance?
   _____Do the management?
   _____Hire the maintenance and management?

9. What amount of cash would you like to invest? _____

10. What would you like to accumulate by retirement in investment property?
Portfolio Value $ _____
Monthly Income $ _____

11. Are you acquainted with a 1031 Tax Free Exchange?
_____Yes _____No

12. What is your total level of indebtedness?
_____ Under $50,000 _____ $100,000 - $200,000
_____ $50,000 - $100,000 _____ $200,000 - $300,000
_____ Over $300,000

13. Do you have a preferred type of investment property?
_____ Single Family (Rent Houses) _____ Timberland
_____ Duplex _____ Recreational Land
_____ 4-Plex _____ Farmland
_____ Apartment Complex _____ Business (If so, what type?)
_____ Hotel/Motel _____
_____ Retail Center _____
_____ Commercial Building _____

14. Is location of property important?
_____ Local
_____ Area (30 mile radius)
_____ Regional (100 mile radius)

15. What is your . . .
Work _____
Title _____
Business (if owned) _____

16. What is your approximate current income (husband and wife)
_____ $25,000 - $50,000 _____ $100,000 - $150,000
_____ $50,000 - $75,000 _____ Over $150,000
_____ $75,000 - $100,000

17. Who is your CPA (if you have one)? _____

18. Who is your attorney (if you have one?) _____

LEASING FEE AGREEMENT

This agreement made and entered into this _____ day of
_____, 2006, by and between:
hereinafter referred to as "LESSOR" and
hereinafter referred to as "AGENT."

LESSOR agrees to pay AGENT a leasing fee for Leasing Services
should AGENT secure a lease for property owned by LESSOR or owned by
any entity of which he is a part, located as follows:

PROPERTY ADDRESS: _____

LEGAL DESCRIPTION: See Exhibit "A"

LEASING FEE: _____

LESSOR hereby employs said AGENT as his sole and exclusive
AGENT to lease the above-described **real property** and hereby grants said
AGENT the exclusive right to lease the same and to accept a deposit
thereon.

Said lease secured by AGENT shall be with terms and conditions acceptable to LESSOR and LESSEE. AGENT may place a "For Lease" sign on
the property.

This Agreement shall be for a term of _____ (   ) **months.** I/We
also agree to refer all prospects to the Listing BROKER.

I/We further agree to pay commission as above stipulated in event of
sale, or lease or option that leads to a sale, of said property by me/us during
the term of the Agreement or within One hundred twenty (120) days after
the expiration of this agreement, provided purchaser has become interested
in said property as a result of the efforts or advertising of said AGENT during the active term of this listing. This agreement shall be enforced in accordance with the laws of the State of Louisiana and shall be binding upon the
respective heirs, successors, and assigns. Should LESSOR fail to pay the
agreed upon Leasing Fee and it is necessary for Tri-State Properties, Inc., to
turn this matter over to an attorney at law for collection, then LESSOR
agrees to pay the Leasing Fee owed, as well as reasonable attorney fees and
all court costs.

Lessor(s) shall agree that lessor shall be bound by, and the terms and conditions would be controlled by, the provisions of the State Licensing Law and Rules and Regulations of the State Real Estate Commission. It is understood that Broker is a member of the _____ Multiple Listing Services ("MLS"). Seller/lessor agrees that this agreement will be filed in MLS and processed in accordance with the rules and regulations of MLS.

I acknowledge that I have read and understand the reverse side of this form regarding Disclosure and Consent to Dual Agency. By my signature below I authorize that the undersigned Agent may act as a disclosed Dual Agent in securing a Buyer or Lessee for the above-listed property.

Other Conditions: _____

RECEIPT OF COPY OF THIS LEASING FEE AGREEMENT IS HEREBY ACKNOWLEDGED:

The parties hereto may rely on a facsimile transmission as to their acceptance of this agreement.

_____   _____
LESSOR: DATE

_____   _____
AGENT: DATE

- -

EXHIBIT "A"

Legal Description

LETTER OF AUTHORIZATION

_____, "Owner," hereby authorizes
_____, "Agent," the Right to Sell his prop-
erty located at _____
at the sale price of _____
($_____).

This "Authorization to Sell" the above property shall continue for a period
of _____ months, or until canceled by either party with a written
notice.

Upon sale of the above property, I agree to pay _____ a
brokerage fee of _____ % (_____ Percent) of the sale
price at closing.

Seller warrants that he is the owner of and has the right to sell the property
described.

Seller acknowledges that this property will not be placed in Multiple Listing Service, will have no sign placed on premises, and will not be advertised.

Seller hereby authorizes that the above Agent may act as a disclosed dual
agent in securing a buyer for property described above. (See Dual Agency
Agreement.)

_____   _____
Owner   Date

_____   _____
Agent   Date

PROPERTY CONDITION DISCLOSURE FORM

PROPERTY: Located at _____
(Municipal Address)   (Subdivision)   (Lot Number)

_____, Louisiana
(City)   (Parish)

PURCHASER may have certain rights under the provisions of Louisiana law regarding undisclosed or hidden defects in the subject property.

For his own protection, SELLER is asked to disclose all conditions that exist in or on the property (land and improvements). SELLER represents and warrants to PURCHASER that SELLER knows of no defects in the subject property, other than those deficiencies disclosed in this Agreement or in the attachments hereto.

As provided in LSA-R.S. 37.1455(27), an agent/broker is obligated "to disclose to a buyer a known, material defect regarding the condition of real estate of which a broker, salesperson, or timeshare interest salesperson has knowledge."

SELLER(S) DISCLOSE(S) THE FOLLOWING INFORMATION WITH THE KNOWLEDGE THAT PROSPECTIVE PURCHASER(S) RELIES ON SUCH INFORMATION WHEN DECIDING WHETHER, AND UPON WHAT TERMS, TO PURCHASE PROPERTY.

SELLER(S) hereby authorize(s) agent/broker to provide a copy of the Disclosure to any person(s) or entity(ies) in connection with any actual or anticipated sale of the property.

SELLER(S) is/are to answer each of the following to the best of his/their knowledge, explaining any affirmative responses below:

PROPERTY CONDITION

1. **What is the approximate age of the principal structure?** _____
   Were there any structures built on this property prior to 1978? (If yes, you are required to Complete the lead-based paint disclosure form.)

   [ ] YES   [ ] NO   [ ] UNKNOWN

2. **During your ownership, has the house, detached buildings, or other structures had termites or other wood-destroying insects?**

    [ ] YES   [ ] NO   [ ] UNKNOWN

    a. If yes, please state the date(s) of any such infestation.

    _____

    b. Are the structures presently under a termite contract?

    [ ] YES   [ ] NO   [ ] UNKNOWN

    c. If yes, state the name of the termite company and the expiration date of the contract. _____

3. **Has the property ever sustained any fire damage?**

    [ ] YES   [ ] NO   [ ] UNKNOWN

    If yes, please state the date(s) of such fire, if known. _____

    _____

4. **Has the home ever sustained any flood damage?**

    [ ] YES   [ ] NO   [ ] UNKNOWN

    If yes, please state the date(s) of such flood, if known. _____

    _____

5. **Does the property have any drainage problems?**

    [ ] YES   [ ] NO   [ ] UNKNOWN

    a. Has the lot or any portion of the land ever flooded?

    [ ] YES   [ ] NO   [ ] UNKNOWN

    b. If yes, please state the date(s) of such flooding, if known.

    _____

    c. Have any of the other structures located on the property ever flooded?

    [ ] YES   [ ] NO   [ ] UNKNOWN

    d. If yes, please state the date(s) of such flooding, if known.

    _____

6. **Has the property ever been classified as wetlands under Section 404 of the Clean Water Act?** (U.S. Corps of Engineers Active enforcement of Section 404 of the Clean Water Act may require certain permits for altering or building upon property that is determined to be wetlands as defined by the Corps. Purchaser or Seller may be charged by the Corps for making this determination. The determination could result in additional fees, charges, and/or mitigation expenses as determined by the Corps for a Section 404 permit prior to any development.)

[ ] YES   [ ] NO   [ ] UNKNOWN

7. **Has Seller made any additions or alterations to the property during the term of ownership?**

[ ] YES   [ ] NO   [ ] UNKNOWN

If yes, please state the additions or alterations and date(s) of such additions or alterations.

_____

_____

_____

8. **Are there any servitudes, easements, rights-of-way, or encroachments, other than typical and customary utility servitudes, that would affect the use of this property?**

[ ] YES   [ ] NO   [ ] UNKNOWN

If yes, please identify: _____

_____

9. **Does the present use of the property conflict with current zoning, building, or safety restrictions, ordinances, codes, deeds, covenants, or subdivision restrictions?**

[ ] YES   [ ] NO   [ ] UNKNOWN

If yes, please identify: _____

10. **Do you know of any title defects with the property?**

      [ ] YES   [ ] NO   [ ] UNKNOWN

      If yes, please identify: _____

11. **Are there any current leases or options on the property?**

      [ ] YES   [ ] NO   [ ] UNKNOWN

      If yes, please identify: _____

12. **Are you aware of any existing or contemplated litigation involving this property?**

      [ ] YES   [ ] NO   [ ] UNKNOWN

      If yes, please identify: _____

13. **Are there any current or pending assessments, dues, liens, or taxes owed on the property?**

      [ ] YES   [ ] NO   [ ] UNKNOWN

      If yes, please identify and state the amount of each: _____

14. **Are there any problems with or defects in the following:** (Please explain any affirmative response regarding any defect in the space provided below.)

    a.   Roof?

      [ ] YES   [ ] NO   [ ] UNKNOWN

    The approximate age of roof is _____

    Roofing material is _____

    b.   Foundation?

      [ ] YES   [ ] NO   [ ] UNKNOWN

    c.   Wall and roof structure?

      [ ] YES   [ ] NO   [ ] UNKNOWN

d.   Flooring and sub-flooring?

[ ] YES   [ ] NO   [ ] UNKNOWN

e.   Electrical system?

[ ] YES   [ ] NO   [ ] UNKNOWN

f.   Heating and air-conditioning system?

[ ] YES   [ ] NO   [ ] UNKNOWN

g.   Plumbing systems (including but not limited to septic systems or private treatment plants)?

[ ] YES   [ ] NO   [ ] UNKNOWN

h.   All other systems and appliances (for example, pool or spa equipment, water softeners, well pumps, security systems, intercom systems)?

[ ] YES   [ ] NO   [ ] UNKNOWN

i.   Any other conditions, problems, defects, including environmental conditions in or around the property, of which Purchaser should be aware (for example, asbestos, radon, etc.)?

[ ] YES   [ ] NO   [ ] UNKNOWN

j.   Fireplace

[ ] YES   [ ] NO   [ ] UNKNOWN

Type of fireplace: _____

Explanation to responses to Question 14 regarding any defect:

_____

_____

_____

_____

Purchaser's Initials	Purchaser's Initials	Seller's Initials	Seller's Initials

Date: _____   Date: _____

Property Condition Disclosure Form
Approved by the Louisiana Real Estate Commission
2/00

General Information

15. **Name of the architect or builder:** _____
_____

16. **Current zoning of the property?** _____
_____

17. **Is the home covered under a home warranty plan currently?**

   [ ] YES   [ ] NO   [ ] UNKNOWN
   a.   If yes, is it transferable?

   [ ] YES   [ ] NO   [ ] UNKNOWN
   b.   Expiration Date: _____
   c.   Deductible per trade call:_____

18. **Amount of annual property taxes for the preceding year?** _____
   a.   Amount of any special assessments:_____
   b.   Is the property homestead exempt?_____

   [ ] YES   [ ] NO   [ ] UNKNOWN

19. **Number of garage door openers? (If applicable)** _____

20. **If applicable, what is covered under association dues?** _____
_____

   1.   Amount of annual association dues? _____
   2.   Amount of any current special assessments?_____

21. **Is an interest in common elements, such as roads, parks, or common areas, included with the property?**

    [ ] YES   [ ] NO   [ ] UNKNOWN

22. **Who owns walls and fences on the property?** _____

23. **What is the flood zone classification of the property?** _____

    a. Does the Seller have flood insurance coverage on the property currently?

        [ ] YES   [ ] NO   [ ] UNKNOWN

    b. Does Seller have a copy of a recent flood elevation survey/certificate?

        [ ] YES   [ ] NO   [ ] UNKNOWN

24. **What are the average monthly utility bills? (Twelve-month period)**

    a. Water/Sewerage? _____

    b. Gas? _____

    c. Electricity? _____

25. **Does Seller have any house plans to transfer to Purchaser?**

    [ ] YES   [ ] NO   [ ] UNKNOWN

26. **Are keys available for all doors/locks?**

    [ ] YES   [ ] NO   [ ] UNKNOWN

    If response is in the negative, identify particular door/lock without keys. _____

    _____

    [ ] SELLER has not occupied the subject property, and no statement of condition is being made.

    [ ] SELLER is the builder of the subject property, and his contractor's license number is _____

I/We state that the above statements and explanations are true and correct to the best of my/our knowledge. This document is made part of the listing agreement executed on the property listed above.

Seller's Signature Date/Time	Seller's Signature Date/Time

By signing below, this document is made part of the agreement to purchase the property listed above and reflects that the Purchaser's has/have read this property disclosure addendum. The signature of the Seller(s) attest(s) that the information contained herein is current as of this date.

Purchaser's Signature Date/Time	Purchaser's Signature Date/Time

Purchaser's Initials	Purchaser's Initials	Seller's Initials	Seller's Initials

Date: _____   Date: _____

Property Condition Disclosure Form
Approved by the Louisiana Real Estate Commission
2/00

REAL ESTATE PURCHASE AGREEMENT EXTENSION

_____, hereafter referred to as "Seller," and _____, hereafter referred to as "Buyer," who have entered into a Real Estate Purchase Agreement on _____ _____ for the purchase and sale of property located at _____ _____ (city and state), hereafter referred to as "The Agreement" have mutually agreed to the following:

1) The Agreement which called for the closing to occur on or before _____ is hereby extended to state "the closing shall occur on or before _____."

2) No additional deposit shall be required.

3) All other terms and conditions of "The Agreement" shall remain in full force and effect on both parties with specific performance.

Buyer(s):

_____

_____ Date

_____

_____ Date

_____

_____ Date

Seller(s):

_____

_____ Date

_____

_____ Date

Property Address _____ MLS# _____

RESIDENTIAL AGREEMENT TO PURCHASE AND SELL

Final Agreed upon Purchase/Sales Price $_____ Date: _____

Date: _____ Time: _____   Received by: _____

Listing Firm and Designated Agent: _____

Office No. _____ Home No. _____ Fax No. _____

Selling Firm and Designated Agent: _____

Office No. _____ Home No. _____ Fax No. _____

PROPERTY DESCRIPTION: I/We offer and agree to purchase/sell the property located at _____
(Muncipal Address)

_____

(Lot No.)   (Subdivision)

_____

(City)   (Parish)   (Zip Code)

Louisiana, with all land and grounds measuring about _____

_____

_____

_____

or as per title, including all buildings, component parts, and permanently installed improvements thereon, together with fences, outside TV antennas, satellite dishes, all permanently installed and built-in appliances and fixtures, including ceiling fans, window A/C units, bathroom mirrors, and window coverings, provided that any and all of these items are in place at the time this agreement is executed, unless otherwise stated herein. The following items are excluded: _____

_____

_____

_____

The following movable items remain with the property, but are not to be considered in the sales price, and no value shall be associated with the movable items that remain with the property: _____

_____

_____

_____

PRICE: Property is to be sold and purchased, subject to title and zoning restrictions, servitudes of records, laws and/or ordinances affecting the property, for the sum of _____

Dollars ($_____).

DEPOSIT: Upon acceptance of this offer, SELLER and PURCHASER shall be bound by all terms and conditions of this agreement, and the PURCHASER shall be obligated to deposit the sum of _____

Dollars ($_____) by [ ] Cash [ ] Check [ ] Other _____ immediately in the Listing Broker's noninterest-bearing sales escrow account with a federally insured bank or savings and loan association, without responsibility on the part of the broker/agent in case of failure or suspension of such institution. Failure to do so shall be considered a breach of this agreement. At the act of sale, this deposit shall be applied to the sales price. This deposit shall not be considered as earnest money.

Notwithstanding any other provision in this agreement, in the event that the sale is not consummated for any reason, including nullity, the deposit shall be returned to the parties in accordance with Louisiana Real Estate License Law and Chapter 28 of the Rules and Regulations of the Louisiana Real Estate Commission regarding deposits.

FINANCING: This sale is subject to the following financial terms:
[ ] All Cash [ ] Conventional Mortgage [ ] VA Guaranteed Mortgage
[ ] FHA Insured Mortgage [ ] Other _____.

IF ALL CASH: PURCHASER will furnish SELLER with written verification of purchase funds within _____ calendar days of acceptance of this offer or this agreement is null and void at the option of the SELLER.

IF FINANCED: This sale is conditioned upon the ability of PURCHASER to borrow the sum of _____

Dollars ($_____) or _____ percent of the sales price by a mortgage loan(s) at an initial [ ] Fixed [ ] Adjustable rate on interest not to exceed _____ percent per annum.

LOAN APPLICATION: PURCHASER agrees to make a good faith appplication, which inlcudes ordering and paying for an appraisal and a credit report if required for loan approval, within _____ days of acceptance of this offer or any counteroffer. Should PURCHASER be unable to obtain loan approval by _____ (date), this agreement shall be null and void. Written commitment by the lender to make loan(s), **without contingencies**, subject to approval of title, shall constitute loan approval.

APPRAISAL: This Agreement [ ] is [ ] is not conditioned upon an appraisal being equal to or greater than the sales price.

OTHER COSTS: SELLER is to pay for the cost of a wood-destroying insect certificate, fees for mortgage cancellation, and any recording fees associated with the cancellation, and SELLER's prorated portion of real estate taxes, unless otherwise stated herein. PURCHASER is to pay all other closing costs, unless otherwise stated herein. SELLER may incur additional fees associated as required by the lender in an amount not to exceed _____ Dollars ($_____).

[ ] PURCHASER   [ ] SELLER agrees to pay discount points not to exceed _____ percent of the loan amount.

[ ] PURCHASER   [ ] SELLER will pay origination fees not to exceed _____ percent of the loan amount.

PURCHASER acknowledges that additional funds may be required to complete the sale of this property, including, but not limited to, other closing costs, prepaid items, and other similar expenses. PURCHASER represents that PURCHASER has the funds necessary to satisfy PURCHASER's obligations, including the down payment, under this Agreement.

CONTINGENCY FOR SALE OF PURCHASER'S PROPERTY: PURCHASER's performance under this Agreement [ ] is [ ] is not contingent upon the sale of PURCHASER's property located at _____ _____ to be closed on or before _____.

EXECUTION OF ACT OF SALE: The act of sale shall be passed before PURCHASER's notary on or before _____ with mutual consent of the parties. Any extension shall be agreed upon in writing and signed by the parties.

SELLER'S TITLE: SELLER's title shall be merchantable and free of all liens, encumbrances, and defects, except those that can be satisfied at the act of sale or insured by title insurance. If bona fide curative work in connection with the title is required, the parties agree to and extend the time for passing the sale by thirty (30) days. SELLER shall pay any cost required to make the title merchantable, including all necessary tax and mortgage releases, certificates, and cancellations, if any. In the event the title is not valid or merchantable and cannot be made so at a reasonable expense, this Agreement may be declared null and void at the option of the PURCHASER. PURCHASER reserves the right to recover from the SELLER PURCHASER's actual costs incurred in performing PURCHASER's obligation under this agreement.

LIENS: All improvement liens and assessments, as well as any other liens of any kind burdening the property at the time of the act of sale, shall be paid by the SELLER.

OCCUPANCY BY PURCHASER: Occupancy will be granted to PURCHASER [ ] upon execution of the act of sale or [_____] days after the execution of the act of sale at _____ o'clock ____.m.

LEASES: The property [   ] is [   ] is not leased currently.

If leased, then this offer is conditioned on PURCHASER's receipt, review, and approval of written leases within _____ (____) days from the date of acceptance of this agreement. Security and pet deposits, keys, and lease agreements shall be transferred to PURCHASER at closing.

PRORATIONS: Real estate taxes, homeowner's association dues, rent income, and any similar items are to be prorated to the date of the act of sale.

MINERAL RESERVATIONS: Mineral rights, if any, are:

[ ] reserved by SELLER [ ] conveyed to PURCHASER. If SELLER reserves the mineral rights, SELLER specifically waives the right to use the surface for any mineral activity. If SELLER conveys the mineral rights, such mineral rights are conveyed without warranty.

BREACH OF AGREEMENT BY EITHER PARTY: In the event of default by either party, the nondefaulting party shall have all right to demand specific performance or damages, at his option. The defaulting party shall also be liable for the brokerage fees and all costs and fees, including reasonable attorney's fees, incurred as a result of the breach of this agreement.

BROKERAGE FEES: The closing notary is authorized to pay brokerage fees at the execution of the act of sale pursuant to the terms of the written brokerage agreement(s).

PROPERTY CONDITION DISCLOSURE: The "Property Condition Disclosure Addendum," signed by all parties is attached hereto and made a part hereof.

SELLER shall maintain the property in substantially the same or better condition as it was when this agreement was executed. SELLER agrees to remove all refuse and personal property from the premises before the date of occupancy. SELLER is not obligated to make repairs to the property except those specifically set forth in the section of this agreement entitled "Other Conditions of Sale," and PURCHASER has no right to demand any other repairs, including other repairs required by the lender.

INSPECTIONS: Commencing with the first day after acceptance of this agreement, PURCHASER may, at his expense, have any inspections made by experts or others of his choosing. Such inspections may include, but are not limited to: inspections for lead-based paint and lead-based hazards, termites and other wood-destroying insects (and damage from same), appliances, structures, foundations, roofs, heating, cooling, electrical, or plumbing systems, and/or square footage. SELLER agrees to provide the utilities for such inspections. PURCHASER's failure to make inspections or respond, in writing, to SELLER (through SELLER's agent/broker) within _____ calendar days of acceptance of this agreement shall be deemed as acceptance by PURCHASER of the present condition of the property.

Upon completion of the inspections, if PURCHASER is not satisfied with the present condition of the property as reflected in the inspection reports, PURCHASER may indicate, in writing, the deficiencies to be remedied by SELLER. PURCHASER shall also provide SELLER (through SELLER's agent/broker) with a copy of the inspection report showing the deficiency.

SELLER shall have seventy-two (72) hours from the receipt of PURCHASER's "Property Condition Clause Response" to respond, in writing, to PURCHASER's list of deficiencies.

Should SELLER refuse to remedy any or all of the deficiencies listed by PURCHASER, then PURCHASER shall have forty-eight (48) hours from receipt for SELLER's written response to do one of the following: (1) accept SELLER's response as written; (2) accept the property in its present condition; or (3) terminate the agreement. PURCHASER's response shall be in writing.

If PURCHASER fails to respond within the deadline set forth above, this agreement shall be terminated.

If the Agreement is terminated as set forth in this section, all parties shall sign a cancellation within twenty-four (24) hours, and the failure of either party to sign the cancellation shall not prohibit either party from making or accepting offers from other persons.

PURCHASER shall have the right to reinspect the property within five (5) business days prior to the act of sale or occupancy, whichever occurs first, in order to determine if the property is in the same or better condition as was present at the initial inspection. If the property is not in the same or better condition, then the SELLER shall be obligated to perform, at SELLER's sole expense, all work necessary to place the property in the ocndition that it was in at the time of the initial inspection.

WOOD-DESTROYING INSECT INSPECTION: At the act of sale, SELLER shall provide a wood-destroying insect report prepared by a pest control company licensed by the State of Louisiana. The report, indicating no visible evidence of active infestation, shall be dated no more than (30) days prior to the act of sale. If either the PURCHASER's inspection or the wood-destroying insect report indicates active infestation or damage from such insects, this Agreement may be terminated, at PURCHASER's option, unless PURCHASER and SELLER agree that SELLER, at his expense, repairs such damage and/or treats such infestation. The repairs of damage from and/or treatment of infestation will be evidenced by a new wood-destroying report.

DEADLINES: TIME IS OF THE ESSENCE, and all deadlines are final, except where modifications, changes, or extensions are made in writing and signed by all parties to this Agreement.

ACCEPTANCE: Acceptance must be in writing. Notice of this acceptance may be communicated by facsimile transmission. The contract date of this Agreement will be the date of final acceptance by the parties.

MEGAN'S LAW: The Louisiana Bureau of Criminal Identification and Information maintains a State Sex Offender and Child Predator Registry, which is a public access database of the locations of individuals required to register pursuant to LSA-R.S. 15:540 et seq. Sheriff's Departments and Police Departments serving jurisdictions of 450,000 also maintain such information. The State Sex Offender and Child Predator Registry database can be accessed at www.lasocpr.lsp.org/socpr/ and contains address, pictures, and conviction records for registered offenders. The database can be searched by zip code, city, parish, or by offender name. Information is also available by phone at 1-800-858-0551 or 1-225-925-6100 or mail at P.O. Box 66614, Mall Slip #18, Baton Rouge, Louisiana 70896. You can also e-mail State Services at SOCPR@dps.state.la.us for more information.

OTHER CONDITIONS OF SALE: If any of the preprinted portions of this agreement vary or are in conflict with any handwritten or other conditions of the sale, the handwritten or other conditions of the sale provisions will control. OTHER CONDITIONS OF SALE include the following:

_____

_____

_____

_____

_____

_____

_____

ADDENDA to be made part of this Agreement include the following.

[ ] Property Condition Disclosure Form   [ ] Leases

[ ] Property Condition Disclosure   [ ] Loan Prequalification
     Response   Response

[ ] Lead-Based Paint Disclosure Form   [ ] Home Inspection

[ ] Home Warranty Disclosure Form   [ ] Other

This offer remains binding and irrevocable until:_____

                                  (Date)   (Time)

_____	_____
Purchaser's Signature Date/Time	Purchaser's Signature Date/Time
_____	_____
Print Purchaser's Full Legal Name	Print Purchaser's Full Legal Name
Marital Status:	Marital Status:
[ ] Single [ ] Married [ ] Separated	[ ] Single [ ] Married [ ] Separated
[ ] Divorced [ ] Co-ownership	[ ] Divorced [ ] Co-ownership
_____	_____
Social Security Number	Social Security Number
_____	_____
Address	Address
_____	_____
Telephone Numbers (Home and Office)	Telephone Numbers (Home and Office)
_____	_____
Name of Employer	Name of Employer

RECEIVED BY: _____
                    Listing Agent/Broker   Date/Time

Property Address _____ MLS# _____

Seller's Response to Agreement to Purchase and Sell

This offer is

[ ] Accepted [ ] Rejected [ ] Countered with Addendum [ ] Countered without Addendum

SELLER'S SIGNATURE Date/Time	SELLER'S SIGNATURE Date/Time
Print Seller's Full Legal Name	Print Seller's Full Legal Name
Marital Status: [ ] Single [ ] Married [ ] Separated [ ] Divorced [ ] Co-ownership	Marital Status: [ ] Single [ ] Married [ ] Separated [ ] Divorced [ ] Co-ownership
Social Security Number	Social Security Number
Address	Address
Telephone Numbers (Home and Office)	Telephone Numbers (Home and Office)
Name of Employer	Name of Employer

Seller's Counteroffer to Agreement to Purchase and Sell

The "Residential Agreement to Purchase and Sell" is acceptable, provided PURCHASER agrees to the following changes: _____

_____

_____

_____

_____

_____

_____

_____

ALL OTHER TERMS REMAIN UNCHANGED

This counteroffer remains binding and irrevocable until _____(Date) ____(Time)

_____   _____
SELLER'S SIGNATURE   Date/Time   SELLER'S SIGNATURE   Date/Time

_____   _____
Print Seller's Full Legal Name   Print Seller's Full Legal Name

RECEIVED BY:

_____
Selling Agent/Broker   Date/Time

Purchaser's Response to Counteroffer

I/We have read, understood, and accept the above counteroffer:

_____   _____
Purchaser's Signature   Date/Time   Purchaer's Signature   Date/Time

_____   _____
Print Purchaser's Full Legal Name   Print Purchaser's Full Legal Name

_____ _____ _____ _____
Purchaser's Initials Purchaser's Initials   Seller's Initials   Seller's Initials

Date: _____   Date: _____

Residential Agreement to Purchase and Sell
Approved by the Louisiana Real Estate Commission
2/00
Used by permission of the Louisiana Real Estate Commission

WOOD DESTROYING INSECT REPORT

Approved by the Louisiana Structural Pest Control Commission (Title 7 Agriculture and Animals Part XXV, Structural Pest control Chapter 141. Section 14116 A.B. and the Louisiana Pest Control Association.

THIS REPORT IS MADE IN ACCORDANCE WITH AND SUBJECT TO THE CONDITIONS ON REVERSE SIDE OF THIS PAGE.

For and in consideration of the price and Sum of $_____

State Fee $_____

Total $_____

A qualified inspector employed by this company has carefully inspected all accessible areas of the structure(s) on the property located at the address below for termites and other wood destroying insects. This disclosure specifically excludes hidden and/or inaccessible areas of damage and the pest control company assumes no legal responsibility for repairs to such damaged areas.

WARNING: THE INSPECTION DESCRIBED HEREIN HAS BEEN MADE ON THE BASIS OF VISIBLE EVIDENCE IN READILY ACCESSIBLE AREAS AND THIS REPORT IS SUBMITTED WITHOUT WARRANTY, GUARANTEE OR REPRESENTATION AS TO CONCEALED EVIDENCE OF INFESTATION OR DAMAGE OR AS TO FUTURE INFESTATION. THIS IS NOT A TERMITE-FREE CERTIFICATE. IF THERE IS ANY EVIDENCE OF WOOD DESTROYING INSECTS IN THE STRUCTURE(S) INSPECTED, IT MUST BE ASSUMED THAT THERE IS SOME DAMAGE.

WOOD DESTROYING INSECT INFORMATION EXISTING CONSTRUCTION	1. HUD/FHA/VA CASE NUMBER	2. DATE OF INSPECTION
PRIVACY ACT INFORMATION - The information requested on this form will be used in evaluating the property for a VA or HUD insured loan and all other real estate sales. Although you are not required by law to provide this information, failure to provide it can result in rejection of the property as security for your loan. The information collected will not be disclosed outside VA or HUD except as permitted by law. VA and HUD are authorized to request this information by statute (38 U.S.C., 1804 (a) and 12 U.S.C. 1701 Et. Seq.)		
3A. NAME OF INSPECTION COMPANY	5A. NAME OF PROPERTY OWNER/SELLER	
3B. ADDRESS OF INSPECTION COMPANY (INCLUDING ZIP CODE)	5B. ADDRESS OF PROPERTY INSPECTED (INCLUDING ZIP CODE)	
3C. TELEPHONE NUMBER (INCLUDE AREA CODE) 4. PEST CONTROL OPERATOR LICENSE NUMBER	5C. STRUCTURE(S) INSPECTED ON PROPERTY	
5D. ONLY STRUCTURE(S) LISTED IN 5 (C)WERE INSPECTED AND ARE INCLUDED IN THIS REPORT. DETACHED GARAGES, SHEDS, LEAN-TOS, FENCES OR OTHER BUILDINGS ON THE PROPERTY, WILL NOT BE INLCUDED IN THIS INSPECTION REPORT UNLESS SPECIFICALLY NOTED:		
FINDINGS		
6. WERE ANY AREAS OF THE STRUCTURE(S) OBSTRUCTED OR INACCESSIBLE? YES ___ NO ___ *(IF "YES" SEE ITEMS 7 & 8)*	7. TYPE OF CONSTRUCTION ___ Slab ___ Raised Pier	

WARNING – COMMON OBSTRUCTIONS AND/OR INACCESSIBLE AREAS INCLUDE BUT ARE NOT LIMITED TO:	
8 A. JOISTS HIDDEN	(a) suspended ceiling (b) fixed ceiling (c) insulation (d) floor over joists
B. WALL COVERINGS	(a) paneling (b) dry wall (c) plaster (d) tile (e) cabinets (f) shelving (g) wallpaper (h) bath trap
C. FLOOR COVERINGS	(a) tile (b) carpet (c) rugs (d) linoleum (e) built-ins
D. PERSONAL POSSESSIONS	(a) stored material (b) boxes (c) pictures (d) clothing (e) furniture (f) appliances
E. ROOF RAFTERS HIDDEN	(a) suspended ceiling (b) fixed ceiling (c) insulation
F. RAISED FLOORING	(a) flooring elevated with sleepers beneath
G. EXTERIOR	(a) dense shrubbery (b) siding (c) window well covers (d) planters
H. PORCH	(a) no access or entry beneath floor surface (b) debris
I. ADD'L ITEMS	(a) standing water (b) debris (c) firewood (d) no access or entry (e) absence of safe or stable access (f) attic (g) leaking roof (h) faulty plumbing (i) earth-wood contact (j) wooden decks (k) hidden expansion joints

9. BASED ON CAREFUL VISUAL INSPECTION OF THE READILY ACCESSIBLE AREAS OF THE STRUCTURE(S) INSPECTED

_____ A.   No visible evidence of wood destroying insects was observed.

_____ B.   Visible evidence of wood destroying insects was observed.
       Evidence found and its location _____

_____ C.   Visible evidence of damage due to _____ has been observed in the following
       areas _____

_____ D.   Treatment was or will be performed by inspection company _____ Yes _____ No If yes, explain

---

10. ADDITIONAL COMMENTS (If necessary, continue on reverse side)

---

11. STATEMENT OF PEST CONTROL OPERATOR

A. The inspection covered the readily visually accessible areas of the structure(s) only. Attention was given to those visually accessible areas which have been shown to be particularly susceptible to attack by wood destroying insects. Probing and/or sounding of visually infested and/or damaged wood members was performed.

B. The inspection did not include areas which were obstructed or inaccessible at the time of inspection.

C. *This is not a structural damage report.*

D. Neither I nor the company for which I am acting have had, presently have, or contemplate having any any interest in the structure(s) inspected. I do further state that neither I nor the company for which I am acting is associated in any way with any party to this transaction.

12. DISCLOSURE STATEMENT PROVIDED TO INSPECTOR _____ YES _____ NO	13. ALL PARTIES SHOULD BE AWARE OF CERTAIN CONDITIONS THAT INCREASE THE POSSIBILITY OF UNDETECTED LIVE WOOD DESTROYING INSECTS. THESE CONDITIONS INCLUDE WOOD TO GROUND CONTACT, SLAB BELOW GRADE, VEGETATION OR VINES GROWING ON EXTERIOR WALLS, BATH TRAPS WITHOUT VISUAL ACCESS AND LIVE WOOD DESTROYING INSECTS UNDER OR WITHIN 12 INCHES OF THE STRUCTURE(S) INSPECTED. THIS SECTION IS FOR INFORMATIONAL PURPOSES ONLY

14. SIGNATURE AND NUMBER OF INSPECTOR		15. DATE
16. REPORT REQUESTED BY	17. REPORT RECEIVED BY	
	18. TITLE	19. DATE
RECEIPT (Signatures not the responsibility of Inspecting Company)		
I have received the original or a legible copy of the front and back sides of this form.		
SIGNATURE OF OWNER/AGENT OF PROPERTY INSPECTED	DATE	
SIGNATURE OF PURCHASER OF PROPERTY INSPECTED	DATE	

LPCA-142 5/98

Appendix B

Measurements and Conversions

Linear Measure

12 inches	=	1 foot
3 feet	=	1 yard
5.5 yards	=	1 rod
40 rods	=	1 furlong
8 furlongs	=	1 mile

Square Measure

144 square inches	=	1 square foot
9 square feet	=	1 square yard
43,560 square feet	=	1 acre
640 acres	=	1 square mile

Cubic Measure

1,728 cubic inches	=	1 cubic foot
27 cubic feet	=	1 cubic yard
128 cubic feet	=	1 cord
24.75 cubic feet	=	1 perch

Measure of Angles and Arcs

60 seconds	=	1 minute
60 minutes	=	1 degree
90 degrees	=	1 quadrant
360 degrees	=	1 full circle

Concise Encyclopedia of Real Estate Business Terms
© 2006 by The Haworth Press, Inc. All rights reserved.
doi:10.1300/5637_23

Surveyor's or Land Measure

1 link = 7.92 inches
1 rod (or pole) = 25 links = 16-1/2 feet
1 chain = 100 links = 4 rods = 66 feet
1 furlong = 40 rods = 10 chains = 1/8 miles
1 mile = 320 rods = 80 chains = 5,280 feet
1 acre = 160 square rods = 43,560 square feet
1 square mile = 640 acres

Engineer's Chain

12 inches	= 1 link
100 links or 100 feet	= 1 chain
52.8 chains	= 1 mile

Chains to Rods and Feet

Chains	Rods	Feet	Chains	Rods	Feet	Chains	Rods	Feet
1	4	66	15	60	990	28	112	1,848
2	8	132	16	64	1,056	29	116	1,914
3	12	198	17	68	1,122	30	120	1,980
4	16	264	18	72	1,188	31	124	2,046
5	20	330	19	76	1,254	32	128	2,112
6	24	396	20	80	1,320	33	132	2,178
7	28	462	21	84	1,386	34	136	2,244
8	32	528	22	88	1,452	35	140	2,310
9	36	594	23	92	1,518	36	144	2,376
10	40	660	24	96	1,584	37	148	2,442
11	44	726	25	100	1,650	38	152	2,508
12	48	792	26	104	1,716	39	156	2,574
13	52	858	27	108	1,782	40	160	2,640
14	56	924						

How to Find . . .

To Find Circumference
    Multiply diameter by   3.1416
    Or divide diameter by   0.3138

To Find Diameter
    Multiply circumference by   0.3183
    Or divide circumference by   3.1416

To Find Radius
    Multiply circumference by   0.15915
    Or divide circumference by   6.28318

To Find Side of an Equal Square
    Multiply diameter by   0.8862
    Or divide diameter by   1.1284
    Or multiply circumference by   0.2821
    Or divide circumference by   3.545

To Find the Area of a Circle
    Multiple circumference by one-quarter of the diameter.
    Or multiply the square of diameter by   0.7854
    Or multiply the square of the circumference by 0.795
    Or multiply the square of 1/2 diameter by   3.1416

Square
    A side multiplied by 1.4142 equals diameter of its circumscribing circle.
    A side multiplied by 4.443 equals circumference of its circumscribing
        circle.
    A side multiplied by 1.128 equals diameter of an equal circle.
    A side multiplied by 3.547 equals circumference of an equal circle.

Bibliography

Armstrong, George M. Jr. *Louisiana Landlord and Tenant Law*, Third Release. Austin: Butterworth Legal, 1989.

Bagby, Joseph R. *Real Estate Financing Desk Book*, Second Edition. Englewood Cliffs, NJ: Institute for Business Planning, 1977.

Black, Henry Campbell M.A. *Black's Law Dictionary*, Fourth Edition. St. Paul: West, 1968.

Casey, William J. *Real Estate Desk Book*. New York: Institute for Business Planning, Inc., 1966.

Halper, Emanuel C. *Ground Leases and Land Acquisition Contracts*, Third Release. New York: Law Journal Seminars, 1999.

Levine, Mark Lee. *Real Estate Tax Shelter Desk Book*, Second Edition. Englewood Cliffs, NJ: Institute for Business Planning, 1978.

Shea-Joyce, Stephanie, ed. *The Dictionary of Real Estate Appraisal*, Third Edition. Chicago: Appraisal Institute, 1993.

Title, Peter S. *Louisiana Practice Library—Louisiana Real Estate Transactions*. Rochester: Lawyers Cooperative, 1991.

Yiannopoulos, M. (ed.) *Louisiana Civil Code 2000*. St. Paul: West Group, 2000.

Index

4-plex units, 169, 174, 233
100 percent mortgages, 87
1031 tax-deferred rule, 154, 233

Absorption rate, 1-2
Access and accessibility, 68-69, 82, 98,
    108, 139, 146, 163, 220
Access easement, 108
Access roads, 185
Acknowledgments, witnessing, 95
Acre, 3
Acre-feet, 86
Acreage, 17
Act of God, 6, 56, 66, 104, 201
"Act of vendor's lien," 171
Action to quiet title, 155
Ad valorem taxation, 3-4, 10
Add-on charges, 4, 54, 55, 60, 111, 193
Additional collateral, 24
Additions to property, 8, 21, 23, 60, 81,
    126, 200, 239
Address
    assignment of street, 17
    property identification, role in, 72
    stating, 234, 237, 246
Adjacent property, 31, 129
Adjustable rate mortgage (ARM), 4-5,
    34, 44, 170
Adjustment charges, 111, 112
Adjustment factors in determining
    market value, 45, 53
Administrative costs, 140
Administrators, 201
ADR (average daily room) rate, 12-13,
    128

ADT (average daily traffic), 13
Advertising of real estate, 55, 82, 83,
    93, 218, 236
Affidavit
    signing, 32
    witnessing, 95
Affirmative easement, 39
After-tax equity yield rate, 69
After-tax profits, 109
Age groups, 36
Agency
    agreement, 6, 16
    definition and overview, 5-6
    designated, 37, 175-176
    disclosure form, 175-177
Agent, profit to, 91, 93, 234
Agent-customer relationship, 32
Agent entrusted with lease, 5
Agricultural land, 64
Agricultural poison, 63
Agricultural use, soils for, 70
Air conditioner unit, movable, 89
Alleys, 146
ALTA Owner's Policy Form B, 222
Alterations of property, 187, 200, 239
Alternative mortgage (AMI), 6
Amenities, physical, 68, 81, 96
Americans with Disabilities Act of
    1990, 98
Amortization
    of building cost, 43
    of debts, 10, 14
    of leases, 6-7
    of loans, 77
    of mortgages, 14, 18, 20, 58, 59
    negative, 90

Concise Encyclopedia of Real Estate Business Terms
© 2006 by The Haworth Press, Inc. All rights reserved.
doi:10.1300/5637_25

Order a copy of this book with this form *or online at:*
http://www.haworthpress.com/store/product.asp?sku=5637

CONCISE ENCYCLOPEDIA OF REAL ESTATE BUSINESS TERMS

_____ in hardbound at $39.95 (ISBN-13: 978-0-7890-2341-4; ISBN-10: 0-7890-2341-5)

_____ in softbound at $24.95 (ISBN-13: 978-0-7890-2342-1; ISBN-10: 0-7890-2342-3)

260 pages plus index

Or order online and use special offer code HEC25 in the shopping cart.

COST OF BOOKS_____

☐ **BILL ME LATER:** (Bill-me option is good on US/Canada/Mexico orders only; not good to jobbers, wholesalers, or subscription agencies.)

☐ Check here if billing address is different from shipping address and attach purchase order and billing address information.

POSTAGE & HANDLING_____
(US: $4.00 for first book & $1.50 for each additional book)
(Outside US: $5.00 for first book & $2.00 for each additional book)

Signature_____

SUBTOTAL_____

☐ **PAYMENT ENCLOSED: $**_____

IN CANADA: ADD 7% GST_____

☐ **PLEASE CHARGE TO MY CREDIT CARD.**

STATE TAX_____
(NJ, NY, OH, MN, CA, IL, IN, PA, & SD residents, add appropriate local sales tax)

☐ Visa ☐ MasterCard ☐ AmEx ☐ Discover
☐ Diner's Club ☐ Eurocard ☐ JCB

Account #_____

FINAL TOTAL_____
(If paying in Canadian funds, convert using the current exchange rate, UNESCO coupons welcome)

Exp. Date_____

Signature_____

Prices in US dollars and subject to change without notice.

NAME_____

INSTITUTION_____

ADDRESS_____

CITY_____

STATE/ZIP_____

COUNTRY_____ COUNTY (NY residents only)_____

TEL_____ FAX_____

E-MAIL_____

May we use your e-mail address for confirmations and other types of information? ☐ Yes ☐ No
We appreciate receiving your e-mail address and fax number. Haworth would like to e-mail or fax special discount offers to you, as a preferred customer. **We will never share, rent, or exchange your e-mail address or fax number.** We regard such actions as an invasion of your privacy.

Order From Your Local Bookstore or Directly From
The Haworth Press, Inc.
10 Alice Street, Binghamton, New York 13904-1580 • USA
TELEPHONE: 1-800-HAWORTH (1-800-429-6784) / Outside US/Canada: (607) 722-5857
FAX: 1-800-895-0582 / Outside US/Canada: (607) 771-0012
E-mail to: orders@haworthpress.com

For orders outside US and Canada, you may wish to order through your local sales representative, distributor, or bookseller.
For information, see http://haworthpress.com/distributors

(Discounts are available for individual orders in US and Canada only, not booksellers/distributors.)

PLEASE PHOTOCOPY THIS FORM FOR YOUR PERSONAL USE.

http://www.HaworthPress.com   BOF06